ART DEPARTMENT
BOWDOIN COLLEGE
BRUNSWICK
MAINE 04011

ART DEPARTMENT
BOWDOIN COLLEGE
BRUNSWICK
MAINE 04011

ART AND ACT

BOOKS BY PETER GAY

Style in History (1974)

Modern Europe (1973) (with R. K. Webb)

The Bridge of Criticism: Dialogues on the Enlightenment (1970)

The Enlightenment: An Interpretation, volume 2, The Science of Freedom (1969)

Weimar Culture: The Outsider as Insider (1968)

A Loss of Mastery: Puritan Historians in Colonial America (1966)

The Enlightenment: An Interpretation, volume 1, The Rise of Modern Paganism (1966)

The Party of Humanity: Essays in the French Enlightenment (1964)

Voltaire's Politics: The Poet as Realist (1959)

The Dilemma of Democratic Socialism: Eduard Bernstein's Challenge to Marx (1952)

Translations with Introductions

Voltaire: Candide (1963)

Voltaire: Philosophical Dictionary, 2 volumes (1962)

Ernst Cassirer: The Question of Jean Jacques Rousseau (1954)

Anthologies and Collective Works

The Enlightenment: A Comprehensive Anthology (1973)

Eighteenth Century Studies Presented to Arthur M. Wilson (1972)

The Columbia History of the World (1972) (with John A. Garraty)

Historians at Work, 4 volumes (1972, 1975) (with Gerald J. Cavanaugh and Victor G. Wexler)

Deism: An Anthology (1968)

John Locke on Education (1964)

ART

AND

ACT

On Causes in History—
Manet, Gropius, Mondrian

Peter Gay

The *Critique* Lectures
Delivered at The Cooper Union

Icon Editions

HARPER & ROW, PUBLISHERS

New York, Evanston, San Francisco, London

ART AND ACT: ON CAUSES IN HISTORY—MANET, GROPIUS, MONDRIAN. Copyright © 1976 by Peter Gay. All rights reserved. Printed in the United States of America. No part of this book may be used or reproduced in any manner whatsoever without written permission except in the case of brief quotations embodied in critical articles and reviews: For information address Harper & Row, Publishers, Inc., 10 East 53rd Street, New York, N.Y. 10022. Published simultaneously in Canada by Fitzhenry & Whiteside Limited, Toronto.

FIRST EDITION

Designed by C. Linda Dingler

Library of Congress Cataloging in Publication Data

Gay, Peter, 1923–
  Art and act.
  (Icon editions)
  Originated as 7 lectures delivered at Cooper Union in Mar. and Apr. of 1974.
  Bibliography: p.
  Includes index.
  1. Manet, Édouard, 1832–1883. 2. Gropius, Walter, 1883–1969. 3. Mondriaan, Pieter Cornelis, 1872–1944.
4. History—Philosophy. I. Title.
ND553.M3G38   759.4   75–12291
ISBN 0–06–433248–9

76 77 78 79 10 9 8 7 6 5 4 3 2 1

To Harvey Potthoff
for sufficient causes

Contents

Preface

This book originated as the Distinguished Lectures of 1974 at Cooper Union. Dore Ashton's invitation came as a fortunate accident: it gave me license to concentrate on art professionally, which proved, in the demands it made on me, very different from the rather more casual, passive spectator's way with which I usually look at buildings or paintings. And it provided unsought-for tests, unanticipated proofs, and welcome general application for ideas about history which I was then trying to clarify for myself. When the invitation came, I had been thinking about history quite directly by thinking about historians; I was completing a book which, like this one, deals with questions that have interested me for many years: the possibility, range, and nature of historical knowledge. *Style in History,* which is being published as I write these lines (May 1974), is brother, almost twin, to *Art and Act.* Inevitably I thought about them, and for some months worked on them, at the same time. Not surprisingly, phrases and ideas from that book have found their way into this one. I have let them stand; together, they propose some solutions to the historian's central epistemological problem, which is also the philosopher's or the social scientist's problem: how to wrest objectivity from one's overpowering subjectivity.

This problem is embedded in a dilemma—in the strict sense of that much-abused word. The historian confronts a choice presenting him with difficulties however he chooses. Like all hunters of knowledge, he must find his way between two persuasive but incompatible theories: the first, that knower and things known are distinct, that there is a firm and fixed reality waiting to be studied and understood; the second, that knower and things known are inextricably intertwined, that our status, our nationality, our character, our religion our very language mould the manner in which we see the world. Of these two fundamental positions, the second, relativist and subjectivist, has secured an almost monopolistic dominance among historians. Much professional criticism takes the form of unmasking, of sniffing for ideology, of convicting others—and, in self-doubting moments, oneself—of incurable prejudice. Whether we quote Goethe or not, most historians accept his sweeping verdict that every perception is already a theory. But, while psychologists, philosophers, and critical historians have amassed impressive evidence of pervasive national, racial, sexual, or social bias in historical writings, they have also amassed evidence (equally impressive though less familiar) that responsible inquirers can muster an arsenal of mechanisms for securing distance between themselves and their subject matter. Science, including the science of history, is an unremitting search for a high and wide, and hence reasonably accurate, vista of the terrain to be surveyed. History can be a progressive science, capable of eliminating errors about, and giving ever better readings of, the past; historical interpretation can be something above the wholly arbitrary assertion of one's private predilections. I wrote *Style in History* to argue that a historian's personal manner of seeing and presenting his material testifies not merely to the subjectivity but also to the objectivity of historical writing; I tried to show that style is more than a symptom of limitations—it is an instrument of discovery as well. I thought then, and I think now, that the objectivist position, despite its apparent naïveté and its insecure reputation, has much to be said for it, and in *Style in History* I said as much for it as I could. *Art and Act* builds on that view and seeks to specify how the historian may explore the dimensions of the past and determine why it happened as it did.

Different as these two books are, therefore, they reinforce one another in more than the obvious way of being the product of a single mind. They represent a continuing conviction. Both are reasonably, I think rationally, optimistic about the historian's capacity to attain reliable knowledge. This optimism places me in opposition to Lawrence Stone who, though himself a practiced untangler of historical causes, has warned fellow historians against harboring high hopes in matters of historical interpretation. In his essay, *The Causes of the English Revolution*, published in 1972, he argues that "in the last resort the imposition of a rank ordering depends not on objective and testable criteria, but on the judgments, sensibility, or bias of the historian." The "task of trying to arrange all the causes in a single rank order" is, as Stone puts it, "futile and intellectually dishonest." This way of resolving—or, rather, of refusing to resolve—the conundrums that cluster about causes strikes me as unnecessarily self-denying, even as evasive. Historians impose rank orders on causes all the time, implicitly if not explicitly; to dismiss this enterprise as futile and dishonest is to give over to private choice, to mere taste, an assignment that belongs to public debate and rational decision. Stone wishes to stop at the very point at which historical inquiry becomes really interesting. Doubtless, historians' attempts to find appropriate hierarchies of causes have often enough proved futile, but this futility testifies only to the difficulty of the effort, not to its intellectual dishonesty.

My argument is in no way specific to art. The form of this book is, as I have already noted, an accident. I chose my illustrative materials from painting and architecture because I thought them appropriate to my host and my audience. I have, in short, written a book on general history, not a book in the specialized history of art. Of course, the evidence I adduce must be accurate, and the inferences I draw must be valid; otherwise, the structure I have built will collapse. But had I tried to make a contribution to art history, I would have said far more than I have about technique, about iconography, above all about style. Art historians have ways of reading pictures or, for that matter, buildings, that I admire but cannot imitate.

I want to underscore this disclaimer because it is, I think, important. Like all modern life, the discipline of history has become enormously specialized, and it is fashionable to deplore the losses that specialization brings. Yet specialization also has its advantages, certainly in history: it permits the expert—the economic historian or the art historian—to address a particular segment of the past with a certain intimacy, a certain confidence. The past is enormously rich and enormously varied; the diversity of its parts does not preclude the unity of the whole. Each branch of history has its way of asking, and answering, its own questions. At the same time, historical artifacts are all of the same kind. Statistics and novels, assassinations and sculptures, politics and portraits are all susceptible to causal inquiry. In 1963, in his vigorous essay on "Western Art History," James S. Ackerman argued that when art historians "study the events that lead to the making of works of art, our methods are nearly indistinguishable from those of the student of political events such as elections and battles; they are wholly in the past and may be reconstructed more or less clearly by means of documents, chronicles, and the like. Indeed, when an art historian engages in the study of events for their own sake, he becomes a social historian: there is no difference in principle or in technique between a biography of Michelangelo and a biography of Luther or of Charles V, or between the publication of documents on the building of Versailles and on the War of the Spanish Succession." Art, in short, inhabits the same past as business, religion, or politics. It is only that the art historian selects his distinct quarter of the past, in his distinct way. I have no intention of lamenting his preoccupations, or of reforming them.

To this disclaimer I want to add another which will, I trust, reassure not only art historians but other historians as well. I have developed a general scheme for causal investigation in history, which divides causes into three distinct kinds, emerging from three worlds: culture, craft, and private life. The Introduction outlines these worlds, and their interaction, in some detail. Now, this scheme, neat as it looks, is not a set of prescriptions but an array of suggestions. It is my attempt to escape the futility that Lawrence Stone fears and predicts. In this attempt, I have followed a fairly simple strategy. I have pursued each of my historical figures through their three worlds, and constructed in each essay an order different from the other two. With Manet, I move from the private sphere to craft and then to culture; with Gropius, from culture to the private sphere to craft; and with Mondrian, from craft to culture to the private sphere. And by design, the hierarchy of causes I discover and present in each of these sequences differs from those in the other two. I want this diversity of results to underscore, once again, the inexhaustible wealth of the human past of which I have spoken. The unity of history is far more evident in the questions we ask of it than in the answers it returns to us. If this book succeeds as a protest against dogmatism I will have accomplished a large part of my assignment. For all my insistence on the crucial importance of psychology, I want also to insist that not even psychology can presume always to supply the principal causes of events, and it can never presume to supply their sole cause. It is worth making this point even though, I think, the danger of doctrinaire claims from the psychologist's quarter is less acute today than the danger of simplistic causal explanations drawn from economics. Whether in its vulgar form (the primacy of economic motives) or its refined form (the primacy of economic structures) Marxism today seems to me more an obstruction to historical knowledge than an aid. I do not mean to gloss over the important share of economics in the making of events, or to minimize the powerful critical contribution that Marxism and Marxists have made to the discipline of history. They have opened new fields to historical inquiry, and added new instruments to historical explanation, and to say this is to say a great deal. But I think that Marxist history has come to occupy the position that Marx and Engels, in the *Communist Manifesto,* assigned to the bourgeoisie: once dynamic, liberating, progressive, it has become a fetter on science. The fish of the past is too large, and too lively, to be captured in its net. But whatever our conclusions on the ultimate place of Marxism in the history of history, I have at all events written these chapters to argue that every historical event has several causes, and several types of causes, and that our capacity to predict which causal hierarchy will eventually emerge is strictly circumscribed. To my mind, these limiting preconditions to the historian's work are anything but disheartening. On the contrary, they increase the interest of the search and the exhilaration of discovery. The rest I may leave to the text.

I have long known that the writing of history is a vast collaboration and the many persons who have helped me in the making of this book have confirmed my conviction. My first thanks go to Dore Ashton, without whose generous and imaginative invitation to be Distinguished Lecturer in the Critiques Series my ideas about historical causation might not have taken publishable form—certainly not this form. The set of seven lectures that I delivered at Cooper Union in late March and early April 1974, were, for me, a pleasing and instructive experience. Everyone at Cooper Union was courtesy and cooperativeness itself; I want particularly to thank Elizabeth Vajda and Marilyn Fish in the slide library for responding to many, often hurried requests.

Several weeks before I gave my lectures at Cooper Union, I had a splendid opportunity to try them out before an audience of my colleagues, friends, and students, both graduate and undergraduate. The occasion was the first set of Charles Domson Memorial Lectures established by Jonathan Edwards College of Yale University to commemorate a former Ph.D. student of mine Before his sudden and untimely death, Charles Domson had made a considerable mark at J. E., arousing widespread, serious interest in the historical discipline during his tenure as Bates Fellow there. I want to thank the History Academy of Jonathan Edwards College–Charles Domson Memorial for a subvention toward the cost of gathering and reproducing pictures. Much to my profit, these lectures were well attended by alert and contentious graduate students and colleagues, especially from art history, whose alert questions and candid dissent gave me great pleasure and much work.

There were many at Yale who assisted me. I am grateful to Rick Brettell, who took out valuable time from his studies to run the slides, find lecture rooms, and otherwise lead me through a stimulating but unfamiliar assignment. I am grateful also to Helen Chillman and Susan Warner-Prouty at the Yale Slide and Photograph Library; both answered innumerable questions, had slides made, and lent me rare slides during critical emergencies. It was an education to work with them. Among colleagues who read my manuscript and commented on my lectures, giving me authoritative counsel and making me feel welcome to art history, I want especially to thank Egbert Begemann, Robert Herbert, and Jules Prown: that my work on this book should have brought me closer to them as scholars and as individuals is one of its far from incidental benefits to me. I am much in debt to C. Vann Woodward, Henry Gibbons, and Susanna Barrows, who all read a draft of the Introduction, and compelled me into significant reappraisals. Yale University Historical Manuscripts and Archives kindly permitted me to reproduce some atmospheric photographs. I was delighted to find that Betty Paine and Heather Anderson could decipher various versions of my manuscript, and I will remember the patience and generosity of

James D. Burke and Denise d'Avella, both of the Yale Art Gallery, in supplying me with information and photographs.

I incurred many obligations outside of Yale. Elizabeth Shaw and Rita Myers at the Museum of Modern Art removed some formidable obstacles to my obtaining illustrations. Professors John Rewald and David Pinkney answered questions. And among those who enabled me to obtain photographs, Lord Raymond O'Neill, Lord Butler, Lady Celia Milnes-Coates, Dr. Christopher White, Dr. L. J. F. Wijsenbeek, Professor Michael Jaffé, Mr. William N. Copley, Mr. Morris Lapidus, and Miss Louise Woods of The Architects Collaborative were particularly helpful. I also want to thank Frau Professor Irmgard Wirth of the Berlin Museum for sending me a brochure on an exhibition of works by the family Gropius. Still others—thoughtful private owners and helpful curators—put me in their debt. Mrs. Ise Gropius granted me a long and cordial interview about her late husband, smoothed my way to the Bauhaus Archives at the Houghton Library, lent me the manuscript of an informative talk she delivered at the Baltimore Museum in May 1974, lent me photographs, and clarified a number of questions by correspondence. Sophie Glazer did some deft detective work on my behalf in Cambridge, Mass., and in Boston. Mr. Norman Leitman of the H. Shickman Gallery in New York graciously supplied me with the photograph of a Thomas Couture. I found Adolf Placzek's reading of the Gropius chapter both informative and encouraging. Mr. Harry Holtzman spent the better part of two days with me talking about Mondrian, allowed me valuable glimpses into materials still unpublished as this book went to press, and lent me some rare photographs without which my chapter on Mondrian would have been poorer. Mr. Martin James, a leading authority on Mondrian, kindly let me read a valuable manuscript article on Mondrian that he had just completed. I have immensely profited from long conversations with Robert Motherwell about Mondrian in particular and modern art in general; my debt to Dick and Peggy Kuhns in this respect (as in others) is equally great. My friend Quentin Skinner, who studied the Introduction much to its benefit, has shared with me for several years his lucid ideas about historical knowledge. My niece Julia Boltin, whose sculpture, *Untitled, 2000,* appears in the Introduction, answered importunate questions about the artistic process as she sees it. My wife, Ruth, my most patient and a most objective reader, heard the lectures and read the manuscript more than once; the book is much the better for it.

I want to say emphatically that all those I have mentioned, important as they were for forming and changing my interpretations, are in no way responsible for what I finally sent to the printer. They will know that this is more than a polite and customary formula, for they are not likely to agree with everything that I have said. The writing of history is not merely a vast collaboration; it is also an unending debate.

PETER GAY

Woodbridge, Connecticut
June 1974

Voor alles is een oorzaak: maar die *kennen*
we niet altijd! Kennen, weten, is geluk—
There is a cause for everything: but we do
not always *know* it! To know, to understand,
is happiness.
    —Piet Mondrian, Sketchbook, ca. 1912

ART AND ACT

ONE

Introduction: Dimensions of Cause

---

1. On Overdetermination

In the course of his work, the historian does many things, but his most difficult and, I think, most interesting, assignment is to explain the causes of historical events. The imperious Why?, which propels children to conduct their earnest investigations, also pursues the historian in his professional researches, as it does all scientists, only less obsessively, more rationally.[1] Marc Bloch, a masterly practitioner, defined history as "the science of men in time." It is the science that makes sense of change. And for the historian to make sense of change is to unriddle its causes, whether he sees them emerging from the hand of God, the imperatives of technology, the conflict of classes, or the will of individuals.

Certainly the historian performs other tasks: he discovers manuscripts and deciphers inscriptions; he defines periods and classifies facts; he explains how things work;[2] and he unearths information and compiles statistics to enrich the reservoir of historical knowledge. In the course of centuries the historian has acquired a cultural role as well. He celebrates what is worth, or, all too often, not worth, celebrating. Except for some glorious liberal intervals when his critical impulses prevail over external and internal constraints and he gives his contemporaries news of their past they may not like to hear, he provides his

---

1. The child, we may say, is polymorphously paranoid, perpetually seeking causal connections, and convinced that these are somehow related to him. Piaget has suggestively called this early conception of causality "magical-phenomenalist." See Jean Piaget and Bärbel Inhelder, *The Psychology of the Child* (1966; tr. Helen Weaver, 1969), 18.

2. "Various senses of 'explain,'" Carl G. Hempel has written, are "involved when we speak of explaining the rules of a contest, explaining the meaning of a cuneiform inscription or of a complex legal clause or of a passage in a symbolist poem, explaining how to bake Sacher torte or how to repair a radio. Explicating the concept of scientific explanation is not the same as writing an entry on the word 'explain' for the Oxford English Dictionary." "Aspects of Scientific Explanation," in Hempel, *Aspects of Scientific Explanation and Other Essays in the Philosophy of Science* (1965), 412–413. The historian is, of course, frequently engaged in offering noncausal explanations such as these.

1. Frans Hals. *The Meàger Company*, begun 1633

culture with the past it wants. The historian, in short, has contradictory ways of being physician to his society: by telling it reassuring lies or sobering truths. He collects and, at best, corrects the public memory.

Much of this handiwork is artistic or, at least, craftsmanlike, for the historian is artist as much as he is scientist. The metaphors that he likes to draw from painting or poetry to describe what he does are unforced, perfectly natural. The historian is a painter: some giants among historical writings, like Burckhardt's *Civilization of the Renaissance in Italy* or Huizinga's *Waning of the Middle Ages,* are crowded canvases, resembling nothing so much as one of Frans Hals's enormous collective portraits [1], in which the historian has compelled narrative and explanation to serve the higher purpose of characterization.[3] And the historian is a public bard: he tells true stories, an activity as indispensable as it is, all too often, despised. Especially in recent years, historians' passion for analysis has grown so exigent that literary craftsmen often think it necessary to remind their colleagues that Clio is, after all, a muse. For my part, I find it self-defeating snobbery to deprecate the transcriber of illegible texts or the dramatizer of stirring events; the division of labor, under which the historian, like all modern intellectuals, must work, gives such craftsmen, too, their valued place in the professional scheme. In the pursuit of the past, pedant, antiquarian, statistician, reporter, thinker, and theorist, all need one another. Yet,

3. "The function of the historian is akin to that of the painter and not of the photographic camera: to discover and set forth, to single out and stress that which is of the nature of the thing, and not to reproduce indiscriminately all that meets the eye." Sir Lewis Namier, "History," in Namier, *Avenues of History* (1952), 8.

after saying this, I return to my starting point: explicitly or implicitly, the historian aims to explain what made something happen. As the science of memory, history places the search for cause at the heart of the historian's business.

Normally, the historian is reluctant to theorize about causes—he prefers to find them. And when he does theorize about them he is not likely to take his instances from art, but to draw his classic examples from portentous catastrophes like the outbreak of World War I or of the English Civil War. Events of this magnitude are as familiar to the historian as a Brahms symphony is to the inveterate concertgoer, and that is why they are so gratifying to explore: they are highly visible. Better yet, they are continuously controversial; the interpretations that historians have offered of their causes have never commanded general assent. And if there is one emotion the historian finds more bracing than the conviction that he is right about causes it is that others have been wrong about them.

This preoccupation with dramatic moments in human history is easy to understand. Historians, like other scientists of man, find a curious satisfaction in the transfer of prestige from the subject under study to its student.[4] With revolutions and invasions, the sinews of cause seem worthy of the anatomist's most strenuous explorations. Yet as I have noted in the Preface, in principle and in practice, the most undramatic work of art presents precisely the same causal puzzles as the eruption of a war, the making of a treaty, or the rise of a class. The historian inquiring into what prompted Leonardo da Vinci to paint his *Mona Lisa* and why he painted it as he did employs the same kind of research and the same logic of proof as he does inquiring into what generated a Progressive Movement in the United States and why it took its distinctive form. Art, I know, invites questions that historical investigation cannot answer. The historian does not render critics redundant; his most exhaustive and most satisfactory causal explanation remains mute on the aesthetic properties, let alone the aesthetic value, of a landscape or a symphony. But I am not here addressing myself to art as an aesthetic object. I propose to deal with art as a piece of history.

There is nothing radical or even new about such an enterprise. After all, for a century and more, artists, writers, and philosophers from Shelley to Nietzsche have claimed art as a significant and revealing clue to the larger world. Stendhal flatly argued that "the arts follow civiliza-

4. My friend Richard Hofstadter used to complain humorously about the figures he had chosen to write about and to compare them invidiously with Voltaire and others who were then my daily fare. "You deal with first-rate minds," he would say, "I have to make do with third-rate minds." His work offers enduring proof that one can write first-rate history about third-rate minds.

tion," and spring from "all its customs, even the most baroque and ridiculous."[5] Marx supplied theoretical underpinning for this claim with his architectonic design for culture: art was one of the "social, political, and spiritual processes of life" which form the superstructure erected upon the "real foundation" of society. Taine, far less committed than Marx to the primacy of any single set of causes, yet insisted that literature and art alike arise from a threefold causal nexus: *race, milieu, moment*—heredity, environment, circumstances. In our day, painters, a self-conscious and voluble lot, have elevated this claim to an indisputable commonplace; with striking and unaccustomed unanimity, they have professed to see threads closely linking their art to its contemporary history. Graham Sutherland has visualized the painter as "a kind of blotting paper": he is "inevitably very much part of the world. He cannot, therefore, avoid soaking up the implications of the apparent chaos of twentieth-century civilization."[6] For Mark Tobey "the content of a painting" is "tied up with time, place and history." Since it is "always related to man's beliefs and disbeliefs, to his affirmations and negations," what and how men "believe and disbelieve" is "mirrored in the art of our times."[7] Picasso, a gifted phrase-maker, once asked rhetorically, "What do you think an artist is? An imbecile who only has eyes if he's a painter, ears if he's a musician, or a lyre in every chamber of his heart if he's a poet, or even, if he's a boxer, only some muscles?" And he answered his own questions: "Quite the contrary, he is at the same time a political being constantly alert to the horrifying, passionate or pleasing events in the world, shaping himself completely in their image."[8] Sutherland and Tobey and Picasso are here affirming the share of social and political realities in aesthetic decisions. Other artists have emphasized the power of art over art: the painter, Robert Motherwell has argued, "carries the whole culture of modern painting in his head."[9]

Most artists, then, are convinced that art somehow "expresses" the worlds in which it was made. And most historians agree. Their argument, however they formulate it, employs, openly or covertly, the language of cause: it understands art to be an effect. But plain and

5. Quoted in F. W. J. Hemmings, *Culture and Society in France, 1848–1898: Dissidents and Philistines* (1971), 2. Shelley spoke of poets expressing "the spirit of the age," while Nietzsche devoted his entire *Birth of Tragedy* to the ties linking art to society.

6. Quoted in Katherine Kuh, *Break-Up: The Core of Modern Art* (1965), 111.

7. Quoted in Kuh, *Break-Up*, 7.

8. Dore Ashton, ed., *Picasso on Art: A Selection of Views* (1972), 149. Again, Claes Oldenburg has said of his drawing that its " 'ugliness' " is a "mimicry of the scrawls and patterns of street graffiti. It celebrates irrationality, disconnection, violence, and stunted expression—the damaged life forces of the city street." Quoted in Leo Steinberg, "Other Criteria," in Steinberg, *Other Criteria: Confrontations with Twentieth-Century Art* (1972), 90–91. But I need quote no further; I think I have made my point.

9. Quoted in Irving Sandler, *The Triumph of American Painting* (1970), p. 202.

2. Vincent van Gogh. *The Night Café*, 1888

persuasive as this claim may sound, I confess that its vagueness and its
highhandedness make me uneasy. To assign the dimensions of breadth
and depth to art is only the beginning of wisdom. Yet it *is*, admittedly,
the beginning of wisdom: both Roosevelt's New Deal and Van Gogh's
Night Café [2] were something of an economic, technological, and
psychological event. A miniature may be as eloquent about art as a
mural; a painting may be as eloquent about causes as a revolution. At
the same time, two witnesses who speak equally well do not necessarily
testify in the same way. Each sort of human activity has its characteristic
cluster and hierarchy of causes. The political historian unraveling the
origins of a piece of legislation can count on finding among its causal
agents a potent admixture of economic interest. The cultural historian
inquiring into the making of a painting is sure to encounter significant
traces of the aesthetic impulse at work. Yet, while the distribution of
causes varies in somewhat expected ways, each event will contain most,
if not all, types of cause in combinations that we can only surmise but
never wholly determine in advance. Art, once again, enjoys no special
status in historical analysis: its causal texture is as rich, as variegated, and
ultimately as unpredictable as the texture of diplomatic or military
events. And even in those rare instances in which causes prove to be
principally of one sort the knowledge of which sort the historian is likely

3. Pablo Picasso. *Guernica*, 1937

4. Pablo Picasso. *Colombe Volant*, 1952

to find also follows, rather than precedes, investigation.

In saying this, I have set out the first point I have written this book to make: a historical event is always the product of numerous causes, immediate and remote, public and private, patent and concealed. The inquirer's impulse to fasten on a single cause appears to be practically irresistible: fame, it seems, awaits that historian who can find one cause where there had been two causes before. But this says more about the explainer and the values of his discipline than about the event he is explaining. We can never, in fact, dogmatically settle, by recourse to some biological or sociological or geographical scheme, which set of causes will ultimately prove the weightiest.[10] Historical events generally have more necessary causes, sometimes even more sufficient causes, than they need. They are, in Freud's valuable word, overdetermined.[11]

The complex of causal determination occasions no surprise when a work of art is crowded with meanings. For a viewer ignorant of the Fascist rebellion in Spain, the career of twentieth-century painting, and Picasso's ambivalence toward politics, art, and himself, Guernica [3] is incomprehensible or, at the least, impoverished. But even when a work of art has a less tormented history than Guernica, even when it is uncluttered in composition and uncomplicated in imagery, the multiplicity of its origins remains. Picasso's dove is more than a pigeon [4], but what else it is and why Picasso chose to paint it must remain unsettled without a grasp of the revulsion against war in Picasso's century, the iconographical history of peace symbols, and the political manipulations with which the international Communist movement victimized its well-meaning supporters.

Cause, in short, is a conjurer, concealing tricks in its capacious bag that even the experienced student cannot wholly anticipate. In the painter, as in the poet and architect—or, for that matter, the imaginative scholar—causes usually move, as it were, from the periphery to the

10. See my comment on Lawrence Stone, p. x.

11. Freud has some emphatic things to say about the multiplicity of causes and of the difficulties in discovering them: "Everything to do with our life is chance, from our origin out of the meeting of spermatozoon and ovum onwards—chance which nevertheless has a share in the law and necessity of nature, and which merely lacks any connection with our wishes and illusions. . . . We all still show too little respect for nature which (in the obscure words of Leonardo which recall Hamlet's lines) 'is full of countless causes ['ragioni'] that never enter experience.'" Leonardo da Vinci and a Memory of His Childhood (1910), in The Standard Edition of the Complete Psychological Works of Sigmund Freud, XI (1957), 137. Defending himself against the "mistaken charge" that he had denied innate factors in favor of infantile experiences, Freud wrote in 1912: "A charge such as this arises from the restricted nature of what men look for in the field of causation: in contrast to what ordinarily holds good in the real world, people prefer to be satisfied with a single causative factor." "The Dynamics of Transference," in Standard Edition, XII (1958), 99 n.

center. The apprentice forms his style on his masters; he paints or sculpts or thinks like others. The motives shaping his work plainly derive from his culture and his craft as transmitted in his lecture hall, his workshop, his studio. For the young, copying is a virtue and, more, a pedagogic necessity. The last place, therefore, where the historian would seek the impulse for the beginning artist's work is in himself. But, like most generalizations about causes, this one is so fragile as to be largely unusable; the greater the artist, the less usable it is. The young Leonardo da Vinci, working in Andrea del Verrocchio's studio, paints an angel so lovely, so unmistakably his own that, Vasari relates, Verrocchio laid down his brush forever [5]. The young Paul Cézanne, compelled by some irresistible urge to make himself into a painter, produces ominous canvases of rapes [6] and murders that owe little to his social environment, little to the tradition transmitted at the academy in Aix-en-Provence, little even to the subversive counsel of his fellow-student Emile Zola, and much to psychological pressures that Cézanne himself did not understand and could only obey. It would be preposterous to argue that Cézanne was in some way more himself before the 1870s than after: he was always himself. But his youthful

5. Andrea del Verrocchio, *Baptism of Christ*, ca. 1472

6. Paul Cézanne. *L'Enlèvement*, 1867

experiments are more visibly—I am tempted to say, more publicly—private than his mature work. Even his early paintings are, of course, far from being pure neurosis; Eugène Delacroix is in them, and Gustave Courbet, as much as Cézanne's buried need for violence and fear of women. These canvases are, like all canvases, overdetermined. But it is instructive that their principal impulsions should run counter to the usual history of causes in art. The historian-detective must be prepared for surprises.

The surprises of cause are not the monopoly of the major masters. Consider a piece of sculpture, made at the age of eight by my niece Julia Boltin [7]. It is, I think, a remarkable success: rigorously simplifying her means, she generates tensions by playing off rounded against pointed elements, and resolves these tensions by cunningly confronting the curve of the hollow with the cluster of right-angled triangles. The point here, however, is not the aesthetic value but the originality of this piece.

Children's art is social in origin; it takes a patient teacher or skilled therapist to make childish paintings or constructions much more than the obedient response to cultural demands. Spontaneity is a burden, or an achievement; there is much truth in the plaintive inquiry of the

7. Julia Boltin. *Untitled 2000,* 1970

first-grader who, in the well-known cartoon, confronts her shop teacher, "*Must* we do what we want to do today?" What children want to do is by and large prescribed by the implacable ideals of progressive educators and the fond importunities of ambitious parents. Julia Boltin's *Untitled, 2000* had a very different history. The children in her class were given eleven pieces of wood scraps and told, in the familiar manner, to do what they wanted to do. For Julia, the usual motives for children's art—the example of her peers and the praise of her instructors—were absent: she was the only one in her class to make an abstract sculpture, and her teacher, as Julia later reported, "thought that it was very stupid, actually, and didn't see the point of it." Nor did she use the full complement of the scraps she had been handed; she confined herself to eight pieces because it seemed to her that "it was complete the way it was and I couldn't add anything to make it better." At the beginning, she did not yet think of her work as a piece of sculpture; she "really began to think" only after she had got under way. And once she began to think, she thought hard, having few, if any models to imitate, and consciously aimed at what I can only call abstract realism.[12]

12. Letter to the author from Julia Boltin, September 13, 1973. Strikingly enough, in view of the resemblance of her sculpture to Constructivist work, Julia dislikes Malevich's *White on White* because "the artist didn't really think about what he was doing," while, in contrast, she likes Eskimo sculpture because it is "very realistic, not in the sense of that's the way it looks but in the sense of that's how I think of it mentally and I feel, sometimes, that's how it should look visually." This is why I am inclined to call her aesthetic point of view "abstract realism."

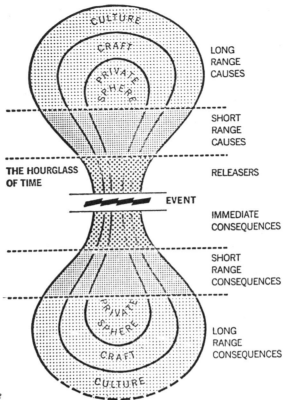

LONG
RANGE
CAUSES

SHORT
RANGE
CAUSES

THE HOURGLASS
OF TIME

RELEASERS

EVENT

IMMEDIATE
CONSEQUENCES

SHORT
RANGE
CONSEQUENCES

LONG
RANGE
CONSEQUENCES

8. *The Hourglass of Time*

Some of her observations, made three years after the event, are, doubtless, a neatened reconstruction. Visits to museums and the taste of her parents surely left their deposit on *Untitled, 2000*; Julia's individual talent, notable though it is, supplied only the most overt of causes. Thus the sources of this little piece, even if less resonant with politics or the artistic tradition than *Guernica*, are quite as mysterious. If we seek a key to the maze of cause, the presumably primitive work of art offers as little assistance as the most sophisticated production.

To reduce overdetermination to a measure of order, we may usefully visualize the historic moment, and all the materials relevant to its origins and its effects, as a cluster of sands in the shapely hourglass of time [8]. The sands of cause converge upon its neck, which constitutes the moment, and spread out from that neck as consequences to the end of recorded history. What the neck of the hourglass represents depends wholly upon the historian's concerns: it may be a single dramatic event, like the firing on Fort Sumter; it may be a network of events, like the American Civil War; it may be a structure, like the society of Beauvais around 1600; it may be a historic actor, like Walter Gropius. No matter who the historian, no matter what his principal interests—whether he is a social historian scornful of narratives or a narrative historian uneasy with analysis—each chooses the neck of the hourglass to stand for the event, the sequence, the structure he wants to understand. But there his freedom ends: the sands in that hourglass are not for him to choose but only to see and to sort out; they adhere to his subject matter by virtue of its character.

The sands of cause are not all of one kind, nor do they all originate at the same distance from the neck. Causal analysis, in fact, takes this diversity into account by proceeding along two different lines of inquiry. One, which moves from immediate precipitating causes to remote general causes, is more familiar; the other, which discriminates among types of causes by their nature rather than their distance, is more controversial.[13] The two lines, of course, often run parallel, though in a far from clear-cut manner: the historian inclined to discover causes in the larger social sphere is likely to look for them in distant preconditions; the historian committed to the influence of world-historical individuals is more likely to concentrate on private wills in action just preceding the event. In this book, I deal with historical actors as clusters of causes and consequences and with the structure of causes rather than their geography. But since causes do not lie side by side, distinct and discrete, I will necessarily and continuously trespass beyond the terrain I have chosen for myself.

This terrain is bewildering enough; it is not a cultivated park but a little-charted jungle. Man lives in several worlds at once, each of them capable of supplying causes. He exists in nature, engaged with physical surroundings that yield food and shelter, bring disease and drought. It is to master the natural exigencies of climate, food supply, and sexual life, that he devises his social technology—the division of labor, machines to multiply his hands, ways of planting crops—and constructs the institutions that make up the second world of human existence: society with its laws, its religious beliefs, its social habits, its codes of conduct and forms of government. Most professional historians at work today— Marxists in Leipzig, *Annalistes* in Paris, or eclectics in New Haven— take it as axiomatic that the weightiest historical causes emerge from these first two worlds, that spacious domain which, for short, I will call

13. For two convergent instances of causal analysis along a temporal axis I note that in 1970 I wrote a lecture on causes in which I took Karl Dietrich Bracher's splendid *The German Dictatorship* (1969) as an example of how a historian moves from long-range causes to relatively remote causes, to recent causes, to what I called "releasers." In the same year, 1970, Lawrence Stone published the first version of an essay on the English Revolution in which he moves from "triggers" (my "releasers") to "precipitants" (my "relatively remote causes") to "preconditions" (my "remote causes"). There is of course nothing very surprising about such convergence. In an early essay in which he tried to lay bare the causes of anxiety neurosis, Freud speaks of what he calls the "probably very complicated aetiological situation which prevails in the pathology of the neuroses: (a) *Precondition*, (b) *Specific Cause*, (c) *Concurrent Causes*, and . . . (d) *Precipitating or Releasing Cause.*" "A Reply to Criticisms of My Paper on Anxiety Neurosis" (1895) in *Standard Edition*, III (1962), 135. Even then the scheme was not new; Taine's famous trio *race, milieu, moment* (which I have cited in the text) bears a close resemblance to these later formulations.

culture.[14] It was in culture, "the social production that men carry on," that Karl Marx discovered the motor that drives history in its dialectical progression. It is in culture—social status, economic oscillations, administrative policies, political leadership, religious sentiments—that historians debating the English Civil War find their principal causes. And it is the clashes within and between these elements of culture that generate most historical events: the uneven development of institutions, the conflict between technological potential and social needs, the pressure of successful inventions on traditional conduct, the struggle for control over the apparatus of patronage and power. They certainly generate most historical debates: the very names of historical specialties (political, economic, military, religious, social history) support the claim of culture to the historian's attention.

Yet, while historians have long, and rightly, focused their analyses on the worlds of culture, there are aspects to them they have slighted. And there are other worlds that they have slighted no less. Men and women live in culture through a series of mediations; they rarely confront society, the economy, politics directly. Habitually they engage in activities that in all ways relate to, and in many ways mirror, the larger world of beliefs and commands. One of these worlds, decisive for most, is that of work: the technological, pedagogic, legal situation in which men and women wrest their livelihood from the soil, the loom, or the typewriter. It is a world contiguous with the world of habit, of training and customary performance, canons of excellence, and the clashes of schools and techniques that make up so much of the shop talk among mechanics and sculptors, farmers and psychoanalysts. For most human beings, work, its possibilities and its frustrations, engrosses the foreground of existence, permeating their fundamental attitudes of hope, patience, rebelliousness, or despair, and invading on one side the public world of culture and, on the other, the intimate world of private life. The study of these domains of work and habit, which I will call the world of craft, have long been the preserve of specialists, the historian of the drama or architecture or agriculture; the general historian has normally treated their preoccupations as somewhat arcane, almost precious, as though it is somehow more profound—or at the least more professional —to explain Edouard Manet's canvases as the work of an alienated artist in philistine bourgeois society rather than that of a craftsman trained

14. The term *culture* is not wholly satisfactory, since it is not used unambiguously. Cultural anthropologists have used it to embrace the totality of human experience within nature; in that usage, what I call *craft* and *privacy* would simply be aspects of culture. In some (I think, unmistakable) phrases I have used the term this broadly. But in general, in contrasting culture with other phases of the human environment, I have given it the somewhat narrower meaning of the social psychologists who contrast culture with personality—as the umbrella under which more specialized institutions and limited environments shelter.

in the conventions of French painting and moved by the Spanish masters.

Historians have treated man's most intimate worlds, those of his family and his inner life—which, together, I will call privacy—as they have treated the world of craft: with a distant and uneasy respect amounting in practice to uncomprehending puzzlement.[15] The power of privacy has, of course, long been recognized, if for the wrong reasons, by popularizers. Helpless before the formidable machinery of economic analysis or demographic reconstruction, they have fastened on to the melodrama of masterful men and seductive women who reshape the world with the exercise of their capricious will. Yet the professional historian, though he may disdain manufacturing great-man romances and seek to identify the deeper forces at play in history, cannot afford to slight the threads of private life in the causal tapestry. That tapestry is opulent in color and mysterious in composition; it discourages simplistic readings. Was it Picasso the political activist, Picasso the anti-Franco Spaniard, Picasso the experimental painter, Picasso the self-conscious autobiographer, or a combination of these Picassos, who painted *Guernica?* It is only at first glance, and from a Romantic perspective, that such a question seems pointless or absurd. The act of creation may appear like a single flash of intuition, a truly indivisible moment. Yet it is never only that. Picasso's many sketches, his deliberation and changes of mind, invalidate this view, at least for *Guernica* [9, 10]. But beyond this, even the most rapid realization of aesthetic intentions—the effortless melody of a Mozart as opposed to the laborious emendations of a Beethoven—is a confluence of many tributaries, a compression of many elements, in the neck of the hourglass of time. Accessible or concealed, overdetermination rules. The historian must therefore never hesitate to split the atom of effect to determine the multiplicity of causes.

2. Minds in History

While the historian's inquiry into the causes of *Guernica* is rational, it is very difficult. And one reason it is difficult is that the worlds I have sketched consist of two dimensions. They are realities, with verifiable qualities and countable quantities, and at the same time subjects of perception. Their characteristics, no matter how patent or stable, are

15. The obvious and important exception is, of course, the psychohistorian; I will comment on his work, pp. 16–32.

9. Pablo Picasso. Study for *Horse's Head*, 1937

10. Pablo Picasso. *Hand with Broken Sword*, 1937

also screens for projection and invite divergent responses and interpretations. Both the objective and subjective dimensions have causal
efficacy; indeed, it is probable that the perceptions are more consequential than the realities, since it is, after all, his perception that
the actor takes as the reality on whose prompting he acts. Realities,
to be sure, have their impact on perceptions: a significant technological invention, a pervasive economic depression, a lost war, or a new
metaphor, affect the way contemporaries think, not only about the
event itself but about its wider environment. The relation of actuali-
ties to perceptions is more subtly stratified than historians are apt to
believe; reality testing is rarely efficient and almost never disinter-
ested. A historian of realities would note that in the late nineteenth
century, the Western bourgeoisie spread across the map of taste.
Some bourgeois depised the new art, others bought it; while many
bourgeois were philistines and many philistines bourgeois, the ranks
of avant-garde artists, critics, dealers, and patrons generally re-
cruited themselves from the same middle-class families and often retained their middle-class values. Yet as the historian of perceptions
will note, many in the avant-garde found it reassuring, indeed in-
vigorating, to employ the word *bourgeois* as an all-embracing term
of abuse; to establish a rigid dichotomy between artists and philistines improved their collective morale even as it distorted their social perspectives. What must matter to the historian of Impressionism is both how the bourgeoisie really treated the Impressionists and
how the Impressionists thought the bourgeoisie treated them. The
craft of history is very much the study of perceptions, and historical
analysis consists in large measure of disentangling and evaluating
them; after all, much history has been made by weighty errors of
judgment. Most historical causes emerge from mistakes that men
make about the world; that is why those historians inadequately prepared to take subjectivity into account make so many mistakes
about causes.

The spectrum of possible perceptions is wide, and that ill-named
discipline, the sociology of knowledge, has by no means identified all of
its fine shadings.[16] Perceptions, we know, vary in predictable ways with
time, place, and social station; that is why individual sets of mind lend
themselves to sociological inquiry. But perceptions vary also with temperament, with unconscious conflicts, with disharmonies among the
public sources of perception. I have already noted that the several
worlds of the individual interpenetrate one another; their interaction
produces hesitation, strain, ambivalence. True: the roles that men enact

16. For a critique of the name, see my essay, "Why Was the Enlightenment?" in Peter
Gay, ed., *Eighteenth-Century Studies Presented to Arthur M. Wilson* (1972), 59–71.

achieve a measure of internal continuity, just as the relations among these roles exact a certain coherence. Cézanne was Frenchman, Catholic, bourgeois, provincial, son, father, friend, paranoid, and painter of genius, and many of these at the same time. But this continuity and coherence of roles are victories scored at the expense of aims inhibited, options rejected, rage repressed. Even historic monomaniacs, those giants of vanity and ambition who seem to have stepped onto the historical stage from the novels of Balzac, have wrested their apparent simplicity from complexity—or, perhaps better, from complexes. Their life, like all life, is a compromise formation, and history must be the account of the compromise in the making quite as much as of the compromise achieved. Historians smart under the oft-repeated and well-deserved reproach that they fail to do justice to losers; they are equally unjust to the Mensheviks of the mind, to impulses repressed in internal conflict, as though these were not as significant a part of the story as its result.

Each world of reality, then, has a world of perception, not as its shadow but as its counterpart. To express it schematically:

Worlds of Reality	Worlds of Perception
Culture	Ideologies
Craft	Traditions
Privacy	Defenses

This scheme has the virtues and vices of any scheme—it clarifies matters and oversimplifies them. It may conceal the extremely diverse pattern of traffic joining all its elements. One set of perceptions shapes, and is shaped by, other sets of perceptions; perceptions and realities teach, and learn from, each other. To enrich and complicate this crisscrossing of influences further: some elements are equally at home in several worlds at once. The family is an institution of culture and acts in most respects as its agent; it transmits and translates social messages by delineating the boundaries of the possible, instilling religious convictions, dictating social norms—it is, in short, the supreme instrument of internalization, which is to say, of socialization. The family is the individual's first culture—it is school, state, and god. In many societies, like the seventeenth-century Dutch Republic, the family may also be an agent of craft, forming artists' dynasties, handing on professional secrets, defining social placement and economic expectations. And the family fits squarely into the world of privacy, giving cultural and craft imperatives a particular, often highly individual, twist. Tolstoy was wrong: happy families are as different from another as unhappy ones.

Similarly, an individual incorporates the shapes of his culture, his craft, and his family; he stretches, as it were, across all his worlds. But his character is a unique mixture of idiosyncrasy and conformity; he is never simply a receptacle for external influences, not always an effect but often a cause. Like the unexpected scarcity of resources, the strategic utility of the submarine, or the financial demands of business interests, the individual too makes history happen: his worlds, both of perceptions and realities, are not solely constraints on his actions, but also so many platforms for the exercise, however circumscribed, of his choice.

I must stress yet another characteristic of my scheme. While, as I have said, reality testing is rarely perfect, and while perceptions are normally incomplete and tendentious reports on reality, it does not follow that the three worlds of perception are simply or merely distortions. They are ways of mastering the world: not all consciousness is false consciousness.[17] An ideology may be a class-bound, self-serving interpretation of social and economic developments but it may also be a coherent way of ordering the plethora of events and impulses. A tradition may be a fanciful mask for sordid motives but it may also be a repository for precious craft wisdom and an authentic defense of threatened standards. And defenses may be the neurotic's way of evading problems but they may also be adaptations to reality, serving rather than subverting reason. Not even clashes within and among these worlds of perception, or between worlds of perception and of reality, need be symptoms of private neurosis or public malaise. Competition, the class struggle, the division of labor, the clash of priorities can contribute to the orchestration of existence. Manet was good bourgeois and subversive painter at the same time but this did not paralyze him as an artist [see 17]. Gropius and van de Velde assessed the same developments in industrial production in markedly divergent ways, but their disagreements did not prevent them from respecting and even cooperating with one another [see 96, 97]. Mondrian was isolated in his culture, his craft, his personal life, but this helped in some way to organize his artistic gifts into an impressive *oeuvre*. The nature of perception is as elusive as the nature of a cause. And we must, as historians, solve the first before we can solve the second.

This argument implies what I want to make explicit now, and with this I have reached my second point. The subjective dimension can never be far from the mind of the historian at work. This is so because that dimension embraces more than the vagaries or the penetration of perception. The social institutions, religious rituals, work habits, and

17. I am here borrowing from an earlier formulation of my own. My *Style in History* (1974) is an extended argument designed to substantiate this point. And see the important essay by Clifford Geertz, "Ideology as a Cultural System," in Geertz, *The Interpretation of Cultures* (1973), 193–233.

moral codes that humans construct over time are all ways of expressing and channeling instinctual demands. No matter how much distance they put between themselves and their psychobiological roots, no matter how elaborate and sophisticated their form, they remain systems for meeting human needs of the most elemental kind, of mastering anxiety, satisfying hunger, and managing aggression. There is some repression in all social relations, some projection in all political activity, some sublimation in all aesthetic enterprise. The fantasies of politicians are historical material quite as much as their economic stakes and their ideals; in fact, their stakes and their ideals derive their shape largely from their fantasies. All individual growth exacts the postponement of some instinctual gratification and the sacrifice of others; all individuals living on the capital of conservative instincts strive to reduce the price of change. All reason, all discipline, all investment in others represents a victory over an alert and vindictive enemy. And, since civilization is but the individual writ large, all civilization is a precarious order imposed on seething disorder beneath. The historian therefore finds himself compelled to be alert, not merely to what humans perceive but also to what they do not perceive. The springs of action that are invisible are often more consequential than those that parade their power. The irresistible conclusion to which I find myself impelled is that psychology is not the sole property of the private world, where its authority is obviously commanding; it forms an essential part of all the worlds from which historical causes emerge. It is active in culture and craft. Therefore, in ways that historians have not yet fully grasped, all history must be in significant measure psychohistory.

To say that all history is psychohistory is not to say that subjective causes are somehow privileged and always determinative. Again and again, theorists of history have posted one-way signs to regulate the traffic of cause and effect: Carlyle his heroes, Marx his relations of production. Yet again and again, other theorists, or the pressure of historical evidence, have compelled their removal. The graveyard of historiography is strewn with the untended monuments of monocausal systems, and I have no intention of adding yet another stone. What I am saying is that all historical explanation must prominently include psychological elements.

By a striking irony, this central place of psychology has been obscured by the very historians who use it as their favored instrument. Much psychohistory has been disappointing—trivial, pretentious, and, worst of all, reductionist. It has explained too much by too little, disregarding Freud's essential, and to us familiar, ground rule that all events are overdetermined. Deceptively modern as their rhetoric may sound, most psychohistorians have done little more than to reinstate Carlyle's old-fashioned great-man history.

While this book is not the place to examine psychohistory in detail, its failures have symptomatic value for the case I want to make. Paradoxically, despite its reductionism, psychohistory suffers less from its absurdities than from its timidity. I have said that its practitioners explain too much by too little, yet at the same time they claim too little rather than too much. Most psychohistorians, to begin with, confine themselves to psychobiography—their subjects are the lives of world-historical neurotics. Only a few have heeded William L. Langer's memorable invitation to study collective behavior, and those who have are treating psychohistory as a distinct branch on a level with diplomatic or economic history, peculiarly equipped to perform rescue operations. As specialists in disasters (intellectual as well as historical) they enter the field when other explanations have failed, when rational and utilitarian motivations seem to be clouded or undiscoverable. They have staked out as their private preserve the charismatic leader, the licensed murderer, the chiliastic movement, the outburst of religious fanaticism.

I am not disposed to deny the point of such investigations. History is only too often the anatomy of unreason, and madness in great ones must not unwatched go. But to restrict psychohistory to psychopathology, whether individual or collective, is to turn back from a supreme opportunity. The historian needs more, and an entirely different kind of, light from psychology than this. He needs theories that will permit him to construct causal explanations of all conduct and all motives, rational and irrational, intelligent or stupid, realistic or projective. And he needs those theories because he renders psychological verdicts much of the time, deriving them, quite unsatisfactorily, from common sense, from bald, rationalistic interest psychology, eked out with bromides about national character.

Periodically, the historian looks out from the niche he has carved for himself to recognize that his real business is not with the bloodless abstractions or the recondite details of his specialty but with past human life in all its profusion. His true assignment, he thinks in these lucid and penitent moments, is to replace the psychological monstrosities that perform on his stage—those single-minded calculating machines, those literally inhuman vessels of greed—with believable human beings working their way through a world that for them is incomplete and partly incomprehensible, human beings who at the moment they act know far less about their situation than the historian who will later judge them from the safe seat of hindsight. He may even reflect that the most accurate history he could ever write would be a history of confusion, of uncertainty and ambivalence. Lucien Febvre, that indefatigable instigator of new enterprises in social history, used to exhort his fellow historians to plunge into the past as into a refreshing pond, to grasp all existence with both hands, to write histories of love, of joy, and of death. I would say, rather, that we need histories incorporating hopes and frustrations, anxieties and fantasies, obsessions and regressions, not segregating them, as though these were isolated or isolable entities, but treating them as forces—*normal* forces—in play at all times and in all humans.

I submit that historians are on the verge of the most fertile of self-appraisals. The materials are rich, the techniques are steadily improving; the time is ripe for historians to realize the ambition they have been voicing ever since Voltaire: to write the history of culture, that comprehensive and judicious account of the past that will give all its elements, its religion and its politics, its technology and its social structure, its play and its art, its statesmen and its mobs their proper place. Like all institutions, the historical profession ossifies, and undergoes recurrent and salutary revolts against the Pharisees, revolts of life against law. The New History in the United States early this century and the social history of the *Annales* school of the 1930s were two such revolts, both necessary, both far-reaching, both partial—partial because once the rebels gained power, they became an orthodoxy. Psychology, the discipline with which most historians have only toyed, seems to me the way beyond these half-way houses of reform. Since, as I have argued, perceptions and projections are pervasive qualities in all historical reality, Nietzsche was surely right a century ago to predict that psychology would come to be recognized as the "queen of the sciences"; after all, it is "the road to fundamental problems."[18] By encapsulating psychohistory within the confines of the irrational, by making it the science of emergencies, historians have postponed the necessary realization of Nietzsche's prophecy.

3. From Id to Ego

A principal reason for the stultification of psychohistory has been its failure to exploit the full resources of the psychology to which it is professedly committed. In contrast with psychohistorians, psychoanalysts are not fixated on pathology; Freud and his followers have attempted to make psychology into a branch of science capable of

18. Friedrich Nietzsche, *Beyond Good and Evil*, Part One, aphorism 23.

supplying laws for normal as well as neurotic behavior, of accounting for successful as well as stunted human development. While the propositions underlying psychoanalytical theory are still incompletely codified, and while its convergence with other psychologies remains a matter of discussion, almost negotiation, Freud's ambition to find the general laws of human nature and human growth persistently occupied him from the beginnings of psychoanalysis and even before. As early as 1888, Freud found Bernheim's work in hypnotism noteworthy precisely because it stripped its manifestations of "their strangeness" by connecting them "with familiar phenomena of normal psychological life and of sleep."[19] And in 1897, in an excited letter, Freud told his confidant Fliess that the value of his new theories about infantile sexuality and repression lay in their linking up "the neurotic and normal processes."[20] This was a conviction, and an excitement, that Freud never lost. He often regretted the historical accident that had made psychopathology his richest source of evidence and his most conspicuous pursuit, and insisted that while the therapeutic encounter had been his starting point, it need not, and did not, constrict his angle of vision.[21] By placing "normal" and neurotic conduct onto a continuum, by finding the sexual "perversions" in everyone, by assimilating dreams to fantasies and psychoses, and by discovering substantial similarities between neurotics and children and primitives Freud elevated repression and regression, displacement and sublimation, projection, ambivalence and anxiety, into something more than neurotic symptoms. He showed them to be part of every man's private history. And it is precisely their ubiquity that makes these mechanisms so indispensable to the historian in search of causes.

The historian uses psychoanalysis not as a clinical specialty but as a way of seeing. There is much for him to see beyond the murky realms of psychotics in power and hysterics in the streets. It is, of course, hard to say just what is normal; if history teaches anything, it is that the unexpected is to be expected, and that supposedly special cases of mental maladaptation are actually as common as erotic desire and as natural as breathing. The irrational—or, better, the nonrational—com-

19. "Preface to the Translation of Bernheim's *Suggestion*" (1888), in *Standard Edition*, I (1966), 75.

20. November 14, 1897, in Sigmund Freud, *The Origins of Psychoanalysis: Letters to Wilhelm Fliess, Drafts and Notes, 1887–1902*, eds. Maria Bonaparte, Anna Freud, Ernst Kris (tr. Eric Mosbacher and James Strachey, 1954), 234. It would be easy to add similar passages from all aspects and periods of Freud's writings.

21. It is probably worth saying once again that the old canard about Freud's system applying only to middle-class Viennese Jewish women is just that—a canard. He analyzed many men, many non-Viennese, many non-Jews. After World War I, he heard less German in his analytic hours than English. And the notion that his ideas are valid only for neurotics is equally ill-founded, if less malicious.

ponent in human experience is, quite simply, pervasive. The lifetimes of Manet, Gropius, and Mondrian prove this point beyond possibility of question. Rapid social change, the traumas of migration, the bewildering effects of technological inventions, the unprecedented exigencies of urban life, the emergence of new political powers and new political classes—these and similar clusters of events, far more general and far less sensational than the usual concerns of psychohistory, were the daily fare of the late nineteenth and early twentieth centuries. Such events require a general psychology for their explanation, more urgently, and, I think, more significantly than Luther's stormy adolescence or Hitler's problematic testicle. The years of Manet, Gropius, and Mondrian span decades in which exhilaration with the new did combat with regret for the old; when an effervescence of thoughts and feelings generated heady designs for Utopia, strange new religious cults, sober proposals for reform, stubborn resistance to innovation, anxious withdrawal from the world, gloomy head-shaking about anomie. That series of overseas invasions, exploitations, and retreats that men were beginning to call imperialism was a vague shape in men's minds before it hardened into policy; it is incomprehensible without a grasp of the strategic, economic, and scientific perceptions, the humanitarian, religious, and sexual impulses that, confused and confusing, strove for clarity and predominance in diplomatic and military action. The emergence of sociological terms like *alienation* and *anomie,* nostalgia for organic society, and programs for the "restoration" of harmonious community were in part rational responses to unprecedented fragmentation, in part concealed defenses of embattled interests. But they were also a collective orgy of regression calling for a psychology which recognizes that mechanism as part of normal, or at least predictable, behavior.

As usual, artists, even those voicing pursed-lipped disdain for the vulgar bourgeois multitude, were in the thick of life, recording, distorting, and in some measure shaping the history of their time. And, as usual, the art they made belonged to their age, to their trade, and to themselves; it was the vector of manifold and conflicting motives. Edvard Munch's lithographs depicting erotic vampires and castrating madonnas [11, 12] join a craftsman's skill to a neurotic's anxieties and to a widespread late-nineteenth-century response to modern feminism.[22] Those affectionate portraits of Paris that Camille Pissarro

22. While there is no point in being reductionist about Munch—or, for that matter, anyone else—J. P. Hodin's refusal to read the obvious testimony of Munch's work also does not help clarity. "Munch," Hodin writes, "does not hate woman, but suffers under the forces to which man is exposed. . . . Munch depicted the spirit of his age; he portrayed the conflicts of modern man and held before him a mirror in which he could recognize himself, even if only after long years of obstinate resistance. . . ." *Edvard Munch* (1972), 87, 99. This tells us both too much and too little.

11. Edvard Munch. *Vampire*, 1894

painted in the winter of 1897 [13] are a highly characteristic and deeply idiosyncratic product of their time; at once cultural monuments, triumphs of mature artistry, and private confessions, they celebrate the urban scene, sum up Pissarro's Impressionist experiments, and served him as consolation in a time of grief for the loss of a beloved son.[23]

23. On December 15, 1897, Pissarro wrote to his son Lucien about the death of another son, Felix, called Titi: "To give way to discouragement would be terribly dangerous, and we must surmount what we could not prevent. . . . Well, my dear Lucien, let us work, that will dress our wounds. I wish you strength, I want you to wrap yourself up, so to speak, in art; this will not keep us from remembering that fine, gentle, subtle and delicate artist,

12. Edvard Munch. *Madonna*, detail, 1895–1902

To understand historic phenomena such as these calls for a psychohistory of a kind that has not yet been explored, let alone practiced. When historians begin to write it, they will profit greatly from the direction that psychoanalysis began to take in the 1920s and has taken ever since, in Freud's late work and in the writings of Heinz Hartmann, Anna Freud, Ernst Kris, Erik Erikson, and others. Without compromising Freud's biological orientation, genetic explanation, or radical propositions about infantile sexuality and psychological strategies, psychoanalytic ego psychology has shed much-needed light on what Hart-

from loving him always. . . . I forgot to mention that I found a room in the Grand Hôtel du Louvre with a superb view of the Avenue de l'Opéra and the corner of the Place du Palace Royal! It is very beautiful to paint! Perhaps it is not aesthetic, but I am delighted to be able to paint these Paris streets that people have come to call ugly, but which are so silvery, so luminous and vital. They are so different from the boulevards. This is completely modern!" Camille Pissarro, *Letters to His Son Lucien*, ed. John Rewald (3rd ed., 1972), 315–316. Needless to say, anyone just looking at the pictures Pissarro painted in these painful days could not possibly deduce Pissarro's state of mind, and their consolatory function.

13. Camille Pissarro. *Place du Théatre Français (Pluie),* 1898

mann has called the "conflict-free ego sphere," in which maturation and adaptation take place.[24] The securing of this sphere for psychoanalysis has been pure gain for the comprehensiveness of psychological theory; it has generalized the mechanisms first discovered in neurotics beyond neurosis, and has shown that fantasies, anxieties, defenses, even conflicts may support rather than obstruct adaptation, aiding the individual in his effort to find his way and make his home in the world of reality. Since much history is made in the conflict-free ego sphere, in the region of goal-directed, effective behavior, the gain for the psychologist has been, at the same time, a gain for the historian: the bridge that ego psychology has thrown from the specialized symptoms of neurotic patients to the general problems of successful individuals is at the same time a bridge between history and psychology.

Since the ego looks outward as well as inward, to the present as much as to the past, adaptation to the world provides the historian with an escape from the monopoly of psychology. And, paradoxically and happily, psychology itself is the means of liberation: Freud's celebrated therapeutic goal, "where id was there shall ego be," is the formula that

24. See Heinz Hartmann, *Ego Psychology and the Problem of Adaptation* (tr. 1958), 5, 8 ff. Significantly, the *Festschrift* presented to Hartmann in 1966 bears the title, *Psychoanalysis—A General Psychology.*

summarizes the route this escape must take. As psychic energies encounter and master the environment, they achieve adaptation by testing reality even more than by gratifying fantasies. This is, in fact, a
definition of growth: to recede from imagined omnipotence, retreat
from impermissible wishes—reduce, in a word, the preoccupation with
self. The serious historian's investigation of cause mirrors this retreat,
for he is quite as much concerned to demonstrate the absence of causal
connections as their presence—the historical sense, Sir Lewis Namier
once said, prominently includes "an intuitive understanding of how
things do not happen." Not every search for profits is strictly derivable
from an unconscious anal compulsion. "We are accustomed," notes
Freud, "to trace back interest in money, *in so far as it is of a libidinal
and not of a rational character,* to excretory pleasure"; but, he adds,
reasonably enough, "we expect normal people to keep their relation to
money entirely free from libidinal influences and regulate them according to the demands of reality."[25] Even that most seemingly private of
dramas, the repression of the Oedipus complex, is enacted on the large
stage of culture: the intimate family triangle does not alone determine
its course, but, also, as Freud explicitly notes, "the influence of authority, religious teaching, schooling and reading."[26] In short, irrational as
much economic and political and social conduct may be, it incorporates
many clues from the world, obeys many "demands of reality." One
need not be a psychoanalyst, or a psychobiographer, to understand the
pressures of a lobbyist on a congressman or of a corporation on a cabinet
officer.

It follows that while all history is in some measure psychohistory,
psychohistory cannot be all of history. This asymmetry follows logically
from the objective dimension of the worlds in which history takes place
and empirically from an inspection of what historians actually do. The
historian of Impressionism neglects at his peril inventions like the paint
tube, aesthetic traditions embodied in the evolution of styles, social
transformations consequent upon shifts in the contours of patronage.
The ubiquity of the psychological element in historical explanation
neither guarantees its primacy nor entails the bankruptcy of rival elements.

There are several reasons why any dogmatic claim for psychology

25. "From the History of an Infantile Neurosis" (1918), *Standard Edition*, **XVII** (1955),
73. Italics mine. See also Géza Róheim: "Primitive economics or economics in general are
certainly what in psychoanalysis we call ego-activity . . . I am not denying that Ego
activities, i.e., activities derived from reality adjustment, have an influence in canalizing
and directing . . . Id trends, or that the economic situation retroactively influences or
limits or transforms the manifestations of our Id drives." "Economic Life," in Róheim,
The Origin and Function of Culture (ed. 1971), 52–53.
26. *The Ego and the Id* (1923), in *Standard Edition*, **XIX** (1961), 34.

must fail on principle. Private motives and responses can never provide the exhaustive explanation of an event because an event never wholly corresponds to the sum of individual intentions, or even to the sum of their conflicts. It is the outcome far less of the realization than of the frustration and distortion of many wills, and of unforeseeable contingencies diverting the most carefully calculated plans. Since a historic event is a compromise formation, psychological causes can provide only part of the impetus resulting in what we, looking back, call history.

Moreover, and more significantly, each historical world generates historical causes of its own, even though each of these worlds initially emerges, as I have noted, to satisfy some elemental urge. Legal codes, social patterns, religious practices, artistic traditions emancipate themselves from their roots and secure a certain autonomy as their distance from these roots increases. Institutions and customs develop an almost instinctive drive to survive for their own sake and do things in their own way. There are many kinds of conservatism, each of them enshrined behind the sheltering wall of habit. The more complicated society becomes, the more intermediate bodies—guilds, parties, professions, coteries—develop loyalties, privileges, and procedures that they jealously guard against attack. And this defensiveness increases the number and the kinds of sources from which historical causes may flow. In our modern world, industrialized, specialized and professionalized, servants have become masters, which is to say, effects have become causes.

Even when a cultural product—a portrait or a piece of sculpture—is demonstrably the child of sublimation, the historian can never supply its complete causal explanation by tracing that product to its remote infantile and repressed causes. Sublimation is, even at its simplest, a long meandering stream that picks up tributaries along the way; the delta that is the event is likely to look very different from the sources that are its ultimate origins.[27] For all but a few, of course—for all but the most original philosophers, statesmen, and artists—the variety of causes for their life's work is not of their own creating; it is an overwhelming fact of their existence. Most men do not make their world; they find it. Most of what they think, feel, perceive, and do is no more than the unreflective reenactment of social habits and cultural stereotypes. The most unfettered innovator is indebted to materials that the past has provided for him. Man is the cultural animal; his culture molds and kneads him, pushes him and pulls at him from the first feeding. Man

---

27. See pp. 224–225. Sublimation is, of course, particularly susceptible to reductionism, but Freud, whose own treatment of it was inconclusive, lends no support to such vulgarity; he noted that energies often moved in unpredictable directions and sublimation seemed rarely a faithful mirror of the passion sublimated. For the complexities of the issue, see Ernst Kris, *Psychoanalytic Explorations in Art* (1952).

without culture is not merely deficient or crippled—he is unthink-able.[28] His very language, including the formulas with which he rejects the past, is anchored in the collective atmosphere into which he is born. The most defiant, unruly avant-garde artist draws strength not from his private psychological sources alone. Nonconformity, too, has its rules and its traditions; antinomianism has become an institution—as the slatternly wife in the *New Yorker* cartoon knows when she berates her avant-garde painter husband, "Must you be a nonconformist like every-body else?"

To enlarge the field of causal explanation beyond psychology is to raise controversial questions about the status of other explanatory agents. In his *New Introductory Lectures* Sigmund Freud said flatly that there are only two sciences, "psychology, pure and applied, and natural science." Sociology, the study of "the behavior of people in society," was, he thought, nothing more than "applied psychology."[29] Some soci-ologists have accepted this view: W. G. Runciman has called sociology parasitic on psychology and the specialized disciplines; and the other social sciences, he has argued, are essentially a "sort of applied psychol-ogy."[30] Even Talcott Parsons has rather defensively admitted that the "ultimate foundation" of sociological theory "must certainly be derived from the science of psychology."[31]

To most readers—except, doubtless, to specialists fighting for their place in the academic sun—this debate must seem a war of words. The operative terms, after all, are "applied" and "ultimate"; they point to the remote ideal of a dependable science of man, a compendious theoretical psychology to which economists, sociologists, anthropolo-gists—and historians—will resort for the causal laws explaining individ-ual and collective conduct. But they also underscore how remote that ideal is. And even if that ideal were to become a reality, the historian would continue to need the social sciences as auxiliary disciplines. The historian lives in the world of the middle range and the middle size. He is in the position of the architect who makes do with Newtonian gravity or Euclidean geometry, since the arcane language of quantum physics and modern mathematics applies to worlds either much larger or much smaller than the prosaic workaday world in which he plies his trade. Ultimate explanations lurk in the background to orient his research and guide his investigations but it is to the applied sciences he most fre-

---

28. See Geertz, "The Impact of the Concept of Culture on the Concept of Man," in *The Interpretation of Cultures*, 33–54.
29. *Standard Edition*, **XXII** (1964), 179.
30. *Sociology in Its Place and Other Essays* (1970), 11.
31. Quoted in ibid., 17 *n.*

quently turns in his perplexities. They contain most of what he needs to know: classifications, noncausal explanations, and generalizations— those useful covert predictions that hover in that dim border region where empirical formulas merge into scientific law.

My argument seems to have drifted toward the exposed and barren position in which R. G. Collingwood came to find himself after all his philosophizing on the nature of history. While Collingwood boldly equated historical knowledge with the "self-knowledge of mind," he conceded at the same time that all the traditional branches of history —military, economic, religious, diplomatic—continued to have a right to exist and their wisdom to impart. Taken simply by itself, my modest claim for the primacy of psychology coupled with my principled permissiveness toward forays into other auxiliary disciplines seems to have produced rather meager results. It reads like a license permitting the historian to keep doing what he has been doing all along: narrate the lives of statesmen, undertake family reconstructions, draw maps of street car lines, study diplomats' papers, and count manors. Surely, Marc Bloch's much-praised excursions into agricultural economics, the science of navigation, and the study of place names deserve all the admiration they have received. But I am saying more than this. I am inviting historians to do the old work in a new temper, to scan and record the surfaces of the past continuously alert to the lava beneath the crust.[32] To write social histories of individuals, histories of the concealed bonds that knit cultures together, histories also of the consequences that habits and traditions of work carry for both individuals in

32. To quote Freud once more: "Writings that seek to apply the findings of psychoanalysis to topics in the field of the mental sciences have the inevitable defect of offering too little to readers of both classes. Such writings can only be in the nature of an instigation: they put before the specialist certain suggestions for him to take into account in his own work." *Totem and Taboo* (1913), in *Standard Edition*, XIII (1955), 75. Responsible historians have not failed to point out, of course, that economic and political behavior cannot simply be equated with the rational search for goals. "Each culture," Thomas C. Cochran has written, "has its own forms of economic irrationality or inconsistency. In some, it is excessive responsibility for the entrepreneur's family. In others, such as in the United States, one form may have been persistent over-optimism. In many others, there has been strong and realistic fear of adverse political change. An actual market, therefore, is a complex made up of the mental images and resulting calculations of those participating in it. Economic or 'market-oriented' decisions depend not on an automatic reaction but on the entrepreneur's interpretation of market forces and trends. Guided by inaccurate views, or local difficulties, average or modal entrepeneurs appear in historic situations to have allocated inputs by decisions based on factors other than marginal cost." "Economic History, Old and New," *American Historical Review*, LXIV, 5 (June, 1969), 1567. And Namier has well said about political ideas: "To treat them as the offspring of pure reason would be to assign to them a parentage about as mythological as that of Pallas Athene. What matters most is the underlying emotions, the music, to which ideas are a mere libretto, often of very inferior quality." "Human Nature in Politics," in Namier, *Personalities and Powers* (1955), 4. I only want to move beyond these scattered insights, to make them systematic and habitual.

14. Honoré Daumier. *Les Paysagistes*, 1865

particular and cultures in general is to pursue a single search in various
ways, the search for answers to that crucial historian's question, Why?,
in new and deeper places, with new and subtler instruments. I have
insisted that history is more than psychohistory; at the same time every
work of history can only be as valid as the psychology that informs it.

I have written these essays to illustrate and to substantiate the arguments I have adumbrated in this introductory chapter. I chose artists,
then, not merely because that was appropriate to my audience, or an
unconventional choice to make. To analyze the structure of historical
causation by means of those who paint pictures and design houses
rather than those who lie for money or kill for glory was to affirm what

I have called the essential unity of historical reality and the unity of method that underlies the diversity of historical investigation. Every human being, insignificant or epoch-making, acts in his world in obedience to the portrait he has made of it. His canvas may be clear in outline or dimly realized; it may be a striking likeness or a distorted caricature. His psychological brushes may be clotted with incompatible hues, his palette inherited, his design academic, his colors somber with depression or lustrous with elation. He may be like Honoré Daumier's second painter, recording nature not directly but by copying another painter [14]. Yet however clumsy his work, however derivative, historians welcome it as an irreplaceable guide to their subject's private experience. When it is illegible, they sort it out; when it is torn, they repair it; when it is incomplete, they restore it with all the tricks their trade has taught them. Whatever a man's picture of his world may be, it is not a quick sketch, not an impressionist bravura piece dashed off with a single application of paint on an unprepared canvas, but laboriously built up, many layered, much revised, thick with impasto, and strewn with pentimenti. It hides as much as it reveals, requiring perhaps more patience and certainly more delicacy to interpret than it took to make in the first place. The artists I chose for these essays make this point graphically; each, as I noted in the Preface, was shaped by the three worlds from which causes can arise, yet each exemplifies a different causal hierarchy. Together—and I have written these essays to be read together—they are my tribute to the wealth of the past and to the pleasure I take in its never-ending surprises. "There is a cause for everything: but we do not always *know* it! To know, to understand, is happiness." After finishing this book my readers will see, I think, why I chose this remark of Mondrian's as its epigraph.

TWO

Manet: The Primacy of Culture

1. An Obsession with Sincerity

Edouard Manet was one of the most personal of painters. All great artists, and many lesser ones, cultivate a particular signature, to make their hand unmistakable.[1] But Manet was so aggressively himself that his art invited the most subjective responses, the most divergent interpretations. It imposed itself on admirers and detractors alike, and left no one indifferent. The bewildered critics who, in the 1860s, felt compelled to reckon with his canvases, reached for terms of personal abuse extreme even for their personal and abusive trade. They found him hard, lazy, unclean. They called his paintings obscene and offensive daubs. They denounced Manet's audacity and resented what they took to be his provocative posture. And the happy few—Thoré, Baudelaire, Zola—who saluted Manet as a fresh face among the stale habitués of the Salons, fastened on the very audacity and provocativeness that so enraged the majority. In 1864, Thoré, the most perceptive and liberal among the critics regularly reviewing the Salons, likened Manet to a savage picador assaulting the public: "His painting," Thoré wrote, "is a kind of challenge." Though Thoré was by no means uncritical of Manet's innovations, he intended these observations on Manet's daring as compliments. A year later Baudelaire told a correspondent, "He has a *temperament;* that's the important thing." And in the following year the young Zola, who had just discovered Manet, consoled him for his isolation by taking that very isolation as the mark, and proof, of his gifts; "I am only interested in temperament," he wrote, unconsciously echoing Baudelaire. His articles allowed no doubt that what he found most interesting about Manet were precisely those qualities that made his work so intensely personal.[2] Even when Manet borrowed, as he did

1. "The whole trick in art is to stay alive," the Broadway cartoonist Al Hirschfeld has said. "Live long enough and it develops by itself. I can't think of an artist who's lived a long time who hasn't developed a thumbprint." *The New York Times,* March 16, 1973.

2. Thoré-Bürger, "Salon de 1864," in *Salons de W. Bürger,* 2 vols. (1870), II, 98–99. Baudelaire to Madame Paul Meurice, May 24, 1865, *Correspondance,* ed. Claude Pichois, 2 vols. (1973), II, 501.

extensively and notoriously in the 1860s, he borrowed with the self-assured avarice of the appropriator; he quoted Velasquez and Francisco Goya to find his own voice.[3] Manet was so much of an individualist that art historians still debate whether to place him among the Impressionists, and their uncertainty is an unwitting tribute to an art that defies classification.

But Manet the insistent individualist was also a thoroughgoing conformist. His emphatic, almost militant, respectability has not escaped his historians; it was equally familiar to his contemporaries. Zola, who knew him well and long, called him "this rebellious painter who worshipped society," who always dreamt of the "success he pursued in Paris, complete with the compliments of women, the flattering acclaim of the Salons, and a breathtaking—*galopant*—life of luxury in the midst of an admiring crowd."[4] Those who wrote about him described a self-conscious bourgeois, dressed with care almost to the point of dandyism; the poet Théodore de Banville portrayed Manet as graceful, subtle, charming and, from head to toe, a gentleman:

> Ce riant, ce blond Manet,
> De qui la grâce émanait,
> Gai, subtil, charmant en somme,
> Dans sa barbe d'Apollon,
> Eut, de la nuque au talon,
> Un bel air de gentilhomme.

Those who painted him—Fantin-Latour, Degas, Manet himself [15, 16, 17]—amply substantiate these verbal portraits. Manet was a rebel, the leader of a whole school of rebels, but all his life he thirsted for the approbation of the establishment. Clamoring for the right to be himself, he wanted to be himself without affronting conventionality, to validate his personal vision by compelling popular acceptance, to wrest from the authorities what his father had proudly displayed: the cross of the Legion of Honor. On the deepest most personal level, it would seem, the psychological mechanism that Freud has called the return of the repressed went into action early in Manet, against little resistance. Manet identified himself with his father and took the supreme sign of his father's success as the supreme sign of his own. His relation to authority was not so much ambivalent as two-sided; intent on pleasing himself he was just as intent on pleasing others. It is poignant to see Manet, even after he had left Thomas Couture's studio in 1856, braving his former

Zola, "M. Manet," *L'Evénement*, May 7, 1866, in *Mon Salon. Manet. Ecrits sur l'art*, ed. Antoinette Ehrard (1970), 66. Henceforth cited as *Ecrits sur l'art*.

3. See pp. 43–47 and 53–58.

4. *Edouard Manet* (1884), in Zola, *Ecrits sur l'art*, 361.

15. Henri Fantin-Latour. *Portrait of Edouard Manet,* 1867

16. Edgar Degas. Study for a *Portrait of Edouard Manet at the Races,* ca. 1864

17. Edouard Manet. *Self-Portrait with Palette,* 1879

18. Edouard Manet. *The Absinthe Drinker*, 1858–1859

teacher's unsparing criticisms by continuing to show him his work; he was, his lifelong friend Antonin Proust recalls, "obstinately bent on overcoming the prejudices"[5] of that surrogate father. No wonder that there were many who simply could not understand him. "The 'artist' wanted to paint like Velasquez," the journalist Firmin Javel wrote shortly after Manet's death, "the 'man' dressed, ate, and lived like Monsieur Bouguereau."[6] Manet, the rebel, was a rebel in a top hat.

The lineaments of Manet's problematic individuality emerged early, in his conduct at *collège* and during his six-year apprenticeship in Couture's atelier. Antonin Proust recalled incident after incident underscoring Manet's clarity of aim, decisiveness of mind, and sobriety of presence. He dates one of Manet's most memorable sayings from his schooldays: *"Il faut être de son temps et faire ce que l'on voit,"* a call for the dignity of the modern and the primacy of the real that would shape and define all his art.[7] And in Couture's studio, though he learned much there, Manet was diligent, intense, and single-minded, which is to say as difficult as he was promising; when he left in 1856, master and pupil felt a measure both of regret and of relief.

Three years later Manet justified the expectations of his friends and the apprehensions of his elders with *The Absinthe Drinker* [18], which, for all its palpable debts, was a declaration of independence. Significantly, Manet submitted the canvas to the Salon of 1859; significantly, the jury rejected it. *The Absinthe Drinker* was Manet's first offering to the artistic establishment of his day and his first rejection—it was to be neither the last of the one nor of the other. What shocked Couture and other professional judges in the painting was not its theme, its pathos, or its modernity; in 1859 the most conventional art lovers cheerfully viewed in the Salons and put on their walls genre scenes depicting miserable rag pickers, destitute peasants, and homeless beggars.[8] What they could not assimilate was the jarring juxtaposition of a contemporaneous subject with traditional handling, a French model with Spanish

5. Antonin Proust, *Edouard Manet, Souvenirs* (1913), 31. This book is a collection of reminiscences that Proust first published in somewhat different and more reliable form in the *Revue blanche*, between February and April, 1897.

6. Quoted in Pierre Courthion and Pierre Cailler, *Portrait of Manet by Himself and His Contemporaries*, tr. Michael Ross (1960), 86.

7. Proust, *Manet*, 7. The saying has its difficulties. "One must be of one's time," seems to have been coined by Daumier. For the remark, see George Boas, "Il faut être de son temps," *Journal of Aesthetics and Art Criticism* (1941), I, 52–65, and Linda Nochlin, *Realism* (1971), ch. 3.

8. See, on this point, Anne Coffin Hanson, "Manet's Subject Matter and a Source of Popular Imagery," *Museum Studies 3* (1969), 63–80; and Hanson, "Popular Imagery and the Work of Edouard Manet," in Ulrich Finke, ed., *French Nineteenth-Century Painting and Literature* (1972), 133–163.

feeling. At least this was Manet's assessment of his failure: "I painted a Parisian character, studied in Paris," he complained, "and I executed it with the technical simplicity I found in Velasquez. Nobody understands it."[9] When, furious at the check to his ambition, he denounced the "bonzes" who had clipped his wings, his friend Baudelaire reasonably enough pointed the moral: "The conclusion is that one must be oneself." It was, as Manet did not fail to reply, a conclusion he had already drawn.[10]

If the affirmation of sincerity is a specifically modern preoccupation, Manet was a modern on that count alone. Being himself was almost an obsession with him. In 1867 when he was not invited to exhibit in the *Exposition universelle,* Manet decided to mount a private one-man show of fifty canvases and a selection of etchings. Through the brief preface to its catalogue Manet threaded sincerity like a leitmotiv: "The artist does not say today, 'Come and see flawless work,' but, 'Come and see sincere work.' " The little manifesto demonstrates that to its author being sincere and being oneself were synonymous: "M. Manet has presumed neither to overthrow the old painting nor to create new painting. He has simply sought to be himself and not someone else." Yet, typically enough, Manet's preface was as conciliatory as it was defiant. "It is the effect of sincerity," he noted, "to give the work a character resembling protest, though the painter has thought only of rendering his impression. Monsieur Manet has never wished to protest."[11] As usual, the two sides of his character were in evidence at the same time.

In his student days he had told his friends that truth and simplicity and clarity were his only masters; while in the course of years his style matured and his palette lightened, his rhetoric remained unchanged. "I render as simply as possible the things I see," he told Antonin Proust in 1876, and in 1880, three years before his death, he praised to Proust the portrait he had painted of him [19], for the same reason and in the same vocabulary: "Your portrait is a sincere work *par excellence.* " Manet's unvarying self-image is that of a candid realist who put on canvas or paper quite directly the impulses he received from the outside world: "Take the *Olympia,* " [20] he told Proust, "what could be more artless—*naif?* I have been told that there are harsh things in it; they are

9. Antonin Proust, "L'Art d'Edouard Manet," *Le Studio,* **XXI** (1901), 7. For the stylistic ingredients composing *The Absinthe Drinker,* see George Heard Hamilton, *Manet and His Critics* (2nd ed., 1969), 23–24; and the sensible comments by Anne Coffin Hanson, in her catalogue, *Edouard Manet, 1832–1883* (1966), 43–45.

10. Proust, *Manet,* 35.

11. For the preface, often reprinted, see Proust, *Manet,* 49–54. (Manet's precise share in the authorship remains uncertain; Zola or perhaps another of Manet's friends, Zacharie Astruc, may have had a hand in it.) The question of sincerity is canvassed by Lionel Trilling, *Authenticity and Sincerity* (1972).

19. Edouard Manet. *Portrait of Antonin Proust,* 1880

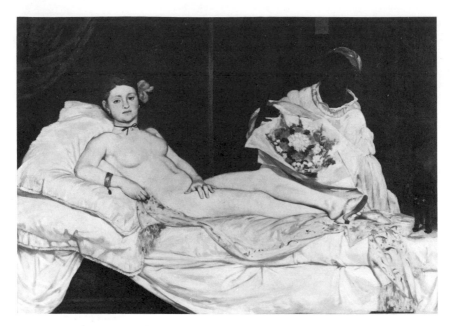

20. Edouard Manet. *Olympia,* 1863

21. Edouard Manet. *Sortie du Port de Boulogne,* 1864

22. Edouard Manet. *The Spanish Singer,* 1860

there, I saw them. I have painted what I saw. And the *Port de Boulogne?* [21] Name me a work more sincere, freer from convention, more life-like!"[12]

Professions of sincerity—especially reiterated professions—are always suspect. They are the protest that all too often protests too much —a screen for conscious doubts or unconscious conflicts. Yet George Moore, Emile Zola, and Berthe Morisot, who saw him working long passionate hours on his canvases or his etcher's plates, soaking up impressions for new painting on his strolls, or talking painting—always painting—to other painters, accepted Manet at his own evaluation.[13] Edmond Bazire, Manet's first biographer, depicted his old friend as a natural phenomenon of sincerity—a concentrated workman, at the easel from dawn to dusk, an intrepid crusader against "traditions, conventions, and divinities," continually striving to achieve "light and truth" and to realize his "personal conception." At the beginning, "he copied; then he was inspired; he groped, he escaped, he found himself; he bloomed, and continued to seek." His motto was fidelity, his contempt for fictions and disguises complete. "He thought himself a primitive."[14]

This collective report is scarcely conclusive. It is composed of claims by an artist who accepted himself and by friends who loved him; it scarcely seems possible to think of Manet—the elegant *flâneur,* self-respecting bourgeois, sophisticated wit, accomplished craftsman—as a *naif* or a *primitif.* The rhetoric is colored by piety, and even by some self-interest.[15] But Manet's performance, which is far more authoritative than the most impressive assessments, supports them. Better still, it gives them concrete meaning. What his work suggests is that, for Manet, sincerity meant free disposal over potent doses of energy and will. Manet's most uncomprehending critics granted him both, though

12. Proust, *Manet,* 80, 102 (the latter in a letter from Manet to Proust).

13. Moore: "Chavannes, Millet, and Manet," *Modern Painting* (new ed., n.d.), 31. Zola called him a "sincere and hard-working craftsman," *Edouard Manet: Etude biographique et critique* (1867), in *Ecrits sur l'art,* 104. Morisot told her sister that she was ready to accept Manet's praise of her work, since Manet "is too straightforward" to permit any misunderstanding. *Correspondance de Berthe Morisot,* ed. D. Rouart (1950), 35.

14. Edmond Bazire, *Manet* (1884), 16, 135. This profusely illustrated biography was published for the posthumous exhibition of Manet's works, for which Bazire prepared the catalogue and hung the paintings.

15. Thus Zola, the first to write about Manet extensively and approvingly, claimed Manet for his own as a naturalist or realist (two terms that Zola used interchangeably). Zola could applaud Manet for displaying traits that he, Zola, himself took pride in: direct observation of nature, uncompromising sincerity, and leading a school that despised schools. For Zola's somewhat self-referential and shifting views of Manet, see Nils Gösta Sandblad, *Manet: Three Studies in Artistic Conception* (1954), esp. 9–10. At the same time, when it was convenient, Zola could offer a purely formal analysis of Manet's work. See below, pp. 78–79.

they treated them as defects. They thought him slapdash, deaf to reason, perverse in his composition, his perspective, his brush work, his color. Not surprisingly, Manet chose to regard his dominant qualities as assets. To be energetic meant to create memorable presences free from the mindless and derivative insipidity, the sheer mendacity of so much art in his time, and to persist in carrying out his artistic intentions in the face of technical obstacles and public resistance. To be willful meant to sustain aesthetic decisions arising from his intensely private judgment of what modern art most urgently needed. Manet was not inclined to see himself as an obstinate man; it was his denigrators who were obstinate—true successors to those self-blinded savants who had refused to look through Galileo's telescope. If he continued to affront the public, he did not want this to be read as proof that he took pleasure in opposition. Manet, in short, sincerely believed in his sincerity. But this much his critics rightly sensed: Manet was an intrusive painter who made his presence felt at all times. The historical events he has made bear the stamp of their maker.

While Manet's performance gained in range and freedom through the years, he remained consistent in the emphatic exercise of his artistic will. This energetic willfulness emerges early, with *The Absinthe Drinker* of 1858–59; it informs his work of the decisive 1860s no less than that of the later years. Just as it was Manet's willfulness that had led him to depict a Parisian rag picker in the Spanish style, it was willfulness that made him choose a lefthanded guitarist to sit for his *The Spanish Singer* of 1860 [22]. And the same willfulness determines his dispositions in his *Mademoiselle Victorine in the Costume of an Espada,* which he painted two years later [23]. *Mademoiselle Victorine* is a painterly game that Manet played for its own sake, and with his own rules. The female matador at center stage is doubly playful: she is a woman dressed, fetchingly but inappropriately, in the costume of a man professionally engaged in a strenuous and deadly sport. She is clearly posing: no one with so slack a hold on cloth and sword could ever hope to survive a single encounter with the bull. Nor is this theatrical matador just any female escaping for a moment her traditional role; she is obviously a model in costume for an assignment. The *espada,* in fact, was Victorine Meurend, Manet's favorite model for over a decade, with her handsome sturdy legs, her solid body, and her experienced, candid eyes. Manet liked to paint this girl looking at men looking at her.

Manet's obligations to Goya were widely canvassed in his own time. Manet made no secret of them, and in *Mademoiselle Victorine* he parades them by quoting frankly from Goya's series of bullfight etch-

23. Edouard Manet. *Mademoiselle Victorine in the Costume of an Espada,* 1862

24. Francisco Goya. *Tauromaquia,* No. 5, ca. 1815

25. Jean Auguste Dominique Ingres. *Le Bain Turque*, 1862–1863

ings, the *Tauromaquia* [24].[16] Yet Manet's *Tauromaquia* is distinctly his own. Goya's etchings are savage reportage, crowded with gored and trampled bodies; Manet's painting is a moment in a Spanish opera. Goya has manipulated the size of his bulls to make them look rather like overgrown and vicious rams; Manet has dramatically dwarfed the battling figures in the middle distance—precisely the group he took directly from one of Goya's etchings—while drawing to scale the crowd pressed against the distant barrier. The perspective in this painting is, in a word, impossible. Distortion was, to be sure, not wholly unknown to Manet's contemporaries. Ingres, a meticulous draftsman, placed an arbitrarily small bather at the left edge of his famous tondo, *Le Bain Turque* [25]. But Manet's distortion is far more deliberate than this; it

16. Etienne Moreau-Nélaton, *Manet raconté par lui-même*, 2 vols. (1926), **I**, 45–46, contains some contemporary comments. For his indebtedness in *Mademoiselle Victorine*, see Jean C. Harris, *Edouard Manet: Graphic Works* (1970), 112.

resembles, not the painting of its day, but the experiments of the Post-Impressionists. It was to be thirty years or more, in the provocative architecture of Cézanne [26], before painters would again so positively assert similar "mistakes." Manet's little bullfight in the middle distance serves purely pictorial needs; so does the dropping horizon in his *Port de Boulogne* [21]. These departures from literal fidelity to nature were, I am sure, intentional. But intended or not, Manet's assaults, in this and other paintings, on the classical laws of perspective were noticed, and aroused the reviewers to their favorite complaint: arbitrariness. Edmond About, analyzing Manet's *Incident in the Bull Ring*, derisively described it as showing "a wooden toreador killed by a horned rat."[17]

Manet smarted under such criticisms but went his way. For his large, ambitious *The Old Musician,* of 1862, he assembled a fortuitous collection of street urchins and ragged bystanders. The musician sits holding

17. In *Petit-Journal,* June 3, 1864, quoted in Hamilton, *Manet,* 53. Manet later partially destroyed this painting. I discuss its largest surviving fragment, the *Dead Toreador,* p. 000.

26. Paul Cézanne. *The Basket of Apples,* 1890–1894

his violin and looking straight out of the canvas, as though he were posing for his portrait; the ill-assorted individuals standing around him are too indifferent to the old fiddler to deserve the collective name of audience. They are as detached from one another, as dissociated as apparitions in a dream. The one thing that unites them is the artist's decision to bring them together [27]. If they are a gallery of quotations, Manet has assembled a most miscellaneous set, borrowing from Jean Antoine Watteau [28], Velasquez, popular French prints—and himself. In fact, almost as though to underscore his mastery over his creations, Manet has introduced into this assemblage his absinthe drinker of 1859 [29, 18], as mincing (or as crippled?) in his stance as he had been in the painting from which he has been so miraculously translated into this indeterminate and perfunctory landscape.

Manet affirmed his mastery early and late. His experiments with color scandalized—or at the least, astonished—his contemporaries quite as much as the nudity in the *Olympia* [see 20] and the *Déjeuner sur l'Herbe* [30]. Even as a young student, Antonin Proust recalled, Manet made the passage from shadow to light the subject of "his constant researches," and he rejected the half tones that painters normally used to ease the transition from darker to brighter areas, since, he argued, they both "weakened the vigor of light" and "attenuated the color of shadows."[18] He painted rapidly and directly on the canvas without a prepared ground, intent on evoking the energy that animated him and the luminosity he saw in the world. He dared to cover large areas of his canvases with unmodulated patches of black or blackish brown; yet the darkest of his paintings are electric in their shadows. And they are heightened in their voltage by applications of brilliant touches, like those small dabs of blue in *The Old Musician*, which move the eye from the baby's frock to the fiddler's shirt to the hills beyond and to that spot of sunlight on the clouded sky. Again, Manet's big, powerfully foreshortened *Dead Toreador*, an almost abstract study in brown, black and white, achieves its macabre vitality with the pink of the fallen bullfighter's cape and the spots of blood on his shirt and by his side. Thoré had this painting in mind when he spoke of Manet's "splendid and bizarre color"—color, he significantly added, which so powerfully 'irritates the 'bourgeois.' "[19] The bright palette of Monet and his fellow Impressionists, which Manet did so much to inspire, make Manet's paintings of the 1860s appear subdued in retrospect. But even before Manet collaborated with the Impressionists to lighten his own colors even more, the public found them dazzling, downright revolutionary.

18. Proust, *Manet,* 16, 31–32.
19. "Salon de 1864," *Salons,* **II,** 98.

27. Edouard Manet. *The Old Musician*, 1862

28. Antoine Watteau. *Gilles*, ca. 1717–1719

29. Edouard Manet. *The Absinthe Drinker*, 1861–1862

30. Edouard Manet. *Déjeuner sur l'Herbe,* 1863

   Like Manet's colors, Manet's spaces were deeply disturbing. They are often vague, ambiguous, mysterious. The ground on which the matador lies fades into an indeterminate distance. The painting, to be sure, is a fragment—it was part of *Incident in a Bull Ring,* which Manet cut into pieces after its failure at the Salon of 1864. But in a slightly later work which is emphatically intact—the *Woman with a Parrot* [31], painted in 1866—a similar spatial ambiguity prevails. The floor on which Manet's model stands becomes at some indeterminable point the background against which her pink shape defines itself; this is a spatial trick far more characteristic of modern photography than of nineteenth-century painting.
   The last of Manet's masterpieces, the *Bar at the Folies-Bergères* [32], painted in 1881, provided academic critics and doctrinaire realists with one more puzzle: the reflection of the bar maid in the mirror lining the wall is severely displaced; it should be directly behind her, while the

31. Edouard Manet. *Woman with a Parrot,* 1866

man she is talking to should appear in the painting itself in front of her. Naturally Manet's implacable detractors complained that the *Bar* was not merely vulgar in its choice of subject, but, worse, illogical in its drawing.[20] While a few allowed themselves to enjoy the still lifes on the counter and the luminosity of the interior, most were appalled at what they thought Manet's ignorance of the most elementary rules and his improbable colors. Even Joris-Karl Huysmans, on his way to becoming a programmatic modernist, could not quite bring himself to like, let alone understand, this strangely exuberant painting. Was this, then, the

20. Raymond Mortimer, *Edouard Manet: Un Bar aux Folies-Bergères* (n.d.), though a suggestive pamphlet, scarcely exhausts the dimensions of this masterpiece. It is perhaps worth noting that the oil sketch he made in preparation for his larger painting is not distorted in any way. Manet did what he did because he wanted to. Ambiguity of spaces is almost a Manet trademark; witness, in addition to the paintings I have mentioned, *Rouvière as Hamlet* (National Gallery, Washington), and his two so-called *Philosophers* (both, Art Institute, Chicago.)

32. Edouard Manet. *Bar at the Folies-Bergères*, 1881

culmination toward which Manet's much advertised sincerity had pointed all along? Here was a bourgeois not merely by origin but by choice who, professing his intention not to offend, persisted in being offensive. Late in 1881, Antonin Proust had secured for Manet the coveted cross of the Légion d'Honneur; was this canvas, painted at about the same time, a wry commentary on the honor on which he had concentrated his life's ambition? When Manet died in 1883 at fifty-one, he received the usual tributes but, outside the familiar circle of friends and admirers, little clear comprehension. Bewildered questions continued to be asked. Together, the man and the work, instead of clarifying one another, only deepened the puzzle. By the time of his death, Manet stood as a paradox in the cultural landscape, as ambiguous as one of his paintings. The most personal of painters took much of his private secret with him.

2. The Cutting Edge of Wit

It may at first appear that Manet's two most salient traits, his sincerity and his conformism, point to a restricted range of causes, the concealed layer of psychological explanation. The struggle for sincerity, after all, is almost by definition a claim to private rights. And conformity, especially in a relatively open modern society, appears less a fate imposed by public forces than a compulsion dictated by private needs. But, like the archeologist and, in another way, the psychoanalyst, the historian in search of causes brings to light strata upon strata of buried cities. Even sincerity and conformity yield the secret of their causal role only within the larger contexts of craft and culture, the arenas of available alternatives, of constricting pressures and inviting possibilities. Hence my inquiry compels me from the world of private into that of public causes, even with Manet—in fact, as I will show, especially with Manet.

For Manet, certainly, the effort to realize his aesthetic aims meant coming to terms with the craft of painting and with the cultural forces that were transforming the world in which he so observantly lived. It is touching to see Manet's most affectionate defenders vindicating his sincerity by seeking to establish his independence from outside influences. Baudelaire argued that, reports to the contrary, Manet did not imitate the Spanish masters—he had not even seen them; the similarity of his work to theirs was a mysterious coincidence. And Zola argued that, whatever the cavilers might say, Manet was not translating the poems of Baudelaire into painting—he was not a man of ideas, but a student of nature.[21] Baudelaire and Zola saw Manet's originality as a kind of autarchy; Manet himself was less exacting in his definition of originality. He sensed that to be in the avant-garde in the late nineteenth century was a demanding enterprise; disgust, even Flaubert's single-minded, elemental hatred for the bourgeoisie was never enough. Politics, morals, traditions, in a word, everything, had become problematical; and the profusion of available life styles— bohemianism, dandyism, monasticism, radicalism, respectability— suggests that the artist's choice among them depended in large part on his assessment of what culture and craft would allow him, or compel him, to be. Manet could not separate his effort to be faithful to himself from being faithful to his art, and this fidelity exacted persistent critical confrontations with artistic traditions, techniques, and tastes.

Manet's engagement with his craft pivoted around two poles: the great tradition preserved in the museums and the academic tradition crowned in the Salons. Both were troublesome to him—as they are for his historian; the first calls for a clarification of his borrowing, the second for a definition of his rebelliousness.

Manet's much debated resort to past masters raises importunate questions about his celebrated originality. I have earlier characterized his quotations as denoting the "self-assured avarice of the appropriator," but is this phrase anything better than a figleaf for Manet's prolonged artistic adolescence? The English Post-Impressionist Walter Sickert was not alone in his skepticism about Manet; he called him, derisively, a "well-bred modest gentleman, who discovered, as it were by chance, that there was such a thing as painting, and who was entirely dependent on previous painters, particularly Ribera and Velasquez"[22] —an accusation of plagiarism as a way of life made presumably more damaging by Manet's ostentatious good breeding. The first, almost self-evident yet still necessary reply is that resemblance does not prove

21. Baudelaire, in a letter to Thoré (c. June 20, 1864), *Correspondance,* **II,** 386. Zola, *Edouard Manet* (1867), *Ecrits sur l'art,* 101. See Hanson, "Popular Imagery and the Work of Manet," 133.

22. Quoted in Alan Bowness, "A Note on Manet's 'Compositional Difficulties,'" *The Burlington Magazine* (June, 1961), 276. Manet's supporters, who fully recognized his borrowings, yet firmly insisted on his originality. The letters of his pupil and sister-in-law Berthe Morisot—who was well equipped to judge—are punctuated with her admiration for Manet's powerful individuality.

33. Edouard Manet. *Madame Manet au Canapé Bleu*, ca. 1878

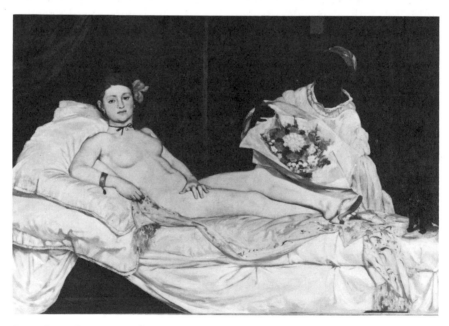

34. Edouard Manet. *Olympia*, 1863

dependence. *Post Velasquez ergo non propter Velasquez.* There are only so many ways in which a painter can render a recumbent Venus, a dead soldier, or a still life with apples. And aesthetic images, like historical causes, are overdetermined. If Manet poses Madame Manet in the posture of his own *Olympia* [33, 34], he was not necessarily quoting himself, or hinting at something scandalous about his wife. He was merely doing a pastel of a woman reclining comfortably on a sofa. Art historians have too quickly assumed that a painter finds his inspiration primarily in art: it must have been the sight of Jean-Léon Gérôme's *Death of Caesar* that moved Manet to paint his dead matador [35]; or, conversely, seized with the impulse to paint a dead matador, Manet must have turned to Gérôme to solve the painterly problem he had imposed on himself [36]. This may be so; it is often so; it need not be so [37, 38]. The causal leap of influence requires demonstration more cogent than a resemblance that the historian finds plausible.

Even after the historian has made a convincing connection between model and imitator, he must recognize that many sorts of currents pass along it. The inheritance of family traits is no guarantee for their respectable employment. Some artists imitate because they lack the gift to shed the dependent habits of their apprenticeship. Painters are born, or rather trained, copyists and their school pieces, designed to sharpen the eye and quicken the hand, sometimes merely bring out the sad truth that their essential talent is for mimesis.

Like other dutiful, well-schooled young artists, Manet also went to the museums to paint his Tintorettos [39, 40] and his Delacroix [41, 42]. But Manet's most intemperate denigrators never denied him individuality; they called him "a Spaniard from Paris," or a "Goya in Mexico, gone native," but they did not aggravate these witticisms, soon grown stale with repetition, into accusations of plagiarism.[23] Those came later. Thoré, for one, recorded Manet's thieveries without disapproval: "Monsieur Manet," he observed in 1864, standing before the *Incident in the Bull Ring*, "has the qualities of a magician, luminous effects, flamboyant tones, which imitate Velasquez and Goya, his favorite masters." And, stopping in the same Salon before the *Dead Christ with Two Angels* [43], he noted complaisantly that here Manet had "imitated another

23. These comments by Paul Mantz and Paul de Saint-Victor, respectively, are to be found in Moreau-Nélaton, *Manet*, I, 45–46. In "Manet's Sources: Aspects of His Art, 1859–1865," *Artforum*, **VII**, 7 (March, 1969), 28–82, Michael Fried has extensively examined the literature and offered a stimulating but unconvincing reinterpretation of Manet's borrowings as being essentially French, patriotic. For a devastating rejoinder, see Theodore Reff, " 'Manet's Sources,' A Critical Evaluation," *Artforum*, **VIII**, 1 (September, 1969), 40–48.

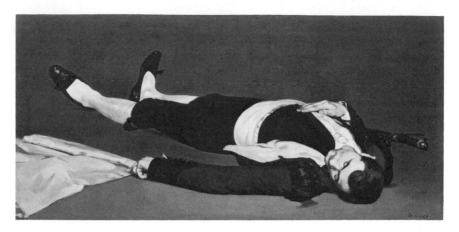

35. Edouard Manet. *The Dead Toreador*, 1864

36. Jean–Léon Gérôme. *The Death of Caesar*, 1867. (The version of 1859, which Manet may have seen, and which showed Caesar alone, is now lost.)

37. Edouard Manet. *Guerre Civile,* 1871

38. Jean Chanfreau of France, after slipping in a match against Mark Cox at Cleveland, April 12, 1973

39. Edouard Manet, *Copy of Self-Portrait of Tintoretto,* ca. 1854   40. Tintoretto. *Self-Portrait*

Spanish master, El Greco, with just as much ardor."[24] Yet he did not like this controversial painting any the less for it. The depressing pall that hangs over truly derivative work never clouded Manet's canvases.

That cluster of attitudes we call, for short, *admiration* is a far more likely candidate for explaining Manet's proceedings than an incapacity to generate his own style. Borrowing and admiration, to be sure, are not inescapably yoked together: an artist may borrow without admiring, or admire without borrowing. Many artists have copied paintings or sculptures because they happen to be accessible; others, because they remind them of something, or pose an interesting artistic problem. And even if appropriation springs from admiration, the unconscious motives that generate this admiration, and the kind of act that this appropria-

24. "Salon de 1864," *Salons,* **II,** 99. There is an interesting problem about this painting: Christ's wound is shown in his left, rather than his right side. Baudelaire called Manet's attention to this "mistake," and later critics have wondered whether the oil was not really designed to serve as a sketch for a graphic work where, of course, the place of the wound would be reversed. (The graphic versions of Manet's earlier painting, the *Spanish Singer,* also make him right-handed, rather than left-handed, as he is in the large oil.) It is true that Manet often made graphics or drawings after, rather than before, his oils. But there is no Scriptural authority for the precise placing of Christ's wound; the "left-side" tradition was simply less prominent than the "right-side" tradition. In an interesting essay, Vladimir Gurevich has argued that this little controversy demonstrates Manet's secularism; he did not even know that viewers might find the painting problematic. "Observations on the Iconography of the Wound in Christ's Side, with Special Reference to Its Position," *Journal of the Warburg and Courtauld Institutes,* **XX** (1957), 358–362.

41. Edouard Manet. Sketch after *The Barque of Dante*, ca. 1854

42. Eugène Delacroix. *The Barque of Dante*, 1822

tion represents, remain to be defined. Some artists imitate to acknowledge, publicly and gracefully, how much they owe to a master; others,
to rival that master in his own domain; still others, to acquire by canni-
balistic incorporation qualities they know they lack. Each of these has
been proposed as a motive for Manet's borrowing; certainly the first two
—the gracious expression of his gratitude and the confident assertion of
his stature—had their share in the making of his art. But there was a pair
of other motives, I think, both congruent with admiration, that princi-

43. Edouard Manet. *Dead Christ with Two Angels,* 1864

pally inspired Manet to quote so copiously from Goya and from Velasquez: polemics and play. Politics and wit, often separate, were con-
joined in Manet's mind and in his work.

To quote from the past can be a mark of cultivation as much as a sign
of respect; it may be politically innocent. In a society whose elite pos-
sesses a common culture, allusions, whether to Cicero or Michelangelo,
are a stylized shorthand with which the educated communicate over
the heads of the vulgar. As Samuel Johnson, himself a master of that
eighteenth-century specialty, the imitation, put it to Boswell: "Classical
quotation is the *parole* of literary men all over the world."[25] Allusion
and quotation were not the private preserve of the snob; they were
artistic and literary devices that heightened the pleasure, by enriching
the signification, of a painting or a poem. An imitation pleased the
knowledgeable both by the way it resembled, and by the way it did not
resemble, the original. The resonances and tensions between the two
could be amusing and subtly instructive; the skillful practitioner of
imitations could convey much in a compressed space by pouring new
acid into old bottles.

The wall between the unpolitical and the political uses of imitation
was crumbling and easily breached. It was frequently breached in the
eighteenth century, and again in the nineteenth, among others by
Manet. But, as so often, overdetermination prevails: Manet, paraphras-
ing the Spaniards in the 1860s, was not at every moment consumed
with making points. He was making pictures. And, I repeat, that even
when he was making points, he was not always making the same point:
to salute Velasquez across two centuries was not simply a polemical
gesture. Imitation, as Manet well knew, was risky. When he finally
reached Spain in 1865, after he had been painting his Spanish subjects
for over five years and had fully absorbed his Spanish lessons, Manet
charged his admired Goya—of all artists!—with imitating the "Master,"
Velasquez, "too much," in the "most servile sense of imitation."[26] Manet was confident that he was not being servile; he was imitating con-
structively, securing his personal mastery by living intimately with the
acknowledged giants of his art. But Manet was imitating for yet another
reason—imitating, I might say, destructively. With his playful allusions
to the great tradition, he was taking sides in the aesthetic debates of his
day. And it is this deliberate double vision that constitutes his wit.

25. For the quotation, and the issue, see Peter Gay, *The Enlightenment: An Interpretation*, vol. I, *The Rise of Modern Paganism* (1966), 39. Amid a vast literature on emulation
and imitation, I single out Ed. de Jongh's suggestive "The Spur of Wit: Rembrandt's
Response to an Italian Challenge," *Delta*, XII, 2 (Summer, 1969), 49–67.

26. Letter from Manet to Fantin-Latour, quoted in Moreau-Nélaton, *Manet*, I, 72.

Artistic wit almost eludes definition and demands exemplification. By no means all imitation is witty, nor is all wit imitation, though the two are often a pair. The artist exercises wit by inventing surprises—by playing with probability, manufacturing illogicalities, awakening reminiscences, parodying cultural monuments. Thus, in *The Human Condition, I* [44], René Magritte has painted a painting cunningly fitted into the landscape it depicts, cleverly confounding art and reality, interior and exterior, and mocked our sense of place. Again, Rubens was practicing typical Baroque wit in his cartoons for tapestries narrating the triumph of the Eucharist [45]. His panels show the central scene as a tapestry; patches of its woven back appear here and there. This "tapestry," held up by *putti,* plainly belongs in a niche framed by columns and other architectural detail visible at the edges of the painting. Thus the painting becomes a sketch for a tapestry that will look like the painting of a tapestry, while the tapestry within the tapestry will appear as a natural product handled by supernatural beings. Rubens plays off one material and one level of reality against another. And Sir Joshua Reynolds (who, not unlike Manet, was accused of plagiarism), by posing Master Crewe as Henry VIII [46], makes play with Holbein, with the patriotic English tradition, and, of course, with his own formal portraits in the grand style [47].[27]

The body of surrealist painting is, of course, a self-conscious, not always very witty, exploitation of visual and verbal ambiguities, startling in its presentations without being always certain in its intentions. We cannot be sure what Magritte meant to suggest with his wicked version of Manet's *The Balcony* [48, 49], a grisly parody made all the more unsettling by the insistent fidelity of detail—the railing, the flower pot, the shutters. What is at work in this exercise of wit—a wry tribute? a sly criticism? a somber moment of mourning for a more liberal, more humane age? In paintings like these, Pirandellian wit reaches for the dimensions of the metaphysical.

Manet's own wit was more worldly, more accessible, than this. But what makes its components hard to disentangle is that it so neatly combines diverse motives. It was playful, casual, opportunistic, admiring, and polemical all at once. To the extent that it was polemical, though, its purpose may be summarized quickly enough: Manet used

27. See Nikolaus Pevsner, *The Englishness of English Art* (ed. 1964), 68, 70, 212. On Reynolds' supposed plagiarisms and a vindication see E. H. Gombrich, "Reynolds' Theory and Practice of Imitation," in Gombrich, *Norm and Form: Studies in the Art of the Renaissance* (1966), 129–134. As Gombrich notes, Reynolds rightly saw a decisive difference between taking a "hint" from another artist for one's own purposes and slavish copying.

44. René Magritte, *The Human Condition, I*, 1934

45. Peter Paul Rubens. *The Meeting of Abraham and Melchizedek*, 1627–1628

46. Sir Joshua Reynolds, *Master Crewe as King Henry VIII*, 1776

47. Hans Holbein. *Henry VIII*, 1537

48. René Magritte. Study for *Perspective: The Balcony of Manet*, ca. 1945

49. Edouard Manet. *The Balcony*, 1868

the art of the past to criticize the practice of the present.[28] His *Young Woman Reclining in Spanish Costume* is mainly a good-humored tribute to Goya, no more [50, 51]. Some of Manet's other tributes were rather less innocent. His *Olympia* compounded its capacity to shock with its unmistakable allusion to splendid models, Venuses by Titian and Giorgione [52, 53, 54]. Even those who failed to recognize *Olympia*'s ancestry saw her family resemblance to the classical Venus. It was permissible to enjoy the earlier Venuses: their eroticism had been exorcised by the lapse of centuries and their stature as classics. *Olympia* was different. With its impudent contemporaneity, its individualized rendering of the courtesan's face and body, its cool presentation of a scene which many Salon goers had doubtless experienced, *Olympia* was an urbane comment on modern manners rather than a moralizing sermon on modern decadence. But the destruction of its erotic distance put the public on the defensive; *Olympia* was an implicit but devastating criticism of the Academic nude, which disguised the sexual *frisson* she gave her viewers with exotic accoutrements, mythological or historical backgrounds, sentimental lessons, or idealized figures [55]. The conventional odalisques, Venuses, or slaves were safe because they were

28. "I think art criticizes art," Jasper Johns has said. "It seems to me old art offers just as good a criticism of new art as new art offers of old." Interview with Vivien Raynor, *Artnews*, (March, 1973), 21. The locus classicus of this conception of how art of all ages interacts is, of course, T. S. Eliot's most quoted essay, "Tradition and the Individual Talent."

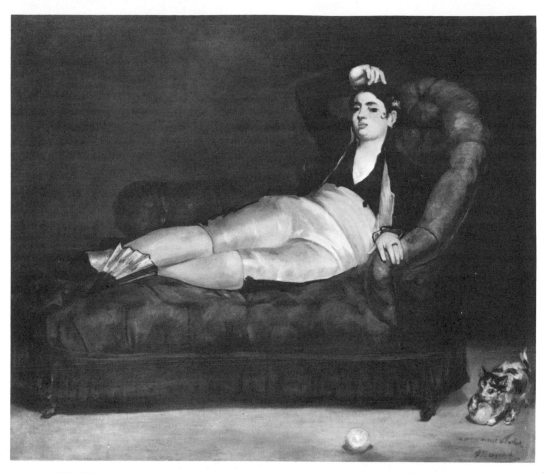

50. Edouard Manet. *Young Woman Reclining in Spanish Costume,* 1862

51. Francisco Goya. *The Maja, Clothed,* ca. 1800

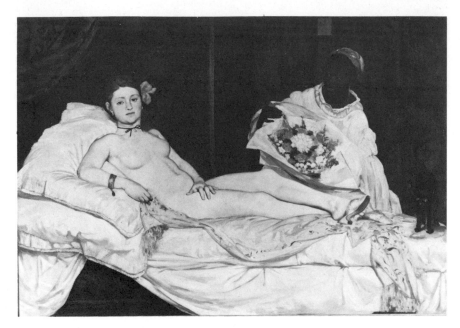

52. Edouard Manet. *Olympia,* 1863

53. Titian. *Venus,* 1511

54. Giorgione. *Sleeping Venus,* ca. 1509

55. Jean–Léon Gérôme. *Pygmalion and Galatea,* ca. 1881

remote, edifying, unreal. Manet confronted the public with modern sensuality in frank undress. To enrich his artistic polemic with a broad hint at the great tradition was to make Manet's point more amusing, but more pointed as well.[29]

In such exercises of Manet's wit, affection and disaffection joined forces to multiply their power. Just as in the eighteenth century, the philosophes had played off the philosophy of pagan Rome against the theology of Christian Europe, Manet played off the honesty and luminosity of the Spanish and Italian masters against the "spoiled cuisine," the affectations, of his contemporaries. And just as the philosophes had found the past useful because they loved it, so Manet, too, put to political uses his own beloved past.[30] If he had not loved it, it would not have been useful.

The evidence for Manet's motives is inadequate but unambiguous. We know enough to say that his experience of the Spaniards was decisive for him. As a young painter in the mid-1850s, Manet traveled to the Netherlands, to Germany and Italy, sketching his impressions and copying the masters. Then, after 1856, he stayed in Paris and went to the Louvre every day "for several years." It was at the Louvre that he discovered the Spaniards [56, 57, 58, 59]. "From the moment he had got to know, and analyzed, Velasquez and Goya," Bazire writes, "new perspectives opened before his eyes." He studied the quality of their light, the vitality of their shadows, "and they overturned all his researches."[31]

This passage contains no surprises; Manet's paintings of these years amply confirm it. But it is of considerable psychological value. Even Bazire acknowledged as early as 1884 that Manet, whom he had called *primitif,* was deeply indebted to the art of the museums—if only for increasing his capacity to pit himself against the successes of the day. Manet continued to respect the past though he lived, intensely, in the present: "The fact is," he said, "our only duty is to extract from our epoch what it has to offer us, without at the same time ceasing to admire what preceding epochs have done."[32] This, we sense, is how Manet must have grown into the painter we know. As a student, he was vaguely if persistently irritated with the tortured poses of the models, the strained search for grand themes, and the incessant laboring for finish that the tastes of Salon juries imposed on aspiring artists. Seeing the Spaniards in the Louvre gave a focus to Manet's discontent. He

29. The literature on *Olympia* is voluminous. See especially Theodore Reff, "The Meaning of Manet's Olympia," *Gazette des Beaux-Arts,* **LXIII** (1964), 111–122.

30. For an exploration of the "useful and beloved past," a double vision, at once affectionate and exploitative, which marked the strategy of the eighteenth-century avant-garde, see Peter Gay, *The Enlightenment,* **I,** *Rise of Modern Paganism,* esp. ch. 1.

31. Bazire, *Manet,* 15.

32. Proust, *Manet,* 66.

56. Edouard Manet. *Philip IV,* after Velazquez, 1862

57. Attributed to Velazquez. *Philip IV*

58. Edouard Manet. *The Little Cavaliers,* after Velazquez, 1860

59. Attributed to Velazquez. *The Little Cavaliers*

came to know not merely what to avoid but also what to do, and he used his wit to correct the one by the other. Only the great masters could overthrow an orthodoxy that was both domineering and persuasive. Only a Titian, a Rembrandt, above all a Velasquez, could improve on a Couture.

These formulas, like all formulas, brutalize historical reality. Their validity lies principally on the level of psychology. Important as his discovery of the Masters was for Manet, his admiring biographers, who enlarged Manet's struggle for independence to heroic proportions and radically simplified its course, translated this psychological truth into a historical error. The early lives of Manet are myth-making on a grand scale. They show Manet, the intrepid David, facing dcwn the Goliath that was the establishment, and fathering an avant-garde that built modern art.

Like other myths, this distortion of the cultural situation had palpable consequences; its deceptive clarity and appealing protagonist made it a reality by polarizing into distinct camps artists who had been engaged in confused battle before, shifting allies and allegiances as the occasion required. The modernist movement was not a mistake, but its origins lie at least partly in a grand misreading. Manet himself was not a doctrinaire; his world was far less savagely torn by ideology than it was to become after his death, and with the Dreyfus case. His most notable literary friends were, like himself, makers of cultural history: Baudelaire, Zola, Mallarmé. His political friends were for the most part, like himself, good republicans: Duret, Bazire, Castagnary. But his artistic associates were a strikingly eclectic lot: Degas, aesthetic innovator and political reactionary; Gérôme, Cabanel, Stevens, Fantin-Latour, Carolus Duran, none of them recorded in the history of art for their contributions to the modernist movement. Manet's much discussed refusal to show in the Impressionist exhibitions was more than negligence or a casual gesture: his brother Eugène and his sister-in-law Berthe Morisot, both of whom he loved, were committed to these shows, and Pissarro, whom Manet respected, urged Manet to participate.[33] His refusal was meditated and in character. It required some strength of mind. As his celebrated little quarrel with Degas suggests, Manet the gentleman was under some pressure to join the Independents and to reject the blandishments of the Salon. Degas had expressed his scorn for the Légion d'Honneur, and Manet had suavely rejoined: "All this contempt, my friend, is just *blague.*" In this "dog's life," where all is struggle, official

---

33. See Eugène Manet to his wife, Berthe Morisot, in *Correspondance de Berthe Morisot*, 108.

decorations are simply "another weapon." To which Degas, furiously raising his shoulders, replied, "This is not the first time I see how much of a bourgeois you are!"[34] Resisting pressure both from the right and the left, Manet had the courage of his conformity.

The truth is, then, that neither the artistic establishment that rejected Manet nor the rebels who claimed him as their leader were monolithic parties during Manet's lifetime. His own artistic practices bear out the essential complexity of the situation. To begin with, his liberating imitation of the masters was not a procedure that Manet or his fellow-rebels monopolized. It was sanctioned, in fact hallowed, by tradition, and in Manet's own day, prevailed generally.[35] The Academy officially sanctioned imitation: to make precise copies or free renderings of the masters led to artistic freedom. Painters who agreed on little else agreed on this. While they differed in the precise reasons for their recommendation, they all copied and encouraged others to copy for the sake of independence. Most significantly for Manet, Couture, too, emphatically belonged to this school of thought. He advised young painters to study anatomy and the laws of physical beauty largely from the classics of painting and sculpture, from the Greeks down to Houdon. "Keep good company," he would say, "which is to say, go to the Louvre."[36]

Agreement covered larger terrain even than this. The painter whom most teachers enjoined their pupils to copy was precisely Manet's Master. Carolus Duran enthusiastically exclaimed: "Velasquez, Velasquez, Velasquez; ceaselessly study Velasquez."[37] Henri Regnault, another gifted Academic painter, unwittingly revealed the magical component concealed in imitation in a heartfelt and hungry message from Madrid: "I should like to devour Velasquez whole."[38] Evidently, the same nourishment had very different effects on different painters; it depended not

34. The story has often been told. See John Rewald, *The History of Impressionism* (4th ed., 1973), 404.

35. Sir Joshua Reynolds had laid it down in his Sixth Discourse that "the study of other masters" should not be restricted to beginners, but "extended throughout our whole lives," since it presented no real danger of "enfeebling the mind, or preventing us from giving that original air which every work undoubtedly ought always to have." "Quite the contrary," Reynolds concluded, it is "by imitation only" that "variety, and even originality of invention is produced." "Discourse Six," *Discourses on Art*, ed. Robert R. Wark (1959), 96.

36. See Couture, *Méthode et entretiens d'atelier* (1867), 47–51; his advice is reported by Cézanne. See John Rewald, ed., *Paul Cézanne: Letters* (1946), 230, and the important article by Theodore Reff, "Copyists in the Louvre, 1850–1870," *Art Bulletin*, XLVI (1964), 552–559.

37. Quoted in Richard Ormond, *John Singer Sargent: Paintings, Drawings, Watercolors* (1970), 16.

38. Quoted in Albert Boime, *The Academy and French Painting in the Nineteenth Century* (1971), 124. On this page, and elsewhere in his important monograph, Boime quotes other academicians to the same effect.

only on the size of the consumer's appetite but also on the state of his palate.

What is more, the call for sincerity and originality that we associate with Manet and his friends was a commonplace in nineteenth-century art. Even conservative Academic teachers cultivated the indefinable quality that would make each painter become essentially himself. Their schools, paradoxical as it may sound, fostered a tradition of originality. While some warned against self-indulgence, against the substitution of facility and emotion for calculated effects, and against the whoring after novelty, Academic and anti-Academic painters alike proclaimed individuality as their ideal. "In the composition of your colors, let yourself follow your inspiration; seek, make mistakes; but above all, acquire the habit of sincerity. . . . Guard against wanting to appear more than you are; guard, above all, against placing the sentiments of others in place of your own: there lies ruin, there is darkness; dare to be yourself: there is the light." These Kantian invitations to autonomy were first published in 1867; they are not from Zola's essays on painting but from Couture's advice to painters.[39] Certainly in rhetoric Manet's teacher and Manet himself were at one. Difficulties arose only when it became necessary to embody sweeping terms like originality or sincerity in specific works; then, one man's freedom became another man's license, one man's individuality another man's eccentricity.

But Couture and Manet agreed on more than words. If Manet consulted his former teacher in the late 1850s, this was not just a filial gesture; these consultations, too, were overdetermined. Couture was neither reactionary Academic nor mediocre painter; to seek his advice was to exercise good judgment. It has been fatal for Couture's posthumous reputation that his most signal success should have come to appear, with the passing of time and the shift of tastes, the most ludicrous of Academic machines. His enormous *Romans of the Decadence*, which won first prize at the Salon of 1847, was a historical composition, just big enough, antique enough, and moralizing enough with its veiled allusions to contemporary decadence, to stand as a splendid example of a dying noble genre, the history painting. The *Romans of the Decadence* at once made, and fixed, Couture's public reputation [60]. It enabled him to found a school, which he advertised to the public in a manifesto striking for an eclecticism much like Manet's later thoughts on art. Couture promised to turn away from "spurious" classicism and "abominable" romanticism, and teach instead a "noble and elevated style" compounded of the Greeks, the Renaissance and the Flemish

39. *Méthode et entretiens d'atelier*, 35, 37. This ill-organized, often absurd collection of aphorisms, short dialogues, and moralizing counsel remains a highly instructive document.

60. Thomas Couture. *Romans of the Decadence*, 1847

masters, and aimed at reproducing "the wonders of nature" and the "ideas of our time."[40] Like his most famous pupil, Couture wanted to be an ancient and a modern at the same time.

Couture was a reformed Academic. In his youth he had done brilliantly in the Ecole des Beaux-Arts and barely missed winning the Prix de Rome for several years running. His failure, particularly galling since he had been so near success, goaded him into independence; while he was willing to play the game of the Salons as the artistic establishment defined it, his hostility to Academic doctrine and ideals was consistent and outspoken. Despite a misplaced confidence in his own genius, he was an informal, generous, and effective teacher. His teaching, diffuse and self-contradictory as it often was, boldly extended or strikingly departed from the Academic line. He told his pupils to master the elements of painting and then to follow their own best instincts; he encouraged spontaneity, which meant rapid painting and imaginative composition. Precisely like Manet later, he discountenanced the mixing

40. For the complete manifesto, see Boime, *Academy and French Painting*, 65–66. The difficulty of placing Couture is dramatically underscored in two catalogues of the H. Shickman Gallery, *The Neglected 19th Century*, Parts I and II (1970, 1971) which refer to Couture as "the perfect example of a so-called 'academic artist,'" who could "almost stand as a symbol of the official academic point of view" (which is inaccurate) and as a painter who "combined the realistic emphasis of the Academy with a bravura and forward-looking freedom usually associated with the Avant-Garde" (which is rather closer to his actual position).

61. Thomas Couture. *Portrait of a Man,* 1856

of colors on the palette; precisely like Manet, he preferred scraping off
the canvas a stroke he disliked to fussing over it with corrections; precisely like Manet, he was skeptical of half tones and taught a variety of
techniques designed to enhance the brilliance of his canvases.[41] While
his own production varies greatly in quality, his best work—his small
portraits in particular—has an appealing freshness of brushwork, ease
of execution, and vitality of line [61]. He was not a Manet *manqué,* he
was Couture. But that was by no means despicable: he was a painter
from whom a Manet could learn.

As the imitator of the masters, then, as the propagandist for sincerity,
and as the pupil of Couture, Manet was not simply an isolated innovator
battling entrenched enemies. Manet's fond biographers, reporting the

41. This, of course, contradicts the appraisal of Antonin Proust, in his *Manet,* 16, 31–32.

intermittent tension and ultimate break between pupil and teacher, did not invent either. But they exaggerated the gravity of the first and misconceived the reasons for the second. On many matters of artistic importance, Manet and Couture were allies; despite his *Romans of the Decadence,* Couture was perfectly willing to ridicule the approved "serious" themes that the Academy set its aspirants and to canvass the modern world for proper subjects. His suggestion that painters include the locomotive among such subjects has evoked some astonished exclamation points from historians.[42] The exclamation points are redundant; Couture was, as I have said, a modern man. The break between Couture and Manet had more subtle and more poignant causes than fundamental disagreements over art. Manet committed a grave offense: he dared to carry out his teacher's program. The man who performs what others promise cannot expect them to forgive him.

I do not intend any of these considerations to minimize the importance of his craft for Manet. He was—need I stress it?—an artist above all, all the time. But the impulses that forced Manet to be free, to take to their limits and beyond the tentative explorations of his teacher, were not confined to his craft. We must dig deeper and more widely still.

3. A Stroller in Paris

When, in 1867, Emile Zola tried to rescue Manet's "new style of painting" from its reputation of immorality, he ingeniously subjected it to a purely formal analysis. Many viewers had professed shock at the "obscene and vulgar" *Déjeuner sur l'herbe* [30]; others had rather enjoyed *Olympia* [52] for these very qualities. Both responses, Zola argued, were misplaced. Manet was an "analytical painter," happily free from the general "preoccupation with subject matter"; he was interested in "vivid contrasts and bold masses." The *Olympia,* to Zola's mind Manet's undisputed masterpiece, was "the most characteristic expression of his talent," the most revealing among his canvases. And what it revealed was Manet's dedication to color and design: "Look at the head of the young girl: the lips are two narrow pink lines, the eyes are reduced to a few black strokes. Now please look closely at the bouquet.

42. See pp. 104–105.

Some patches of pink, blue and green. Everything is simplified, and if you want to reconstruct reality, you have to step back a little. Then an odd thing happens: each object falls into its proper place." It was Manet's need for a dark patch that had dictated his choice of the servant, his need for luminosity that had induced him to give her a bouquet. The scandalous contents of *Olympia,* as of the *Déjeuner,* about which there had been so much debate, was of no importance, and the debate therefore irrelevant.[43]

Zola's intentions were unimpeachable, but his stratagem had unfortunate consequences. His interpretation of *Olympia* signals the fashion of identifying Manet's modernity with his presumed indifference to subject matter. Oddly enough, Zola, the chief of the realists, was a founder of formalism. In our century formalist critics have seen the artist's emancipation from nature as an indispensable ingredient in our modern sensibility and, following Zola's lead, Manet as the great emancipator. For André Malraux he is the painter who turned his back on imitation and idealization, and thus participated in the making of modernism which meant, in art, "simply—painting."[44] Manet's share in this revolution was large but subtle: "The green of *The Balcony* [49], the pink patch of the dressing gown in *Olympia*. . . ."[45] And Lionello Venturi has described Manet as an unconscious revolutionary, whose "free creation" was guided by "a principle of which the artist himself was unaware but which opened the way to modern art—the principle of the *autonomy of art.*"[46]

This dubious procedure, which isolates one aspect of Manet's art at the expense of the others, obstructs our vision of the whole. On the one side, Manet was by no means the first painter to discover that his principal loyalty belonged to the painterly aspect of his craft. Painters before Manet doubtless obeyed religious, literary, or historical imperatives more than he was to do, but we cannot derive, say, Caravaggio's or Rembrandt's dramatic chiaroscuro from such imperatives. These artists, and countless others, were principally making pictures.[47] Their stylistic devices did not serve reportage or history; they served painting. And on the other side, to reject illusionism was, at least for Manet, not to reject objectivity. Illusionism, the literal and meticulous transcription of detail that popular nineteenth-century artists like Meissonier and

43. *Edouard Manet,* in *Ecrits sur l'art,* 108–110. Thoré has a similar formal analysis in *Salons,* II, 531.

44. See Leo Steinberg, "The Eye Is a Part of the Mind," in Steinberg, *Other Criteria: Confrontations with Twentieth-Century Art* (1972), 289.

45. Malraux, *Museum Without Walls,* tr. Stuart Gilbert and Francis Price (1967), 42.

46. *Four Steps Toward Modern Art: Giorgione, Caravaggio, Manet, Cézanne* (1956), 53.

47. On this issue, see Steinberg, "The Eye Is a Part of the Mind," in *Other Criteria,* 289–306.

62. Sir Lawrence Alma-Tadema. *A Roman Amateur,* 1868

63. Edouard Manet. *Théo-dore Duret,* 1868

Alma-Tadema [62] practiced with such seductive skill was only one version—a debased version—of the antique ideal of mimesis. In academic prescriptions, the call for fidelity to nature had degenerated into the fetishism of finish. It was only against this degenerate form of imitation that Manet rebelled, not because it created illusions of reality but because it destroyed them.

Certainly Manet was something of a *tachiste*—a passionate painter of colored patches—who permitted his subjectivity a prominent share in his aesthetic decisions. We have a delightful circumstantial account of the way in which Manet permitted aesthetic needs to impose themselves on him. In 1868, Manet painted a small standing portrait of his friend Théodore Duret [63]. He began with the face and figure—a man in a grey suit on a grey background. Duret was content; Manet was not. Something indefinable was missing. "He seemed eager to add something more," Duret recalled. Manet made Duret take up his original post once again, then put a stool with a garnet-colored cover next to him and painted that. Then he put a book with green binding on the stool and painted that. Still not satisfied, he placed a lacquer tray on the stool, then a decanter, a knife, and a glass. This "unpremeditated" still life was a great surprise to Duret and, one suspects, to Manet. But this was not yet enough. Manet finally added, even more unexpectedly, a lemon on a glass placed on a tray. When he asked himself why Manet had made these successive additions to his portrait, Duret "understood that here I had a practical instance of his instinctive, as it were inherent way of seeing and feeling. Evidently the picture entirely in monochromatic greys did not please him," and so Manet introduced, element by element, a multicolored still life which satisfied some undefinable urge.[48] Doubtless, this is what made Manet so refreshing to those who had grown impatient alike with the jeweled but hollow perfection of the Salon pieces on the one hand and the sentimental agrarianism of Millet or the polemical virility of Courbet on the other—impatient, that is, both with being dazzled by technique and being lectured through pathos.

Yet there is more to Manet's art, and to his modernism, than his kind of impulsive subjectivity. Antonin Proust reports—it is perhaps the most famous anecdote in his repertory—that one day in Couture's studio, Manet laughingly rebuffed a fellow student who had suggested that he finish one of his rapid sketches. "You take me," he said derisively, "for a history painter."[49] Manet, of course, was distancing himself from

48. Théodore Duret, *Histoire de Edouard Manet et de son oeuvre* (new ed., 1919), 88–89.
49. Proust, *Manet*, 29.

64. Edouard Manet. *The Execution of Emperor Maximilian of Mexico,* 1867

65. Francisco Goya. *3rd of May, 1808,* 1814

66. Edouard Manet. *La Barricade*, 1871

pseudo-antique compositions like Couture's *Romans of the Decadence*.
But in a very distinct sense, Manet too was a history painter. With all
his devotion to art as a pure and autonomous discipline, he never turned
his painter's eye from the contours of the outside world. He did not
always simply report: the firing squad in his *The Execution of Emperor
Maximilian of Mexico* owes much to Goya's *3rd of May, 1808* and to
his imagination; in turn, his etching, *La Barricade*, owes more to his
The Execution of Emperor Maximilian of Mexico than to a specific
event [64, 65, 66]. But even in these works, where fantasy and reconstruction take the place of literal reporting, reality retains its primacy
for Manet. He functioned, in short, as history painter to future generations by being, more than anyone else, "the painter of modern life."

This epithet inescapably brings to mind Charles Baudelaire who in
December, 1863 somewhat eccentrically bestowed it on Constantin
Guys, facile sketcher of contemporary society [67]. It is a matter of
record that Manet's association with Baudelaire meant much to him;
certainly the two were intimate enough for Baudelaire to worry affec-
tionately about Manet's sensitivity to criticism and to exhort his friend
to accept the burden of originality [68]. Zola, to be sure, did not see

67. Constantin Guys. *The Café*, ca. 1860–1870

Baudelaire's poems in Manet's paintings.[50] And Antonin Proust, more jealous of his friend's originality than Zola ever was, even suggested that the current of influence ran not from poet to painter but from painter to poet.[51] But that the two made a difference to each other no one has ever denied.

Antonin Proust's claim appears to us extravagant. After all, Baudelaire had discovered the "heroism of modern life" in the mid-1840s, at least fifteen years before Manet began to record and to exemplify it. Yet his formulation hints obliquely at the wealth of French cultural criticism in the 1860s. Baudelaire was far from alone in his wry but genuine appreciation of modern dress, modern professions, modern styles of life, or in his advocacy of modern subjects as suitable to high art and literature. While the guardians of Academic ideals harangued the Salons at prize-giving ceremonies to remain faithful to the time-honored hierar-

50. See pp. 52–53.
51. Proust, *Manet*, 39. Sandblad, *Manet: Three Studies*, 56 and passim, is exceptionally lucid on the relationship between poet and painter.

chies, to remember the dignity of historical and religious subjects and to cherish, by emulating, the glories of classical art, the painters they exhorted to follow the ways of tradition were increasingly turning from history to genre.[52] While popular artists depicted milliners and drunkards, influential critics urged painters to find their subjects in their own environment. The Goncourt brothers assiduously propagandized for candid and contemporary realism; they explicitly designed their novel, *Germinie Lacerteux,* published in 1864, to continue the assault on traditional literary pieties that Flaubert had undertaken seven years before in *Madame Bovary.* They wrote their novel, which explores the decline and fall of a servant, to enlarge the domain of fiction in a world that had grown into modernity: "Living in the nineteenth century, in a time of universal suffrage, democracy, and liberalism, we asked ourselves

52. See Joseph C. Sloane, *French Painting Between the Past and the Present: Artists, Critics, and Traditions from 1848 to 1870* (1951), passim, esp. 45.

68. Edouard Manet. *Baudelaire de Profile en Chapeau,* 1862

whether what are called 'the lower classes' did not have a right to the novel, whether the world beneath a world, the people, must remain under literary interdict and the disdain of authors."[53] Three years later, in *Manette Salomon*, the Goncourts applied their programmatic modernism directly to art. The protagonist of this novel, Coriolis, is a painter of modern life, intent on recording "the modern physiognomy"—life, in a word, "as it is."[54] While others remained uncertain and continued the struggle, Zola, himself an untiring advocate of the modern, could as early as 1868 declare its victory secure. "I do not have to plead the cause of modern subject matter," he observed with real satisfaction. "This cause was won long ago." With a sigh of relief Zola noted that modern Frenchmen were rid of the Greeks and Romans and finished with the Middle Ages. The nostalgic medievalism of the Romantics had fortunately failed. "Today we find ourselves faced with reality. In spite of ourselves, we encourage our painters to depict us on canvas, just as we are, and in modern dress."[55]

In the very year that Zola made this somewhat self-satisfied appraisal of the cultural situation, Manet exhibited his portrait at the Salon [69]. It showed Zola, perhaps not just as he was, but most emphatically in modern dress, and surrounded by the attributes, less of Zola's than of Manet's struggle for self-definition and autonomy: a photograph of the *Olympia*, a Japanese print, a Goya etching after Velasquez, and, as if to underline the painter's debt to his sympathetic critic, a copy of Zola's pamphlet on Manet. Zola was inclined to give painters much of the credit for the victory of modernity. "The remarkable works of Manet and Courbet," he wrote, had proved that "contemporary life" is a "worthy subject matter for the painter's brush."[56] Manet of course had been painting contemporary subjects for some years; Courbet, aggressive in everything he did, not content with painting stone breakers and fat, thoroughly unclassical nudes, explained his aims in pamphlets and aphorisms. He refused to paint angels, he said, because he had never seen any. And Degas, though down to the mid-1860s he turned out historical and mythological canvases, began painting racing scenes as early as 1862, complete with factory chimneys in the distance.

This was the atmosphere when Thomas Couture published his *Entretiens d'atelier*. The year was 1867—the year of Baudelaire's death. Significantly, he dedicated the book to *"l'Amérique,"* that monumental

53. This Preface has often been reprinted; it is conveniently available in George J. Becker, ed., *Documents in Modern Literary Realism* (1963), 117–119.

54. That the evidentiary value of this novel is not yet exhausted emerges from a recent study of French artists' life-style of that age, Jacques Lethève, *La vie quotidienne des artistes Français au XIXe siècle* (1968).

55. "Les Actualistes," *L'Evénement illustré*, May 24, 1868, in *Ecrits sur l'art*, 151.

56. Ibid.

69. Edouard Manet. *Portrait of Zola*, 1867–1868

exemplar of modernity, the country without a past but, he hoped, with an unlimited future. "Why this antipathy toward our soil, our manners, our modern inventions?" Couture asked. "What can justify it?" If the ancients had not depicted modern subjects, there was sound and simple reason for this: these subjects had not existed then. In a rhapsodic outburst, he asked young painters to visualize the locomotive: "At the moment of departure, all are at their post; the powerful machine lets its copper glitter in the sun; its brazier sparkles, seemingly wanting to light up the route it will travel. Look at the man in the center; he is in control; hand placed on the lever, he awaits the signal. How proudly he stands planted there! his mission has made him grow taller. He knows that the slightest error can endanger the lives of those of whom he is in charge. See those stokers reflected in the furnace, then the headlight, then the inspector who watches . . . On that grandiose and modern chariot, I see intelligence, force, watchfulness . . . What a handsome picture—*Quel beau tableau!*"⁵⁷ What Couture here envisages is the heroism of modern life, complete with its heroes.

Couture's poetic commendation of modern subjects and naive rhetorical questions are instructive in their very mediocrity. They suggest that Baudelaire's vigorous and lucid aesthetic ideas had drifted down to a wider public. In formulating his own artistic aims, therefore, Manet did not need to draw solely on Baudelaire's writings or conversation. And this was just as well, for, much as Baudelaire appreciated Manet, he signally failed to see how magnificently Manet embodied the modernism he had been advocating since the mid-1840s.⁵⁸ Yet, being at once so intelligent and so widely accepted, Baudelaire's aesthetic position serves as an informative commentary on the cultural sources of Manet's work.

Baudelaire published his first "Salon" in 1845. It is shorter, less adventurous and more tentative than his later observations on painting and painters. He was still groping. The "heroism of *modern life,*" he wrote, "surrounds us and presses in on us"; men are looking for "the true painter" who will use modern subjects and modern colors to make a modern epic.⁵⁹ Yet he also noted, with a residue of timidity, that in calling for *"originality"* and for the employment of "more modern ideas," he was referring not to subject matter but to "the manner in which subjects are comprehended and depicted."⁶⁰

This was still a hesitant, somewhat vague prescription for artistic renewal. But in the "Salon of 1846" Baudelaire found his footing. In that piece of bravura journalism, as in his writings on art of the 1850s and in his lyrical tribute to "The Painter of Modern Life," Baudelaire stood on the liberating doctrine that beauty is both multiple and relative. There are many kinds of beauty and "Since all centuries and all peoples have had their beauty, so inevitably we have ours." The Academic schools have denied this, for they have a strong interest in "ceaselessly depicting the past."⁶¹ But in their love of "general beauty" they have neglected "particular beauty," the "beauty of circumstance."⁶² That is the lazy road to beauty. The true road is far more strenuous; it is to see the beauty of one's own day not in military or political events, not in

57. *Entretiens,* 100.
58. Baudelaire's only published comment on Manet was appreciative but too short, and too general, to amount to anything like a serious assessment. It simply praised Manet's "decided taste for reality, modern reality." "Peintres et Aquafortistes," (1862), *L'Art romantique,* in Œuvres complètes, ed. Jacques Crépet (1925), 112.
59. "Salon de 1845," *Curiosités esthétiques,* in Œuvres (1923), 77.
60. "Salon de 1845," *Curiosités esthétiques,* 36.
61. "Salon de 1846," 196–199.
62. "Le peintre de la vie moderne," *L'Art romantique,* 50.

"public and official subjects," but in the "spectacle of fashionable life." Officers, dandies, prostitutes are all proper subjects for the painter. Even that "much-abused garb," the seemingly drab black frock coat, is really the cloak of "the modern hero"; it has its "beauty and its indigenous charm."[63] While beauty partakes of the eternal, it is its transitory aspect that the modern artist must see and capture. "Modernity" lies here, in "the ephemeral, the fugitive, the contingent."[64]

Baudelaire's theory of modern art thus culminates in a theory of the modern artist, and this itself, with its exaltation of the craftsman over his craft, was modern. The artist must learn to look and forget what the schools have drilled into him: "Parisian life is prolific in poetic and marvelous subjects. We are enveloped and soaked in the atmosphere of the marvelous; but we do not see it."[65] The "heroism of modern life" will disclose itself to the open-eyed stroller; only the "passionate observer" who "sets up house in the heart of the multitude" can contribute his bit to "that immense dictionary of modern life." In short, the modern artist—or, better, the artist of the modern—is a sophisticated man of the world without being a blasé cynic: "He marvels at the eternal beauty and the astonishing harmony of life in the capitals"— after all, London, like Paris, is an "immense picture gallery." There the artist "contemplates the landscapes of the great city—landscapes of stone caressed by the mist or buffeted by the blows of the sun. He enjoys splendid carriages; proud horses, the dazzling smartness of the grooms, the dexterity of the footmen, the undulating stride of the women, beautiful children happy to be alive and well dressed—in a word, universal life."[66]

But Baudelaire's call for modernity also sounds a contrasting note. His delight in originality of vision and spontaneity of execution did not incline Baudelaire to favor the dictatorship of the subjective. He objected to Academic finish, to the infinite effort at rendering detail, solely on the grounds that it reduced paintings into mere artful reports of brickwork or wallpaper. He valued intuitive perception: a portrait, he finely said, is "a model complicated by an artist." But intuition never excused hasty work: "The first quality of a draftsman is . . . the slow and sincere study of his model."[67] Imagination is "the Queen of the Faculties"; its lack is fatal to art. But it must never act alone. The most formidable weapon the artist can command in his "battle with the ideal" is "a fine imagination disposing over an immense store of obser-

63. "Salon de 1846," 198–199.
64. "Le peintre de la vie moderne," 66.
65. "Salon de 1846," 200.
66. "Le peintre de la vie moderne," 62, 57, 105, 63.
67. "Salon de 1846," 144.

70. Gustave Courbet. *Hunter on Horseback*, 1867

vations."[68] And, in addition to facts, the imagination needs skill; the true artist is a thoroughly trained artist. That is why Baudelaire found Delacroix [see 42] such a great painter: he was at once natural and calculating, free and controlled; he was, "like all the great masters," an "admirable mixture of science—that is to say, a complete painter; and of naiveté—that is to say, a complete man." That is why Baudelaire found the old romanticism—all imagination and no technique—so unsatisfactory, or Courbet's robust rendering of nature [70] "fanaticism." That,

68. "Salon de 1859," *Curiosités esthétiques*, 272, 276.

71. Horace Vernet. *Mohamed Ali Pacha, Vice-Roi d'Egypt,* 1818

finally, is why he found Horace Vernet [71], "a soldier who makes paintings" and improvises his art "to the roll of the drum," so detestable: "I hate this man because his pictures have nothing to do with painting, but are a nimble and frequent masturbation, an irritation of the French skin."[69] In one of his last essays Baudelaire puts his principles a little less inelegantly: neither the exclusive reliance on reason nor the exclusive reliance on imagination can produce the art that the modern age deserves: "What is pure art according to the modern idea? It is to create a suggestive magic, containing at the same time the object

69. "Salon de 1846," 112, 162.

72. Edouard Manet. *Femme en Costume de Voyage,* 1880

and the subject, the world external to the artist and the artist himself."[70]
This text sums up the sources of Manet's achievement to perfection.

Baudelaire's writings on art read like a prescient analysis of Manet's
character and catalogue of Manet's work. Like Baudelaire's ideal modern artist, Manet responded intensely to the colors and shapes of daily
existence. He was Baudelaire's *flâneur* with a sketchbook. "With Manet," Antonin Proust reports, "the eye played such a prominent part
that Paris has never known such a stroller—*flâneur*—or a stroller strolling more usefully." Manet's sketches bear him out [72]. When the
temperature or the light impeded work in the studio, Manet and Proust
would "take off," to walk the boulevards, and there Manet would "draw
in his sketchbook a nothing, a profile, a hat, in a word, a fugitive impression."[71] And, unlike the Academic painters, Manet would retain the
vitality of his sketches in his paintings.

During the 1850s and 1860s—decisive years for the growth of Manet's art—the vitality of Paris and the vitality of Manet were perfectly

70. "L'Art philosophique," *L'Art romantique,* 119.
71. Proust, *Manet,* 29. In his novel about a modern painter *L'Œuvre* (1886), Zola
describes him, on the first page, as *"artiste flâneur, amoureux du Paris nocturne."*

matched. These were the decades when Haussmann, seconded by Napoleon III, transformed Paris from an unsalubrious and stinking warren of crooked streets, congested slums, and open sewers into a showplace of wide boulevards, generous parks, and healthy plumbing. Haussmann found Paris medieval; he left it modern [73]. The activity he generated was vertiginous. Between 1850 and 1870, the population of Paris nearly doubled while at the same time the crowding of houses and streets markedly diminished; in the 1860s, the reconstruction of Paris occupied one in every five of its working population. "Let no one be afraid to make things too beautiful, too rich, too vast," wrote Théophile Gautier about the projected new opera house early in 1861. "Paris is in process of growing, and God knows where it will stop. The monument that is adequate today will tomorrow appear small, mean, poverty-stricken. Let us think of this prodigious future and build, with stone, marble, brass, iron, and gold, without saving on space, a colossal theatre."[72]

Manet strolled through this city during these dramatic years watching the demolition of slums, the cutting of boulevards, the planting of parks [74]; the process itself, with its enormous élan and unprecedented speed, was as exhilarating to his imagination as the results—sometimes, in fact, more exhilarating since some of the results, like Garnier's Opéra, were rather disappointing [75]. The *boulevardier* of Manet's youth was something of an adventurer: before Haussmann began to clear away the thousands of obstructions that impeded circulation, Paris was a maze aspiring to be a labyrinth. Few Parisians ventured out of their districts; they were born, grew up, worked, and died, within a confined circle of a few streets. If, by the 1860s, it was easier and safer to walk long distances across the changing city the practice remained the distinguishing mark of the *flâneur*.

The *flâneur* was more than a stroller in an urban landscape; he was engaged in a stylized activity appropriate to Baudelaire's superb dandy. It involved alert promenading, social encounters, visits to favorite parks and certain cafés. But while Manet shared in the easy sociability that men of the world then cherished, strolling meant something more to him. It supplied material for his pencil. Many of his drawings, etchings, and paintings explicitly record what he saw; they are, in addition to being great art, superior reportage. His *La Musique aux Tuileries* [see 85], first exhibited in 1863, informally collects his friends and acquaintances at a fashionable spot not far from the Emperor's palace.[73] His *Ballet Espagnol* [76], painted in 1862, immortalizes the Paris engagement of a popular Spanish ballet troupe. His lithograph of the same

72. Quoted in A. Tabarant, *La vie artistique au temps de Baudelaire* (1932), 321.
73. See Sandblad, *Manet: Three Studies,* 19. In my account of Paris in these years, I have depended on the scholarly treatment of David H. Pinkney, *Napoleon III and the Rebuilding of Paris* (1958).

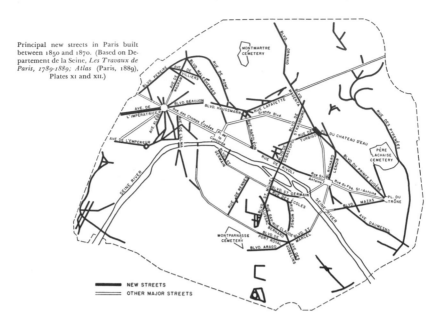

Principal new streets in Paris built between 1850 and 1870. (Based on Departement de la Seine, *Les Travaux de Paris, 1789-1889; Atlas* (Paris, 1889), Plates XI and XII.)

73. Principal new streets in Paris built between 1850 and 1870

74. Edouard Manet. *Rue de Berne*, 1878

75. Charles Garnier. *Opera House, Paris,* 1861–1875

year, *Le Ballon* [77], takes for its subject a popular and thoroughly modern entertainment.[74] His *The Battle Between the "Kearsage" and the "Alabama"* [78] is first cousin to a journalist's photograph posed after the event with real materials: Manet did not actually watch the battle between the Union corvette *Kearsage* and the Confederate ship *Alabama* off Cherbourg but went to Boulogne shortly after the encounter to see the victorious *Kearsage* at anchor. His *The Execution of Maximilian of Mexico* [64] occupied Manet as soon as he heard, early in the summer of 1867, that the hapless Emperor had been shot. His last major canvas, the *Bar at the Folies-Bergères* [79], painted from sketches the ailing Manet had made on the spot, immortalizes one of the new pleasure palaces of Haussmann's city; it had been opened as recently as 1869. The Folies-Bergères was a favorite place for watching acrobats, drinking champagne, and picking up girls. If the sensual delights it advertised have a very long history, its style of procuring them was unmistakably modern.

This catalogue gives only the most superficial account of Manet's commitment to the contemporary. His paintings of top-hatted Parisians, with their nervous line, flat black planes, and irresistible informal-

74. See Harris, *Manet: Graphic Works,* 83.

76. Edouard Manet. *Ballet Espagñol*, 1862

77. Edouard Manet. *Le Ballon*, 1862

78. Edouard Manet. *Battle between the "Kearsarge" and the "Alabama," 1864*

79. Edouard Manet, *Bar at the Folies-Bergères,* 1881

80. Edouard Manet. *At the
Café*, 1878

ity, answer Baudelaire's call for artistic attention to that modern cloak,
the frock coat.[75] His lovingly observed scenes of restaurants and bars
breathe an atmosphere of unbuttoned conviviality, of men and women
on the town, intent on their drink, their pipe, their amorous plans [80].
His portraits of poets and politicians offer a small gallery of contemporary heroes: a slouching Mallarmé rather abstractedly smoking his cigar
[81], a stern Clemenceau firmly folding his arms [82]—modern men in
modern poses. In fact, the manner in which Manet often posed or
captured his subjects reinforces his essential modernity: the casual,
negligent Berthe Morisot on a sofa [83],[76] or the equally casual George
Moore musing in a cafe [84], owe in their postures nothing to tradition.
And when Manet the reporter does quote from the classics, his witty
double vision underscores not his debt but his self-confidence: *La
Musique aux Tuileries* [85] is a loose paraphrase of what he thought was
a Velasquez, *The Little Cavaliers* [86], in which he believed Velasquez
had portrayed himself and his artist friends. Like its model, *La Musique
aux Tuileries* is a group portrait: it includes Manet himself, Baudelaire,

75. See pp. 83–86. Hanson has some interesting comments on Manet's "new and
personal" handling of black. *Edouard Manet*, 25.
76. Interestingly enough, the poet Théodore de Banville thought the painting particularly modern. (See Sandra Orienti, ed., *The Complete Paintings of Manet* [1967], 99.)

81. Edouard Manet. *Portrait of Mallarmé,* 1876

82. Edouard Manet. *Portrait of Clemenceau,* 1879

83. Edouard Manet. *Le Repos*
(Portrait of Berthe Morisot),
1870–1871

84. Edouard Manet. *George
Moore (au Café)*, ca. 1879

85. Edouard Manet. *La Musique aux Tuileries,* 1860

86. Attributed to Velazquez. *The Little Cavaliers*

87. Edouard Manet. *Rue Mosnier, Paris, Decorated with Flags on June 30, 1878,*
1878

Gautier, Offenbach, and other accomplished *boulevardiers.* Clearly,
Manet thought his own and his friends' faces worthy of being immortal-
ized in the manner of the great tradition.

These, then, were some of the pictorial precipitates of Manet's strolls
in Paris, a picture gallery of modern life observed with affection and
transcribed without pathos. Not even the cripple who looms so prominently in Manet's painting of the flag-bedecked rue Mosnier imposes
pathos on it in any way [87]. It was not proper for a dandy to be pathetic.
Nor was it proper to be lubricious; Manet's eroticism is frank and relatively uncomplicated. Equally remote from the brutal perversity of
Félicien Rops, the paralyzing anxiety of Edvard Munch [12], or the sly
suggestiveness of Gérôme [55], Manet did few nudes after his early
Olympia, but those he did are tributes to the flesh. They are (at least
for male viewers) sexual beings, unashamed of their attributes and
unambiguous in their appeal [88]. One of Manet's last masterpieces,
Chez le père Lathuille [89], is subtler in its sensuality than his nudes but
similar in its erotic honesty. The protagonists are at lunch in an outdoor
restaurant, bathed in Impressionist daylight. The young man's ardent
gaze and the young woman's ambiguous expression invite the viewer
to speculate on the outcome of this little drama of seduction. The

88. Edouard Manet. *Blonde Nude*, 1878

89. Edouard Manet. *Chez le Père Lathuille*, 1879

homely details on the table and the impassive waiter in the background emphasize that Manet is here deliberately immortalizing a most ordinary moment in the lives of two most ordinary people. When he showed the painting at the Salon of 1880, the critics by and large detested it and what they detested was its modernity: its "untrue" colors and its refusal to lend an amorous scene the distance of history, the detachment of humor, or the sedative of refinement. Huysmans, whose taste was nothing if not unpredictable, voiced his dissent from the general disapproval: the painting exemplified the modernism he was seeking in art. Huysmans was right, but then the modern view of the erotic was still the privilege of a restricted avant-garde. In 1877, Manet had submitted the painting of a courtesan dressing in the presence of her admirer, and the nervous jury had first accepted, then refused to hang, this immodest canvas [90]. Manet, we cannot doubt, was a proper bourgeois, but in his treatment of the sensual we glimpse, not for the first time, a certain heroic dimension.

The principal component in Manet's modernity was his emphatic acceptance of the contemporary world. His daylight vision of the erotic was one prominent instance of this acceptance; his positive view of the machine was another, and he embodied that view in one of his greatest paintings, *The Railroad* [91]. In 1867, as we know, Couture had argued that the locomotive was worth painting and insisted that previous efforts to paint it had been failures: "that strange and mysterious power which hides a volcano in its flanks; that monster in bronze carapace and snout of fire which devours space" needs "larger canvases" and "more robust talents" than have been devoted to it so far. "Believe me, the locomotive has not been done."[77] Perhaps he did not know Turner's *Rain, Steam and Speed,* or Inness' *Lackawanna Railroad,* but in any event, the best railroad painting lay ahead: Monet's famous series on the St. Lazare station dates from 1876 and 1877.

Emotionally, even geographically, Manet's *The Railroad* belongs to this series; it reads like a response to the challenge that his old teacher had thrown out, or to Théophile Gautier's paean to the railroad stations as "the new cathedrals of humanity."[78] The painting is the subtlest of tributes to the locomotive since no locomotive appears in it; all we see is its product: steam. *The Railroad* is the record of a response to the machine which is representative of Manet's response to his culture. Exhibited at the Salon of 1874, it called forth comments and cartoons as hostile as those that had greeted Manet's scandalous pictures of the

77. Couture, *Méthode et entretiens d'atelier,* 255.
78. Quoted in Phoebe Pool, *Impressionism* (1967), 161.

90. Edouard Manet. *Nana,*
1877

early 1860s. One prominent critic, Ernest Duvergier de Hauranne,
suggested that despite the "innovations" Manet had introduced, he was
"an essentially bourgeois painter," perhaps the "most profoundly bourgeois of all the contemporary painters who have succeeded in stirring
up a little excitement on their own account." Manet, bourgeois painter,
and his allies, he wrote, lacked all capacity to "recognize beauty," and
consequently they had "made a new ideal of triviality and platitude."[79]
Duvergier was both right and wrong. Manet was bourgeois. And
The Railroad does represent a new ideal, though not of triviality
and platitude. It is an urban, industrial ideal: I think it is not extravagant to read this painting as Manet's manifesto in behalf of
modernity. The train that has puffed out all this steam has just
passed by in the cut below on its way to the tunnel leading to the
Gare St. Lazare. Through the grating and around the edges of steam
we glimpse Paris; the scene, though sunny with green trees and
purple grapes, is unmistakably urban. The figures form a family in
color and in feeling, but Manet organizes the composition with the
grating, which boldly stretches across the canvas like an anticipation
of Mondrian, and even more, with the steam. The steam is the hero
—the modern hero—of this painting.

79. In the *Revue des deux mondes,* quoted in Hamilton, *Manet and His Critics,* 179.

91. Edouard Manet. *The Railroad,* 1873

Execution matches intention. Though more carefully finished than some of his marines and his self-portrait, Manet's *The Railroad* employs his bright late palette and his customary dash: he has sketched in the sleeping puppy with a few broad strokes, and indicated the still life of grapes, the low parapet, the neglected book, and the urban scenery in the background with supreme sureness and Impressionist rapidity. The painting, considered simply as painting, is a triumph of color as well as design: the blue on dress and apron, the spots of red on bonnet, fan and earrings, the shades of white on a variety of textures testify to the beauty that Manet could discover in this little scene. In manner as in matter, *The Railroad* is a poem about speed contemplated in tranquility.

I know of no nineteenth-century painting that celebrates modernity more unreservedly than this. The young woman, the little girl, and the little dog are a commentary on its pleasures and its possibilities. The puppy sleeps, oblivious to the noise, the smell, the smoke of the train. The girl is riveted to her spot; she is watching the passing train, possibly with interest or, more probably, with the calm indifference that habituation brings. The young woman sits like a monument to serenity, looking at the world with her clear dark eyes. The book she holds so casually and the grapes on the parapet are accessories testifying to the peaceful quality of this urban pastoral.

I am not imposing this interpretation on Manet. In his later years, he had a studio on rue Saint-Petersbourg and, as a visitor reports, the floor would shake as the trains went by on their way to St. Lazare, evidently without disturbing its tenant.[80] Manet, in fact, was a great admirer of the railroad and other modern inventions. In a much-quoted letter to the Prefect of the Seine, he proposed to decorate the Municipal Council Chamber of the new Hôtel de Ville with scenes from public and commercial life, including markets, railways, bridges, tunnels, race courses, and public gardens—a typical proposal to which, typically, he never got a reply. But he himself never wavered. Shortly before his death, he recalled that not long ago he had climbed onto a locomotive, next to the engineer and the stoker. "What a magnificent spectacle, these two men!" he exclaimed. And he promised himself, "When I am well again I'll take them as a subject for a painting."[81] It is not a painting he lived to paint. If he had, he would have made a companion piece to *The Railroad,* his tribute to "modern heroes." Manet the modernist found

80. See the account by the journalist Fervacques, quoted in Hamilton, *Manet and His Critics,* 173.

81. See Courthion and Cailler, *Portrait of Manet,* 11. On October 22, 1881, an official of the Compagnie des Chemins de fer de l'Ouest wrote to Manet granting him permission to "make studies in one of our depots of a locomotive with driver and stoker."

his values, and the principal impulses for his work, in the urban industrial society growing around him.

This definition of Manet's modernism suggests which forces principally shaped his art. And it suggests why the purely formal analysis of
his work misrepresents not only its effects but also its causes. Manet
simply does not fit into the interpretation of modernism that dominates
in our day. That interpretation sees a great transvaluation of values
beginning, roughly, with the Impressionists and ending, roughly, with
the Surrealists, as the impassioned protest of civilized artists and think-
ers against the mechanization, the ugliness, the rootlessness, the sheer
vulgarity of technological mass civilization. Modernism, in this view, is
the hatred of the modern world, the rebellion of culture against culture.
Its name is the Waste Land; its dominant emotions are alienation, ambivalence, and anxiety; its principal victims the illusions of liberalism;
and its chief adversaries those supreme representatives of the genteel
age, the bourgeois. Its chosen language is subtle, suggestive, esoteric,
deliberately difficult; the incoherence of Expressionist drama, the im-
pudence of Dadaist anti-art, and the hermeticism of abstract painting
all participate in the modern revolt of despair. Only a self-deluded
optimist could find relevance, let alone delight, in traditional styles, or
interpret the modern artist's rejection of nature and form as a sign of
independence. The riot of modern subjectivity is a symptom of dreadful
freedom, the outcry of lost men in an incomprehensible world in which
standards have decayed and reason has abandoned its claim to order the
chaos of experience. From this perspective, Manet's quarrel with
Academicism makes him a great forerunner in that somber procession,
the makers of modernism, a pioneer on the long trek to a world in
which self is divided from its culture and the artist from his public.
But the modernist movement was not only an expression of hostility.
It was also an act of affirmation. Sometimes, in fact often, it was cheerful.
Many among the avant-garde—including, as we know, Manet's friends
and biographers—chose to remember the bitterness of rejection and to
forget the exhilaration of making things new. Unfortunately, historians
have taken their intemperate, often self-serving reminiscences as serious appraisals rather than partisan pleas. In truth, modernism was as
much the heir as the adversary of liberalism, as much the climax as the
nemesis of bourgeois life. The modern metropolis, the most monumental witness to technological civilization, served modernists as an ambiguous metaphor: for Manet's friend Baudelaire as for his contemporary Dostoevsky, it exercised a fascination that was far from simple
horror. Science and technology were sources of confidence quite as
much as for dismay. Realism and Impressionism, with their loyalty to

surfaces and the outside world, were as modern in their sources, their intentions, and their consequences as Symbolism and Expressionism, which practically abandoned the object for the exploration of inner states. Not all those who ventured into the dark realms of the irrational, the unconscious, the perverse did so for the sake of celebrating these forces; Sigmund Freud, the Columbus of unreason, was a thoroughgoing rationalist, a nineteenth-century positivist, only better. The modern temper, our style of seeing, feeling, and thinking, emerged from the divergence and confluence of two streams, the conflicts and compromises between two parties.

Most modernists opted for one party or the other: Seurat worshiped science, Gauguin detested it; Zola wanted to obey nature, Wilde to tame it. But some few masters compelled the divergent directions of modernism into a single order. Manet was one of these. He departed from Academic finish and middle-class gentility without despising the Salons or bourgeois respectability. He chose contemporary themes without abandoning the great tradition. He found pictorial inspiration in the works of science without minimizing the claims of art. His notorious departures from classical verisimilitude—his eccentric colors and equally eccentric perspective—were not steps toward Expressionism or Abstraction; his work was a synthesis that Baudelaire had anticipated by his definition of modern art as an "evocative magic" that gives equal attention to "the object and the subject," to the "world external to the artist and the artist himself." The quality of Manet's work stems from his capacity to synthesize formal and substantive elements into immortal moments of beauty.

The recognition of Manet's synthetic power gives us access to the sources of his art. In the course of this essay I have called Manet a personal painter, a self-aware artist, and a painter of modern life. These names are shorthand designations for the major strands—person, craft, and culture—in the texture of cause. Each worked in Manet to produce a series of unique historical events, a Manet drawing, etching, watercolor, or painting. It was Manet's character, that mixture of independence and conformity, that enabled him to select from the past what most suited his talent, and to seek the success that others had defined as success, though on his own terms. It was his craft that gave him his technique and his problems. Nothing is easier than to trace these two causal elements in all his work. Yet in the end culture bulks largest. It was a culture that produced both the bourgeois as philistine and the bourgeois as hero; mediated through his private and artistic milieu, it offered Manet just enough resistance and just enough encouragement to give him the incentive for his own style and a wealth of materials on which to exercise his gifts. It is a commonplace to say of great artists—

especially of those who, like Manet, suffered neglect and ridicule—that they were ahead of their time. But Manet was in his time; he was the painter that Gautier and Taine called for, the painter who (in Taine's words) represented the "moral temperature" of his age to perfection. Concluding a set of lectures to the Ecole des Beaux-Arts in 1864, Hippolyte Taine exhorted his listeners to follow Goethe's advice: "Fill your mind and heart, however large, with the ideas and sentiments of your age, and the work will follow."[82] This is what Manet did. His work is the fulfillment of the program he had laid down for himself in his youth, though interpreted in the most individualistic way. In being of his time and in painting what he saw, he acknowledged and asserted in his rich and varied work the primacy of culture.

82. Taine, *Lectures on Art,* tr. John Durand (1875), 165. Zola told his school friend Cézanne in an early letter: "In the artist there are two men, the poet and the workman. One is born a poet, one becomes a workman." Rewald, *Cézanne,* 17. He should have added a third dimension—the social being, the citizen.

THREE

Gropius: The Imperatives of Craft

1. The Cathedral of the Present

Walter Gropius earned his international reputation with his commitment to social principles. Society, of course, impinges on architecture at decisive points, and architecture responds to social pressures in the most visible way: court houses and churches, banks and prisons are only the most conspicuous memorials to its engagement with the world. Nor do private dwellings ever wholly escape the public dimension. Many seekers after shelter are admittedly undemanding: as aesthetic illiterates, they restrict their fantasies to domestic memories of their childhood and are satisfied with duplicating the tastes of their parents.[1] Most men's homes are their father's castle. Yet the most pathetic, most passive consumer, content as he may be with some nondescript apartment, monotonous development house, or cliché-ridden palace is touched, no matter how fleetingly, by the shaping hand of the architect.

Architecture, in short, is the most emphatically public of all the arts. But Gropius' work was anchored in culture far more firmly than this. It is striking but not accidental that his most enduring monument, the Bauhaus, should have been a school—a school, moreover, founded on the ground of a social philosophy [92]. The materials compel the historian of Gropius to begin his inquiries in the realm of cultural causes. It will emerge that he cannot end there.

While Gropius' career took its unmistakable political turn only after the end of World War I, it never suffered, or enjoyed, the dubious blessings of splendid isolation. The decade before 1914 saw an impassioned struggle for the soul of German design, and two of its critical dates, 1903 and 1907, conveniently match the terminal points in Gropius' architectural education. In 1903, the year that Gropius began his studies at the Technische Hochschule in Berlin, the architect Hermann Muthesius returned to Germany after seven years in England, a

---

1. Walter Gropius speaks of the *"visuelle Analphabetentum—visual illiteracy"* that afflicts the average modern man. "Tradition und Kontinuität in der Architektur" (1964), *Apollo in der Demokratie* (1967), 53.

92. Walter Gropius. *The Bauhaus,* Dessau, 1925–1926

prophet seeking honor in his own country. And in 1907, the year that Gropius left the Technische Hochschule in Munich, Muthesius moved from polemics to organization—or, perhaps better, to organization for the sake of polemics—by founding the *Deutsche Werkbund.* While Gropius was training himself to be an architect, his elders were conducting a debate unsurpassed in volume and vehemence. It was not lost on him.

Muthesius, public servant and skillful publicist as well as trained architect [93], had been attached to the London embassy with the assignment of studying English housing. While the English in those closing years of the nineteenth century admired the Germans' way of designing their social services, the Germans in return admired the English way of designing their domestic environment. Muthesius was singularly fortunate in the timing of his English investigations: he witnessed the vocal, exhilarating rebellion against the oppressive comfort, stifling decor, and unapologetic eclecticism that had dominated Victorian design for decades [94]. The passionate denunciations that Ruskin and Morris had launched against the hideousness of their urban world lived on in Voysey's intense search for the clean English vernacular [95] and Lethaby's energetic denunciations of inauthenticity. English designers were not free from incoherence or extravagance in their pronouncements—designers, English or otherwise, rarely are. But foreign visitors

93. Hermann Muthesius. *Haus Freudenberg*, Berlin–Nikolassee, 1907–1908

94. Gilbert Scott, *St. Pancras Hotel*, London, 1865

95. Charles Voysey, *"Broadleys" on Lake Windemere*, 1898

found English practice, even more than English programs, an enviable and eminently portable model, and, like other Continental explorers of the English aesthetic landscape, Muthesius was bursting to impart the good news he had learned.[2] His shibboleth was *Sachlichkeit*, design stripped of timid historicism and gratuitous ornamentation—in short, functionalism.[3]

Muthesius perceived his task to be a "struggle against existing conditions."[4] Not unexpectedly, "existing conditions" defended themselves, and their opposition, in turn, moved Muthesius to join forces with likeminded manufacturers, designers, artisans and educators to construct a forum for his ideas. The *Werkbund*, an association devoted to the "ennoblement" of design through the "collaboration of art, indus-

2. "It was as if Spring had come all of a sudden," the Belgian designer Henry van de Velde said about C. F. A. Voysey's wallpapers. Quoted in Nikolaus Pevsner, *Pioneers of Modern Design from William Morris to Walter Gropius* (rev. ed. 1960), 148.

3. See Walter Gropius, *The New Architecture and the Bauhaus*, tr. P. Morton Shand (ed. 1965), 23. Mrs. Gropius has noted that "Gropius never liked the term functionalism the interpretation of which seemed too narrow and rigid to him, and the word was taboo in the Bauhaus." Ise Gropius to Peter Gay, July 1, 1974.

4. "Die Bedeutung des Kunstgewerbes," (1907), in Julius Posener, ed., *Anfänge des Funktionalismus: Von Arts and Crafts zum Deutschen Werkbund* (1964), 180.

try, and artisanship"[5] became that forum. Its members saw their age as, indisputably, an age of quantity; the point was to endow quantity with quality. The best means at their command was, as it were, to democratize German aesthetics, to lavish even-handed attention on all elements of the man-made environment. In the process, they generated a controversy that soon reached down to fundamentals of modern life: the nature of work, the potentialities of the machine, the disharmonies of urban existence. The young Gropius swam in a sea of words, many of them portentous, even pretentious words, which bestowed on mundane objects the unaccustomed stature of a metaphysical problem.

Gropius witnessed this solemn self-searching from a privileged vantage point: from 1907 to 1910, he worked in the atelier that the prominent architect Peter Behrens had just established in Berlin. Behrens was a one-man Werkbund. Talented, versatile, and articulate, he taught design, gave speeches, drafted projects, and built whatever came his way. In 1907, the year he settled in Berlin, he enlarged his already impressive scope by joining Emil Rathenau's Allgemeine Elektrizitäts-Gesellschaft, Germany's largest supplier of electrical equipment, as its artistic advisor [see 149, 150]. In making Behrens *künstlerischer Beirat* to the A.E.G., Rathenau, famous father of a more famous son, made a most imaginative appointment; it exemplified the collaboration between art, craft, and industry for whose sake the Werkbund was being launched.[6]

By 1910, when Gropius set up his own office in Berlin, he had the first "presentiment" of his future social philosophy, his position in the great debate. Later he remembered how uneasy he had been with the general denial of "naked facts," how much he had disliked seeing architects restrict their practice to "the small circle of the affluent." All too few of his fellows seemed responsive to the requirements of modern industry and modern transport; by pandering to the rich, they labored to secure for themselves that comfortable title, "arbiter of good taste." Intense and critical, Gropius found the architectural atmosphere around him polluted by mendacity and snobbery. The need, at least to him, was plain: if architects really wanted to "develop a genuine, historically valid form of expression" they would have to "revolutionize the visual education of the young" and at the same time make intensive studies of mass-production in housing. "Even before World War I," Gropius recalled, "I and some other architects grew alarmed to see that, more and more, the members of our profession were putting them-

5. "Satzung," paragraph 2, in *Die Durchgeistigung der deutschen Arbeit, Jahrbuch des deutschen Werkbundes, 1912* (1912), not paginated.
6. It is less likely that Rathenau himself was responsible for the invitation than the director of his enterprises, Paul Jordan.

selves into a straitjacket."[7] From the outset of his career, rather in the style of Manet, Gropius saw himself as liberator.

A memorandum that Gropius submitted to Emil Rathenau in 1910 supports this retrospect; his social conscience was alert even before the war, which would give it a new intensity and larger assignments. Gropius criticized speculative builders for turning out housing at once shoddy and hideous; the huckstering clamor of commercialism, he complained, entailed neglect of architectural fundamentals and a corresponding excess in externals: "Overloading and false romanticism in place of good proportions and practical simplicity have, for all purposes, become the tendency of our age." He saw one way back to "quality and style": an organization that would apply industrial techniques to the building trade. Mass production had proved beneficial in combining the "highest quality of raw materials and labor" with "low prices"; to treat houses as industrial products would be to employ technology in the service of cultural ends. A return to handicraft, Gropius concluded, was impracticable, in fact unthinkable; the road to the future lay in the intelligent application of prefabrication and standardization.[8]

In Gropius' proposal to import "industrial simplification" into architecture we seem to hear the Gropius familiar from the textbooks—the utilitarian, the functionalist. In fact, this memorandum of 1910 is strikingly prescient; it adumbrates the aesthetic and social convictions that would dominate the Bauhaus from the early 1920s on, once it had found its direction. And it is an instructive document for its own time as well; it displays the beginning architect joining the side of the moderns in the battle over German design.

Yet in this very memorandum, in which he appears as the cool engineer, Gropius also sounded a different, less modern note. In tune with most German cultural historians, educators, and philosophers, he professed himself dismayed at the disharmony—*Zerrissenheit*—of his age, and lamented its incapacity to develop its own appropriate style— *Zeitstil*. It has become a cliché to say that a functionalist is a repressed Romantic. Gropius certainly had his moments, early and late, when he advocated the very views he is famous for detesting. The noisy debate between Expressionists and rationalists, between adversaries and advocates of the machine, between champions of the solitary genius and those of the anonymous designer—in short, between ancients and mod-

7. "Tradition und Kontinuität in der Architektur," *Apollo*, 52.

8. The memorandum is partially reprinted in Hans M. Wingler, ed., *Das Bauhaus: 1919–1933, Weimar Dessau Berlin* (1962), 26–27. From the beginning, Mrs. Gropius rightly notes, "The main difference between Gropius' prefabrication proposal and all later ones made in different countries, was the fact that he did not want to prefabricate *whole* houses but *parts*, so that all deadly monotony would be avoided by combining an infinite variety of house types." Ise Gropius to Peter Gay, July 1, 1974.

erns—was in fact anything but the clear-cut combat that the spectacle of public discord made it appear. It was often a civil war in the soul of one designer, a private quarrel in which no position was pure and no victory permanent. The rise of the machine and the attendant emergence of mass production had raised complex problems to which only the simpleminded would offer a simple solution. Hence the nostalgic interludes in Gropius' career as teacher and polemicist are not alien intrusions, momentary aberrations, or casual experiments: they are part of his history as a German architect.

Like Gropius, others in the *Werkbund* flavored their assessments of modern *Zivilisation* with a dash of yearning for that picturesque, traditional Germany when men had lived companionably in accepted hierarchies, when architect, craftsman, and builder had still been one person, when art had not yet been torn from utility. That this past was largely imaginary did not lessen its appeal. The cheery medievalism that Richard Wagner had conjured up for his *Meistersinger,* the small-town concord that warmed the poignant tales of Wilhelm Raabe, idealized a past that had never existed to deprecate a present that was all too real. The hunger for wholeness that would mark, and distort, social perceptions and political judgment during the Weimar Republic already plagued many thoughtful, troubled Germans before the World War.[9] Cultural nostalgia, of course, never swamped the *Werkbund;* the organization had, after all, been formed to face rather than to deny technology. But nostalgia invaded the deliberations even of this self-consciously modern organization.

It is fair to add that when Gropius struck this fashionable note of discontent and regret he did so with reasonable restraint.[10] In an essay he wrote in 1914 for the *Jahrbuch* of the *Werkbund*, Gropius begins like the other critics of "mass civilization": he denounces "crass materialism" and deplores, in familiar language, the "splintering" of cultural

9. See Peter Gay, *Weimar Culture: The Outsider as Insider* (1968), ch. VI. And see pp. 126–129.

10. Gropius, too, saw the "artisan" as the "typical bearer of medieval culture," who had been, "in one person, technician, artist, and tradesman." See "Der architekt als organisator der modernen bauwirtschaft und seine forderung an die industrie" (1927); Gropius Papers, Ordner 18/2. It is significant that in 1911, speaking to the *Werkbund,* Muthesius invoked Julius Langbehn's antirationalist diatribe, *Rembrandt als Erzieher,* which had enjoyed an immense popularity in the 1890s and continued to be widely read. Muthesius, to be sure, said nothing of Langbehn's bloodthirsty anti-Semitism; rather, he cited the book for its defense of "old truths," for its championship of artistic against scientific culture, and for its insistence that "rational activity alone could neither satisfy man, nor be the ultimate realization of his yearnings." "Wo Stehen Wir?," *Durchgeistigung der deutschen Arbeit, Jahrbuch des Deutschen Werkbundes, 1912,* 14–15. In this benign reading, Langbehn the antimodern chauvinist becomes the prophet for a new aesthetic age. This was not the only curious political coupling for which the *Werkbund* provided a genial forum.

life. In this essay as in others Gropius does not hesitate to use that vague
and popular word *Einheitlichkeit*—more than unity and less than uni-
formity—to characterize the quality that contemporary German culture most conspicuously lacks. But while Gropius' perception of the
modern malady resembled the perception that other cultivated com-
plainers were retailing in these years, his prescription for its cure differed decisively. For Gropius, the "gigantic tasks" that industry and
transport were imposing on society were in themselves evidence of an
"immense social will." And the designs of modern automobiles, railways, and steamships, he suggests, foreshadowed the emergence of a
new "development of form."[11] Like Behrens, Gropius found the sales-
men of the past less than persuasive. He did not see the machine as the
enemy; he saw it, rather, as a potent and two-edged instrument which
had torn open wounds that it alone could heal. In his most depressed
or most exalted moments Gropius did not turn his back on technology.
At worst the machine was a necessary evil with which modern man
must learn to live; at best it was the diligent servant of the good life.

Gropius' discriminating appraisal of technological civilization was his
own, but others too groped toward the complexity of the issues. The
much-discussed debate over standardization that divided, and almost
destroyed, the *Werkbund* in 1914 was a famous, acrimonious, but, in
the end, inconclusive fight.[12] The most outspoken advocate of standard-
ized production—*Typisierung*—was, as always, Muthesius, but he was
at the same time a self-proclaimed champion of spirituality. The most
outspoken advocate of artistic individuality was van de Velde who, for
all his abiding suspicion of industry, did not reject modern materials or
techniques. And, to compound complexity, Gropius, who had defended
mass production for several years, found himself in van de Velde's
camp. If anything, Gropius was angrier at Muthesius' dogmatic proposals than van de Velde himself, and agitated for secession from the
Werkbund should Muthesius' views prevail.

Gropius' vehemence had a personal component: he did not like Muthesius and he did like van de Velde. If Gropius and van de Velde
ultimately diverged in the directions of their work [96, 97], they retained the liveliest admiration for one another.[13] Van de Velde was a

11. Gropius, "Der Stilbildende Wert Industrieller Bauformen," *Der Verkehr, Jahrbuch
des Deutschen Werkbundes, 1914* (1914), 29–32.

12. I dissent here from the summary account of the Cologne debate offered by Nikolaus
Pevsner, who speaks of "the victory of Muthesius." *The Sources of Modern Architecture
and Design* (1968), 179.

13. For the situation in 1914, see Marcel Franciscono, *Walter Gropius and the Creation
of the Bauhaus in Weimar: The Ideals and Artistic Theories of Its Founding Years* (1971),
ch. 2; esp. p. 77. As late as 1924, van de Velde vigorously defended the "radicalism" of
Gropius' Bauhaus in a formal statement to the provincial minister at Weimar, D. Hart-

96. Walter Gropius with Adolf Meyer, *Deutscher Werkbund Exposition.* Cologne, 1914.

97. Henry van de Velde. *Werkbundtheater,* Cologne, 1914

professed Utopian, Gropius a professed realist. But both were artists, and the polarity of their positions was more rhetorical than real: van de Velde mixed a good measure of realism into his aesthetic fantasies, while Gropius, for all his commitment to utility, paid consistent tribute to artistic inspiration. It is not enough to say that architecture makes strange bed-fellows; the mutual esteem of the last great practitioner of Art Nouveau and the future apostle of functionalism was neither merely casual nor simply tactical. Gropius' rationalism was not hostile to deeper impulses. His alliance with van de Velde in 1914, therefore, is an instructive clue: it helps partially to explain, in advance, the cheerful coexistence of craft, art, and mechanization in the Bauhaus that has baffled so many observers; and it displays different, but far from incompatible, aspects in the character of its founder.

The *Deutsche Werkbund* was strenuously nonpartisan, an attitude which invites the Marxist gloss that it was objectively conformist. Its ideal of collaboration between art and industry amounted in practice to the patronage of artists by industrialists. Muthesius and his supporters liked to picture their struggle for good design as the assault of an avant-garde on an entrenched establishment; this is not the first time, nor the last, that an ascendant party has recognized the tactical value of presenting itself as a brave minority.[14] Actually, in the German high culture of these days supporters of quality and a new aesthetic held strategic spots: Karl Ernst Osthaus and Harry Graf Kessler were millionaires with a passion for art and a generous purse; they subsidized Behrens and van de Velde, innovative Expressionist artists, and little avant-garde magazines that would have gone under without their support. Bruno Paul, the imaginative designer of machine-made furniture, was appointed director of the Gewerbeschule in Berlin in 1907; Alfred Lichtwark, one of the founders of the *Werkbund*, directed the museum in Hamburg. Muthesius and his fellow-reformers entered combat with far better chances of victory than they found it prudent to admit.

The pressure for good design was not all quality for quality's sake. The A.E.G. was only one of many industrial firms to employ advanced designers in the interest of higher sales as well as higher prestige. The leaders of the *Werkbund*, those mortal enemies of crass commercial-

---

mann; see his letter of October 16, 1924, Gropius Papers, Ordner 2/24–28.

On February 6, 1964, in a conversation with Stanford Owen Anderson, Gropius referred to himself as the "enfant terrible" in the confrontation of 1914; he saw Muthesius' championing of *Typisierung* as a symptom of Muthesius' total lack of artistic feeling. Anderson, "Peter Behrens and the New Architecture of Germany, 1900–1917," Columbia University dissertation (1968), 411.

14. For similar useful distortions of perception in the worlds of Manet and Mondrian, see above, p. 42, and below, p. 176.

ism, shamelessly employed crass commercial arguments to recruit support; they frankly conceded that the shoddiness of German industrial products reduced their appeal abroad, and that the purification of design was the prerequisite for the enlargement of markets.

This blatant, almost innocent, oscillation between spirituality and materialism characterizes much German culture of the time; it pervades the speeches of Wilhelm II quite as much as those at the *Werkbund*. The Emperor's call for a place in the sun conjured up fantasies not merely of German flags flying but also of German cash registers ringing.[15] Not even Gropius wholly disdained the appeal to economic self-interest: "It has already become clear in practice," he wrote in 1913, "that it is shortsighted for the manufacturer to think he can save himself the expense of an artist. Leading big business has proved—and this is decisive—that in the long run it pays to care about the artistic value of its products, as well as about technical perfection and reasonable prices." Products as handsome as they are well-made and cheap will carry good taste to the masses; this will earn manufacturers "not merely a reputation for furthering cultivation, but pecuniary gain as well," a financial return which, Gropius a little naively explains, has as much significance in commercial life as does its missionary work in behalf of *Kultur*. Plainly, as van de Velde was quick to point out, the practical idealism of the *Werkbund* had its rapacious side.[16]

With its peculiar mixture of woolly philosophizing and hardheaded calculation, the *Werkbund* assiduously avoided any kind of social analysis. Gropius in 1910 had come closer than most—closer than he himself was to come for years—to identifying the agents of modern ugliness by pointing at speculators and entrepreneurs as profiteers in bad taste. Rudimentary as this was, it was yet rare in his circles. Apart from chauvinistic claims for the virtues of the German character and the need for German world power that dotted the speeches of Muthesius, the speakers in the *Werkbund* confined their politics to what they called cultural politics—*Kulturpolitik*.

15. One of the dogmatic *"Leitsätze"* that Muthesius presented to the Werkbund Congress at Cologne in 1914 read: "The world will call for our products only when they speak with convincing stylistic expression." His ten points are reproduced in Posener, *Anfänge des Funktionalismus,* 205.

16. Gropius, "Die Entwicklung moderner Industriebaukunst," *Die Kunst in Industrie und Handel, Jahrbuch des Deutschen Werkbundes 1913* (1913), 18. In the pointed counter-theses that he offered to Muthesius' *"Leitsätze"* at the Congress of 1914, van de Velde said flatly: "Never has anything good or magnificent been created from sheer concern with exports." And he stigmatized the self-serving arguments of his opponents as the "opportunism" of industrial and business interests intent only on "bringing in the harvest at last." See Henry van de Velde, *Geschichte meines Lebens,* ed. and tr. Hans Curjel (1962), 364–368. Since Gropius and van de Velde remained friends through it all, van de Velde must have taken Gropius' excursion into commercialism as merely marginal.

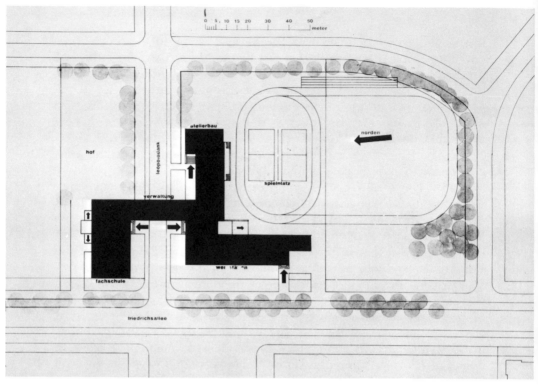

98. Walter Gropius. *The Bauhaus*, plan, Dessau, 1925–1926

The war changed all this, at least for Gropius. "The full consciousness of my responsibility as an architect," he said later, "came to me as a result of the First World War, during which my theoretical premises first took shape." The "violent eruption," he noted with commendable exaggeration, made "every thinking man" feel "the necessity for an intellectual change of front." Each, he added, still exaggerating, "each in his own particular sphere aspired to help in bridging the disastrous gulf between reality and idealism. It was then that the immensity of the mission of the architect of my own generation first dawned on me."[17] What the shock of the war began the shock of the revolution completed. On furlough from the Italian front in the Fall of 1918, Gropius witnessed the outbreak of the November Revolution and the assaults of crowds on German officers. They confirmed and clarified his earlier ideas: "This is more than just a lost war," he told himself. "A world has come to an end. We must seek a radical solution to our problems."[18] Gropius' radical solution was the Bauhaus.

17. *The Scope of Total Architecture* (ed. 1962), 19.
18. Gropius to James Marston Fitch in conversation. See Gay, *Weimar Culture*, 9.

99. Wassily Kandinsky. *Abstraction*, ca. 1925

100. Paul Klee. *Red-Green Steps*, 1921

101. Lyonel Feininger. *Church in the Woods, II*, 1921

I have no intention of rehearsing once again the brilliant history of the Bauhaus, its meteoric career, its solid achievement, its life after death. Its history *is* impressive. The Bauhaus persuaded designers to adopt a new, clean vocabulary in lamps, in chairs [see 123], in typography; it changed the face of modern architecture with its exhibition houses and with that model of modernity, the Dessau Bauhaus of 1926 [98]; it propagated its views with enthusiastic shows and striking pamphlets; it earned the gratitude of modern art by appointing artists like Vasily Kandinsky, Paul Klee, Lyonel Feininger [99, 100, 101], Josef

Albers, László Moholy-Nagy, and others to its staff; it undertook an experiment in aesthetic education unprecedented in its imaginative sense for the whole person. Its poignantly short life span and its principal dates parallel the course of the Weimar Republic, of which it was a famous manifestation and to which it remains an unforgettable monument. Founded in early 1919, half a year after the flight of the German Emperor and half a year before the adoption of a republican constitution [102], it moved in 1925 from the obstructiveness of the city of Weimar to the fostering environment of Dessau at a time when the republic seemed to be enjoying a measure of stability [103]; it moved to Berlin in 1932, to constricted quarters, in the midst of the Depression; and it was compelled to close in the Summer of 1933 some months after Hitler had come to power. Possibly the most influential school of design since men began to teach design, the Bauhaus has enormous intrinsic importance. But my assignment here is to exploit the Bauhaus, not to praise it, to trace the contours of the causes that made Gropius. And therefore since Gropius overcame daunting obstacles to make his Bauhaus into the lengthened shadow of himself, the school he founded and directed supplies dependable clues to the impulses that drove him on. That it was never a one-man show makes it no less instructive, for this, too, reflects his impulses, which were consistently antiauthoritarian.

The particular moment of its founding is as critical for the meaning of the Bauhaus as the general ideas of its founder. The exalted tone of its first publications, the extravagant hopes and missionary fervor of its early days, the prominence of mystics on its staff, and its programmatic efforts to become a way of life for masters and pupils alike were all sensitive responses to the political upheavals, the institutional disorder, and the spiritual effervescence of republican Germany in its founding years. It is easy now, in hindsight, to deprecate the November Revolution as not very revolutionary, to point at the persistence of the old centers of power and the timidity of the new rulers. In late 1918 and early 1919 there were many, Gropius included, who saw these times, though burdened with disaster, as equally rich in possibilities; the end of empire fostered heady speculations about a radical renewal in political and social life.

It was this sense of potentialities that gave the fledgling Bauhaus its confidence in the face of low budgets, its resilience amidst abject poverty, its courage in confronting implacable opposition, its very capacity for survival. In 1923 when the Bauhaus first faced a wider public by mounting an ambitious exhibition, the masters' wives eloquently testified to the poverty of the Bauhaus, and to its high morale, by serving

102. Henry van de Velde. *School of Applied Arts*, Weimar, 1904

103. Walter Gropius. *The Bauhaus*, Dessau, 1925–1926

as charwomen. "The spirit," Gropius fondly remembered much later, "was simply excellent, and some of the informal activities, like our celebrations—the *Feste*—when someone would set a theme, like 'black and white,' or 'square,' were splendid occasions." The machinations of *völkische* political circles and of traditionalist architects threatened by innovations compelled Gropius and other Bauhaus masters to waste time in tedious and interminable correspondence; they had to refute slanders here, reply to newspaper libels there, and enlist support among patrons, politicians, artists everywhere. Looking back at this decade, Gropius later said in some discouragement: "I spent ninety percent of my time fighting off the right radicals, ten percent on design."[19] It was under the guns of hostility and the persistent threat of starvation that the Bauhaus revolutionized design and the teaching of design.

The unexpected and melodramatic collapse of Germany's Imperial regime infused Gropius with a sense of urgency he had not felt before. He shrewdly recognized that he could not expect whatever opportunities the fluid revolutionary situation might hold to fall into his open hands. It would not do only to stand and wait. Upon his discharge from the army, Gropius became a moving force in the *Arbeitsrat für Kunst*, founded late in November, 1918 to celebrate and consolidate the revolution. "I came here," Gropius wrote from Berlin on December 23, 1918, "in order to take part in the upheavals. The atmosphere is highly charged and we artists, too, must strike while the iron is hot."[20] The new artists' organization was earnestly, if rather imprecisely, radical; it dedicated itself to fostering and propagating an art worthy of the pure democratic polity of the future. As one of the "revolutionaries of the spirit," Gropius joined fellow enthusiasts to make all things new and beautiful. By late February, 1919, Gropius was chairman of the *Arbeitsrat*, and in early April, he succeeded in uniting its three sections— painters, sculptors, and architects—into a "unified circle of artists," who, he thought, in collaboration alone could do the necessary constructive work.[21]

In the same Spring, without severing his connection with the *Arbeitsrat*, Gropius realized the opportunity to put programs into practice. His long-drawn-out negotiations with the government of Saxony had finally

19. Walter Gropius to Peter Gay, see *Weimar Culture*, 100; Ise Gropius in conversation with Peter Gay, December 10, 1973; Gropius, "Der 'Baum des Lebens' und die 'Verkaufsspirale' " (1961), *Apollo*, 31.

20. Quoted in Wolfgang Pehnt, "Gropius the Romantic," *Art Bulletin* (September, 1971), 379.

21. For a careful chronology of events, see Franciscono, *Gropius and the Bauhaus*, Appendix D, esp. pp. 277–278.

brought results: merging an academy of art with a school for applied arts Gropius established the new Staatliche Bauhaus in Weimar. Whatever else he left behind in Berlin, he brought with him his pedagogic ambitions and his Utopian rhetoric. In April, 1919 he published the program of his new Bauhaus, fittingly prefacing it with a one-page manifesto; just as appropriately, Lyonel Feininger decorated the little pamphlet with a suggestive woodcut depicting a stylized Gothic structure lit by three stars which symbolized the sculptor, the painter, and the architect working together to build the secular cathedral of the future [104].

Gropius' manifesto was resonant and appealing; it would also prove rather confusing. It called for the reuniting of design and craftsmanship, artisan and artist, whom the "salon art" of the recent age had separated: "The artist," Gropius wrote, "is an exalted craftsman—*Der Künstler ist eine Steigerung des Handwerkers.*" Painter, sculptor and architect must all return to craftsmanship: "Let us then form a new *guild of craftsmen,* without the presumptuousness of class distinctions, which sought to raise an arrogant wall between artisans and artists! Let us together will, invent, create the new building of the future, which will be *everything in a single form:* architecture *and* sculpture *and* painting, which will one day rise toward heaven as the crystalline symbol of a new, emerging faith."[22] A manifesto is not a monograph, and Gropius principally intended his ringing words to set a tone of self-confidence for a venture as untried as the republic taking shape at the same time. Still, Gropius' insistence on craftsmanship and silence on industry suggested, at least to some readers, that Gropius was on his way to becoming Germany's William Morris. They raised the spectre of medievalism, a spectre that Gropius and the Bauhaus would make strenuous efforts to banish in later, soberer years.[23] In Gropius' mood of the time this rhetoric was perhaps inescapable, but even in those days he had no desire to restore medieval conditions. He believed in 1919, as he had believed in 1910

22. Program, Manifesto, and the Feininger title woodcut are reproduced in Wingler, *Bauhaus,* 38–44; I am quoting from p. 39.

23. The German word *"Handwerk*—handicraft," to which Gropius often appealed, does not necessarily mean work done manually, but may, and often does, refer to work done in small shops, where the division of labor is less marked than it is in factories. For a good definition, see Franciscono, *Gropius and the Bauhaus,* 24, 24 n. Among the few books Gropius mentions in his correspondence of these years is Heinrich Tessenow's little polemic, *Handwerk und Kleinstadt* (1919), a vigorous defense of the organic wholeness that attaches to *Handwerk* and small-town life. See Gropius to von Forell, April 3, 1919. Gropius Papers, Ordner 10/256. One reason for Gropius' emphasis on craft was political. "Any inkling on the side of the crafts organizations that the 'uplifting' of the crafts was not his only aim," Mrs. Gropius has written, "would have immediately produced financial consequences for the budget of the Bauhaus, because these organizations were extremely powerful in the legislature." Ise Gropius to Peter Gay, July 1, 1974.

104. Lyonel Feininger. *Cathedral*, title page for *Bauhaus Proclamation*, 1919

and would believe in 1930, that the separation of artisan from artist was a loss and that the modern machine, incompletely mastered, was a threat. But he also believed, with equal persistence, that Ruskin's solution was an "intellectual mistake," and that man must understand, utilize, and dominate the instruments of the modern industrial age for the sake of his own, higher humanity.[24]

The uncertain debut of the Bauhaus, then, faithfully reflected the high hopes and vague thinking of the *Arbeitsrat für Kunst.* It was true, as Gropius had optimistically noted in January, 1919, that almost all the artists and patrons "on the radical side" had joined the *Arbeitsrat.* But its wealth in prominent names barely concealed its poverty in coherent principles. These organized radical artists envisioned a better world— communal, egalitarian, and lovely. But the articulation of this vision, no matter how attractive, scarcely told people how to vote. In a characteristic manifeṣto, which Gropius wrote in the late spring of 1919 with the architect Bruno Taut (whom he greatly admired) and the architectural critic Adolf Behne (who greatly admired him), the political aim of this circle emerged as "true ṣocialism."[25] But true socialism meant, at least for these three authors, not partisanship so much as the triumph of benevolent attitudes like idealism and fraternity. This was politics for the unpolitical.

Not surprisingly, impatience with practical politics soon gave way, even for Gropius, to detestation of all politics. As early as 1919, in the midst of his most animated radical polemicizing, he longed for a kind of Epicurean withdrawal from the real world. In June, 1920, disgusted with the gains of *völkische* demagogues, he wrote to Behne from Weimar that these right-wingers were dragging cultural matters into politics and that this vice disfigured all public debate of the day: "That is why I am turning away from it, whatever its name." And he predicted that intelligent and spiritual individuals—*die Geistigen*—would all keep away: "the destruction of politics must come."[26] In January, Gropius had already told Behne, with unaccustomed bitterness, that German parties of all description were nothing but "dirt." Politics, he wrote, "generates hatred and more hatred. We must destroy parties. I want to found an unpolitical community here."[27]

Gropius' antipolitical politics has overtones of a corporate ideal.[28] But his aversion to parties was far more significant than his indeterminate, occasional aspiration for a social order based on guilds. He was speaking

24. On Ruskin's *"denkirrtum,"* see Gropius, "der architekt als organisator," Gropius Papers, Ordner 18/1.
25. See Pehnt, "Gropius the Romantic," 379.
26. Letter of June 26, 1920. Gropius Papers, Ordner 10/173 x.
27. Quoted in Franciscono, *Gropius and the Bauhaus,* 148 n.
28. See again, letter of June 26, 1920, quoted above; Gropius Papers, Ordner 10/173 x.

more wisely, in fact, than he knew. He had poured a good deal of radical passion into his work for the *Arbeitsrat* and into his early propaganda for the Bauhaus; the communal organization of his school, its mixture of Utopian ideas and realistic work, had audible political resonance. Yet essentially the community that Gropius was establishing was precisely what he said it was: unpolitical. The time for detachment was scarcely propitious; in a decade as feverish as the 1920s, in a country as frag- mented as the Weimar Republic, everything from the colors on the nation's flag to the shape of a designer's chair could become a rallying point for rancorous partisanship. The men and women of the Bauhaus, whom many execrated as living symbols of cultural bolshevism, could never escape this charged atmosphere. But, some notable exceptions apart, Gropius and his associates did not seek politics; they had politics thrust upon them. It is not without significance in this connection (and it has not gone unnoticed) that when his Utopian correspondents in- vited Gropius shortly after the war to adopt a *nom de guerre*, he chose "Mass—*measure*" for himself.[29]

I am not saying that Gropius was unpolitical on principle. To build low-cost public housing [105] or to experiment with mass-production, as he did during the 1920s, was something of a political act, a realization of an old social ideal dating back at least to 1910 [106]. Gropius was no political theorist, nor even a political thinker; he borrowed freely from the vocabulary of others, sometimes echoing Marxist and sometimes conservative formulas. But Gropius' political impulses were coherent and consistent enough to support a political position. He was an in- dividualist and a libertarian; he was a democrat by instinct. Nothing is more instructive than Gropius' dismay at Frank Lloyd Wright's cult of

29. On the nickname *"Mass"* and the others see the good appraisal by Pehnt, "Gropius the Romantic," 381. For two instances of the kind of political adroitness Gropius felt called upon to exercise, see his letter of March 7, 1924, to Friedrich Paulsen, editor of the *Bauwelt*. Paulsen had evidently complained about the predominance of aliens and Jews in the Bauhaus and Gropius took two tacks in reply: first, he defended the right of foreigners like Kandinsky to work at the Bauhaus: "everyone who helps in the good work is welcome"; and he refused to exclude either foreigners or Jews on principle. But, secondly, he noted that in fact there are no Jews among the masters and few among the students. And while he will not reject anyone, "it will happen of itself that precisely those akin in tendency and in racial heritage—*Sinnes- und Artverwandte*—will work to- gether." (Gropius Papers, Ordner 2/362–362 x). And in March, 1934, Gropius appealed to Eugen Hönig, boss of the Nazi Reichskammer der bildenden Künste, to protect the "new architecture," then under strong attack by Alfred Rosenberg, and to achieve at last the "valid union of the two great spiritual heritages of the classical and the Gothic tradition," a synthesis Schinkel had sought in vain. (Quoted in Barbara Miller Lane, *Architecture and Politics in Germany, 1918–1945* [1968], 181.) Such tactics are impossi- ble to appraise without intimate knowledge of the surrounding circumstances. It is signifi- cant that Gropius volunteered the second of these pieces of evidence to Lane, and kept it in a folder entitled "Eigner Kampf mit Nazis," strongly implying that he took some pride in his resistance. (Lane, *Architecture and Politics*, 263.)

105. Walter Gropius. *Siemensstadt Housing Development*, Berlin, 1930

106. Walter Gropius. *Prefabricated House for the Werkbund Exhibition*, 1927

personality—*Ich-Kult*—and at Wright's tendentious version of individualism which, Gropius reluctantly concluded, amounted in practice to a claim for the rights of a single lordly individual. Visiting Frank Lloyd Wright's school in 1969, some years after Wright's death, he observed that the sketches of about fifty students were, "without exception," copies of the master. Such an "autocratic method of pedagogy," he concluded, "cannot be called creative, for it invites imitation"; it makes a "horde of assistants, not independent artists."[30]

It was this set of political impulses that enabled Gropius to give a democratic interpretation to his cherished principle of "totality." There is striking originality in such a reading of this principle since, in general, the call for totality was the counterpart of the regressive longing for a rooted stratified community. Its analytical animus sprang from a sense of loss and the corresponding need for restoration. Schiller and Hegel had indicted modern culture for destroying the organic personality of the ancient Greek and the versatility of the Renaissance man. Critics of nineteenth-century culture—Carlyle and Ruskin and others—variously identified the enemy of wholeness as the division of labor, the rise of industry, the explosion of cities, the decay of religion, the intrusion of Jews, the triumph of traders, or the imperialism of reason. Protean as it was, the force that had reduced man to a mere fragment and degraded him into a machine, was a single, if many-headed monster: modernity.

But Gropius, with fair consistency, held to the conviction that the malaise of modernity would yield only to more, and better, modernity. It was in this spirit that, in 1916, he proposed to the government of Saxony a scheme for architectural education that would bring together art and industry, mass production and craftsmanship; and in the same spirit that he developed his organic pedagogical scheme of the Bauhaus.[31] That is why Feininger's famous woodcut for the 1919 manifesto [104] symbolizes Gropius only in a passing mood. When the exaltation was gone, Gropius' concern was less Utopian and more tough-minded that that: he cared to build not the cathedral of the future but the cathedral of the present, not abstractly through schemes and plans but concretely in houses, offices, and schools. However much politics was in Gropius' mind in one form or another, it was as an architect that he practiced it—which is to say, as an artist.

30. "Frank Lloyd Wright," *Apollo*, 126.
31. For the memorandum, see Wingler, *Bauhaus*, 29–30.

2. On Individuality and Collaboration

Once when Walter Gropius was a small boy a visitor asked him about his favorite color. "The colors of the rainbow," Gropius replied: *"Bunt ist meine Lieblingsfarbe."* His family condescended to find this answer amusing, as families will; Gropius himself, more perceptive than they, took it seriously. And what makes this scrap of childhood memory significant is precisely that he later found it significant. At seventy, he held it up as a comprehensive symbol of his architectural ideal: "The strong desire to *include* every vital component of life," he said, "instead of excluding part of them for the sake of too narrow and dogmatic an approach has characterized my whole life."[32] His boyish preference for motley suggests more than his suspicion of the doctrinaire and his commitment to totality: it is emblematic of his self-recognition as an individualist and as an artist.

Modern artists find that imperious inner voice they call *inspiration* a highly problematic endowment. Those who find it desirable—and many artists, though by no means all, do—see it as the source and mark of their originality. And that originality in turn defines their personal talent, their relation to the public and to the tradition. When the artist is an architect, this private voice grows no less imperious; its imperatives only grow all the more problematic. For, unlike the painter, the poet, or the novelist, the architect is by definition a collaborator. Other artists, to be sure, are less self-sufficient than they may wish, or seem, to be. Like the architect, they too maneuver across the minefield of approval and neglect; consciously or unconsciously, they incorporate at least some caprices of their patrons and tastes of their critics. But what is concealed or marginal with them is candid and central with the architect: the wishes of others touch every facet of his assignment.

For good reason, the architect's engagement with his client has long been the stock theme of lay sermons in the architectural literature; it is crucial to his self-definition. From the initial moment, the client's program is both spur and constraint; after its completion, the building must work. And the judgment whether it fulfills the program and whether it works is in large measure the prerogative of those who use it. Some of the most self-assertive of modern architects have acknowledged their public's share in the making of architectural art. "Sculpture," Paul Rudolph has said, "is never architecture and architecture is never sculpture. There has to be a balance. Buildings have to be

32. Gropius, *Scope of Total Architecture*, 11.

used."[33] That familiar list of three qualities, which Vitruvius thought every building must have, implicitly recognizes that prerogative: "durability, convenience, and beauty" do not add up to an architect's license for aesthetic willfulness. They are, on the contrary, injunctions to internalize the needs of the clients, by means of what Gropius once picturesquely called "a sensitive, built-in thermometer which registers the crises and doubts, enthusiasms and fancies of their contemporaries."[34] The architect may elect to disregard these doubts and refuse to gratify these fancies, but he works in full view of their manifestations.

Gropius' thermometer, I might note, is hard to read, not merely for the architect, but also for the historian disentangling the causes that make the architect into an artist. Both the assertion and the failure of individuality have personal sources; the most autocratic innovator, diplomatic team worker, or slavish hack has reasons for making or evading choices that lie buried in the recesses of his psyche. But if an architect has a distinctive, forceful talent, it would offer a persuasive argument, if not conclusive proof, that his private vision has played a significant part in his public performance. To determine Gropius' stature as an artist would, therefore, be to move a long way toward determining the relative distribution of causes for his work.

Yet, oddly enough, after a long life crammed with commissions and punctuated by reaffirmations of his architectural creed, after a great mass of analysis, Gropius' stature remains in doubt. He has his enthusiasts, notably among influential architectural historians, who esteem his work as a decisive juncture in modern design. Nikolaus Pevsner has called Gropius a "genius" of our age and predicted that his "sublime" work will retain its validity. And Sigfried Giedion, explicitly recalling T. S. Eliot's gloomy diagnosis of the modern "dissociation of sensibility," hailed Gropius' Fagus factory of 1911 [125] as a cure for this cultural disease: "The break between thinking and feeling which had been the bone-sickness of European architecture was healed."[35] In sharp contrast, practicing architects have denigrated Gropius' work as anti-individualist in essence and soul-destroying in effect. Paul Rudolph, who studied with Gropius at Harvard, has called him "a very powerful, but not a very good, architect." Robert Venturi, though pleased at the collaborative spirit in his own office, has repudiated the term "team action" because, he said, that sounded "too much like a Walter Gropius

33. John W. Cook and Heinrich Klotz, *Conversations with Architects* (1973), 96.

34. "Unity in Diversity," in *Four Great Makers of Modern Architecture: Gropius, Le Corbusier, Mies van der Rohe, Wright* (Record of a Symposium at the Columbia School of Architecture, May, 1961), 216.

35. Pevsner, *Pioneers of Modern Design*, 215–217; Giedion, *Space, Time and Architecture* (1941), 390. I suppose I need scarcely add that I regard Eliot's notion to be an interesting and in its way instructive fiction, but a fiction nevertheless.

architectural collaborative."[36] The ultimate appraisal of Gropius' architecture has been complicated by the proliferation of the boring glass
cages and concrete prisons that have come to dominate the office districts of our great cities—mindless white-collar factories that compul-
sively copy earlier buildings, only slightly less mindless, all in the name
of the International Style. Gropius himself in his last years repeatedly,
vehemently, denounced these doctrinaire constructions as perversions
of his ideas,[37] but architects have insisted on treating them as Gropius'
children. Whether legitimate or illegitimate hardly matters: either way
they have been taken to reflect on their putative father.

It is an old maxim, widely cited and generally ignored, that the
historian must not judge masters by their disciples. Nietzsche's stric-
tures against the epigone are only the most emphatic in a sizable literature. Disciples trivialize; they apply, humorlessly and by rote, the pre-
cepts that the master intended to be playful and experimental. Often
a master will get the disciples he deserves: the monotonous replication
of Frank Lloyd Wright's unmistakable spaces by his pupils reflects the
master's imperial presence, at once tyrannical and needy. But other
masters are more innocent; they are unfortunate enough to be persuasive, lucid, and easy to imitate. Gropius was one of these; derivative
designers have copied his forms without understanding his intentions
and have used his name in vain. This is not without irony, for Gropius'
most consistent pedagogic aim was to train architects who would be,
above all, themselves.

"My intention," he wrote in 1937, upon assuming his post at Harvard,
*"is not to introduce a, so to speak, cut and dried 'Modern Style' from
Europe, but rather to introduce a method of approach which allows one
to tackle a problem according to its peculiar conditions."* He wanted
"a young architect to be able to find his way in whatever circumstances"; to have him create, independently, "true, genuine forms out
of the technical, economic and social conditions in which he finds himself instead of imposing a learned formula onto surroundings which may
call for an entirely different solution." Gropius repudiated any wish to
teach "ready-made dogma," and called instead for "an attitude toward
the problems of our generation which is unbiased, original and elastic.
It would be an absolute horror for me if my appointment would result
in the multiplication of a fixed idea of 'Gropius architecture.' What I do

36. Rudolph, in *Conversations with Architects*, 96; Robert Venturi, ibid., 261.
37. See Gropius' vigorous comment on "the marvel of glass curtain walls (today misused
and therefore discredited) . . ." "Unity in Diversity," *Four Great Makers*, 219. While it
is customary to single out Mies van der Rohe as the father of these glass boxes, Gropius
is often blamed as well. Thus Bertrand Goldberg speaks of Gropius' imitators, the "func-
tionalists who made dogmas out of the Bauhaus ideas"; Goldberg holds them "largely
responsible for the boring city-scapes of today." *Conversations with Architects*, 138.

107. Walter Gropius and Adolf Meyer. *Deutscher Werkbund Exposition*, Administration Building, 1914

108. Walter Gropius. *The Bauhaus*, Dormitory Wing, Dessau, 1925–1926

want is to make young people realize how inexhaustible the means of creation are if they make use of the innumerable modern products of our age, and to encourage these young people in finding their own solutions."[38] He had said the same thing in similar words during his years at the Bauhaus and would say them later, as the vital center of the Cambridge Architects' Collaborative. It was in his spirit that Cooper Union went to school to the Bauhaus in the 1930s. While the "entire art school admitted its debt to the principles laid down at Weimar and Dessau," yet, to the "extent of the ability of its students and its teachers,

38. *Scope of Total Architecture*, 17.

it tried never to copy end results." Rather, it embraced Gropius' general philosophy of design.[39]

No one, least of all Gropius, would deny the existence of a recognizable Bauhaus idiom. That, after all, was inescapable, given his principled acceptance of modern technology and rejection of applied decoration [107]. But Gropius liked to think of the Bauhaus as a "laboratory," an open-minded school hospitable to experimentation, a nursery of talent that cherished the gifts of each collaborator while subjecting their work to unsparing criticism [108]. All that the Bauhaus imposed on the *Bauhäusler* was "objective principles of universal validity" that could be "derived from the laws of nature and the psychology of man."[40] In anxious moments, when Gropius' need to cajole and persuade overrode his natural inclinations, he would speak of a Bauhaus style; most of the time, though, like the embattled Naturalists in late-nineteenth-century France, Gropius feared labels like *school* or *style* as straitjackets fatal to all creativity.[41] The architectural problem was always paramount.

One way of resolving the tension between the architect as private artist and as public servant was to insist that the designer learn to trust himself: "The creative spark," Gropius said, "originates always with the individual." But his much-quoted slogan, Unity in Diversity, shows that individualism was only half his prescription. If the need for unity must not snuff out individuality, the claims of talent must not degenerate into willfulness. The creative spark originates with the individual, but his "close collaboration with others," their "stimulating and challenging critique," will help his work to mature more rapidly.[42] Some of Gropius' gifted and impatient students thought this doctrine baneful, calculated to stultify self-expression, perhaps even to stifle genius. But whether this kind of collaboration fosters aesthetic vitality or drowns it in no way depends on the principle, which is defensible enough; it depends on the

39. Esmond Shaw (then professor of architecture at Cooper Union), "The Influence of the Bauhaus," *Four Great Makers*, 244. There are revealing and affectionate memories of Gropius' pedagogic procedures in Eckhard Neumann, *Bauhaus und Bauhäusler: Bekenntnisse und Erinnerungen* (1971).

40. "Unity in Diversity," *Four Great Makers*, 224; and see Gropius' declaration of the early 1920s, addressed to the Berlin journal, *Die Glocke*, "Die geistige Grundlage des Staatlichen Bauhauses in Weimar," in which he defends the creative freedom of his school, calls attention to the candid self-criticism that helped the young to overcome their doctrinaire "constructivism, romanticism of the machine, and cubic stylization—*Konstruktivismus, Maschinen-Romantik, Quadratstilisierung*," and then adds, rather pointedly: so far, the Bauhaus "has happily steered past the cliffs of German dogmatism." Gropius Papers, Ordner 2/233–234.

41. See Thomas H. Creighton, "Walter Gropius and the Arts," *Four Great Makers*, 247–258, esp. 253.

42. "Unity in Diversity," *Four Great Makers*, 227.

109. *View of Yale University,* 1960s

kind of criticism the collaborators give and get and the kind of architect they are.[43]

For Gropius, the collaboration of architect with architect was counterpart to the collaboration of architect with client. The general record of twentieth-century architects on this score is fairly consistent and fairly bad. The most celebrated designers of our time have given the public not what it wants but what they have been grimly confident it ought to want. They have assumed the mantle of the courageous cultural critic, the misunderstood innovator, the lonely prophet who defies the public for its own good, showing it the way out of the swamp of timidity and vulgarity. Looking at the cities, the universities, the suburbs built in our century, we can hardly dismiss this posture as mere pose, or the architects' dismay as mere self-pity. In the United States, down to very recent years, collegiate building has amounted to little more than twentieth-century American copies of nineteenth-century English copies of Gothic structures built centuries earlier, often for other purposes [109]. And American suburbia, populated by prosperous

43. Thus Paul Rudolph could write: "Gropius may be wrong in believing that architecture is a cooperative art. Architects were not meant to design together; it's either all his work, or mine." Cranston Jones, *Architecture Today and Tomorrow* (1961), 175.

110. Don Metz. *Gay Residence*, Woodbridge, Connecticut, 1971

families who can afford to build what they like rather than having to buy what they must, presents a depressing spectacle of helpless and expensive eclecticism: near-French provincial or Tudor ranch "homes," punctuated at rare intervals by an honest house that it is a never-ceasing exhilaration to come home to by day or by night [110]. Nor has Europe been much more receptive to good innovative design than the United States: Gropius reports that his good friend Le Corbusier was permanently embittered by lack of recognition. Too few commissions came his way to enable Le Corbusier to show, and to develop, his talents. He was, he told Gropius sadly, "all too far ahead of his time."[44]

No political-aesthetic choice seems easier or more necessary than to side with the embattled modern artist against the obtuse vulgar philistine. Yet many modern architects have taken the resistance of popular taste as an excuse for utter self-indulgence. The buildings they have ostensibly designed to educate their public have been statuary actually intended to glorify themselves. Exasperated users have been tempted to call them monuments to monomania. James Stirling's highly praised History Faculty building at Cambridge University, irreverently nicknamed "the greenhouse," [111] has been celebrated as a modern masterpiece, but mainly by those who only know it from dramatic photographs. Its internal spaces and external aspect are indeed breathtaking,

44. "Le Corbusier," *Apollo*, 129.

111. James Stirling. *History Faculty Building*, Cambridge, 1964–1968

but most of the Cambridge history faculty refuse to inhabit it, since its uninterrupted glass facades alternately broil and freeze its occupants and its badly insulated cells afford no effective privacy. The cramped and drafty quarters in the old colleges seem infinitely preferable; their discomfort is at least familiar.

The archetypal instance of the artist's contempt for his client is Mies van der Rohe's account of the Tugendhat family. "Mr. Tugendhat came to me," Mies later recalled. "He was a very careful man. He did not believe in one doctor only—he had three." He chose Mies—or so Mies claims—because he had seen an early Mies house that he thought well built. "I went there and saw the situation. I designed the house [112]. I remember it was Christmas Eve when he saw the design. He nearly died." But Mrs. Tugendhat had some interest in modern art; she owned some van Goghs and she induced her husband to think it over. "On New Year's Eve he came to me and told me that I should go ahead. He said he did not like the open space; it would be too disturbing. People would be there when he was in the library with his great thoughts. He was a business man, I think. Later on he said to me, 'Now I give in on everything, but not about the furniture.' I said, 'This is too bad.'" Mies then instructed the foreman to accept the shipment of furniture he would send out from Berlin to Brno; then, " 'Shortly before lunch, call him out and say you are at his house with the furniture. He will be furious, but

112. Ludwig Mies van der Rohe. *Tugendhat House,* exterior, Brno, Czechoslovakia, 1930

you must expect that.' Tugendhat said, 'Take it out!' before he saw it. However, after lunch he liked it." [113] And Mies drew the conclusion, without rancor and without hesitation: "I think we should treat our clients as children."[45]

The issue cannot, I think, be drawn more firmly than this. It is consoling to know that the Tugendhats came to enjoy living in their house after a time.[46] And it is true that the architect blessed with a new sense of space, a new grasp of materials, a new perception of form needs more than the drawing board or the scale model to test his ideas. Moreover, he lives not only in a world of clients but in that of other architects as well, and his innovations, suitably mediated and modulated, often find their way into public favor through the designs that other architects have derived from his original uncompromising vision [114, 115].[47] The

45. See James Marston Fitch, "Mies van der Rohe and the Platonic Verities," *Four Great Makers,* 157. It is significant that the Tugendhats' own recollection is quite different: Mrs. Tugendhat (who had Renoirs, not van Goghs) had actually seen the Mies Pavilion in Barcelona. Mies' later recollection, by making his clients far more philistine than they were, only makes his own lordliness all the more extreme.

46. Mrs. Tugendhat told Howard Dearstyne who, as a young student of architecture, came to see the Mies house in the early 1930s: they had had some trouble adjusting to it at first, " 'But now,' she added, 'we are beginning to enjoy this way of living.' " "Miesian Space Concept in Domestic Architecture," *Four Great Makers,* 130.

47. Thus the fashionable American architect Morris Lapidus (who built the Fontainebleau Hotel and other pleasure palaces in Florida) testifies that Mies' Tugendhat house with its free flow of space and curved interior wall deeply influenced him. Cook and Klotz,

113. Ludwig Mies van der Rohe. *Tugendhat House,* interior, Brno, Czechoslovakia, 1930

innovator must, almost by definition, offend reigning taste. Yet the
question remains whether the architect acts with his client as autocrat
or as educator, as tyrant or as teacher.

Gropius found this question easy to answer. He was committed to
certain general principles which, he knew, would arouse the anxiety,
and hence the hostility, of the traditionalist. While he never adopted
Adolf Loos' rallying cry, "Ornament is crime"—such apodictic language
made him singularly uncomfortable—he shared Loos' central conviction that decoration plastered onto a facade or historical echoes gratui-
tously sounded are obstacles to man's necessary conquest of the machine. But just as Gropius tried to educate other architects without
forcing them to become copies of him, he tried to educate his clients
without forcing them to fit into a doctrinaire sculptural vision. The
modernist slogan, functionalism, which is associated with Gropius'
name, has obscured his essential flexibility. Dogmatism in fact was his

Conversations with Architects, 150. See also Leonard K. Eaton, *Two Chicago Architects
and Their Clients: Frank Lloyd Wright and Howard Van Doren Shaw* (1969) which, for
all the naiveté of its categories and sentimentality of its tone, is a valuable study.

114. Ludwig Mies van der Rohe. *Tugendhat House,* interior, Brno, Czechoslovakia, 1930

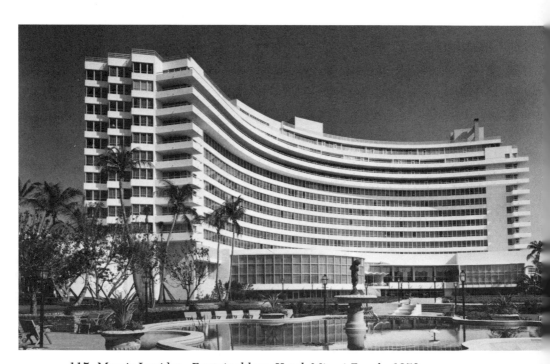

115. Morris Lapidus. *Fontainebleau Hotel,* Miami Beach, 1952

enemy, construction of a livable space his overriding consideration.[48]

The functionalist prescription seems abstract, rationalist, impersonal —architecture that works only on the draftsman's table. But functionalism, though in appearance rigid, is in application strikingly elastic. The ultimate shape of a functionalist design depends, after all, on the function it is intended to perform. It may satisfy not some fancied ideal of practicality but snobbery, self-satisfaction, or the thirst for pure form. One man's utility is another man's beauty. Whatever the interpretation of functionalism in other architects' minds, Gropius consistently interpreted the term in the most generous, most human way possible: it included comfort, intimacy, aesthetic satisfaction. It meant frankness to him, unabashed modernity, but he did not equate these with bareness or monotony. In Gropius' architectural vocabulary, less was not always more. While, he thought, the beautiful is always truthful, the truthful is not always beautiful. To be expressive and flexible with spaces, to deploy materials candidly, was only half of the architect's assignment. The aesthetic, though inseparable from the useful, could not properly be reduced to it. "The liberation of architecture from a welter of ornament," he wrote in *The New Architecture and the Bauhaus*, probably the best-known exposition of his principles, "the emphasis on its structural functions, and the concentration on concise and economical solutions, represent the purely material side of that formalizing process on which the *practical* value of the New Architecture depends." But, he immediately added, "the other, the aesthetic satisfaction of the human soul, is just as important as the material. Both find their counterpart in that unity which is life itself. What is far more important than this structural economy and its functional emphasis is the intellectual achievement which has made possible a new spatial vision."[49] Beauty,

48. In this connection, it is worth exploring Gropius' relations with the mystic Johannes Itten, who conducted the first introductory Bauhaus course, and the dogmatic Theo van Doesburg, artistic prophet of the De Stijl group, who made a brief and tempestuous appearance at the Bauhaus in 1921. Gropius, despite an early admiration for the first, broke with him and took care not to invite a similar type again; and, despite interest in De Stijl, he repudiated, early and late, van Doesburg's claim that his vision of art had in any way influenced the Bauhaus. See Gropius' important letter of August 1, 1966, to George Rickey: "My design of the Chicago Tribune Tower has certainly nothing to do with van Doesburg. When you look at my early buildings which became landmarks in Germany, the Fagus Factory, Alfeld, 1911; and the Factory and office Building at the Werkbund Exhibition, Cologne, 1914, you will see that the character of my buildings had been developed already before I even knew the name of van Doesburg and the De Stijl in Holland." Rickey, *Constructivism: Origins and Evolution* (1968), 85. Mies has also vehemently repudiated van Doesburg's claims as "absolute nonsense." See Peter Blake, "A Conversation with Mies," *Four Great Makers*, 101.

49. *New Architecture and Bauhaus*, 23–24. Toward the end of the nineteenth century, the great Dutch architect H.P. Berlage already utilized uncompromising (and ultimately confusing) utilitarian rhetoric when he predicted that a "pure art of utility" would become *"the* art of the twentieth century." Quoted in John Summerson, "Architecture, Painting and Le Corbusier," in Summerson, *Heavenly Mansions and Other Essays on Architecture* (1963), 184.

116. Walter Gropius with Adolf Meyer. Design for *Chicago Tribune Building*, 1922

117. John Howells and Raymond Hood.
Tribune Tower, 1922–1924

he reiterated very late in his life, as emphatically as he could, *"is an essential component of all of life, and cannot be isolated as a special privilege for the aesthetically initiated; it is a fundamental need of all men."*[50]

Perhaps the most convincing demonstration of Gropius' commitment to beauty is the design he submitted in 1922 to the international competition for a new *Chicago Tribune* office tower [116, 117]. Its utility was never tested for it did not win the prize and was never built. But its beauty is striking. The drawings are exemplars of rationality; they are uncluttered, eloquent, and immediately appealing. The wide, vigorously articulated windows bear a family resemblance to the famous "Chicago windows" that Burnham and Root first used in local skyscrapers; their rhythm firmly underscores the formal structure of the steel skeleton and complements, in a highly individual way, the fenestration of the neighboring, earlier *Chicago Tribune* printing works. Yet, though emphatically rhythmic, Gropius' design escapes the monotony that would afflict so many later skyscrapers by introducing a blank surface to separate and balance the two halves of the building and, even more, with cunningly spaced, boldly cantilevered balconies. As a totality, the design matches Mondrian's artistic aim of "dynamic tension" by inscribing diverse, interacting forms within regular, controlling rectangles. By themselves the Gropius drawings are immensely gratifying; compared with the winning entry by Howells and Hood, chosen from no fewer than 263 entries, they stand as a triumphant response of functionalism to historicism. They achieve formality without suffering from the deadly chill of formalism.[51]

But an unbuilt building, tantalizing and suggestive as it may be, must remain an incomplete test of an architect's real capacities. Gropius, especially in the critical Bauhaus years, had fewer commissions than he liked, and than the historian, in retrospect, needs. But he built enough to put his artistry to the trial of use. And in full accord with his humane principles Gropius' best completed buildings were, and are, eminently satisfying to look at, walk through, and live in. The famous Bauhaus complex and its related clusters of houses for masters and pupils were by all accounts handsome and livable dwellings [118, 119, 120, 121].

50. "Apollo in der Demokratie," *Apollo*, 16. This democratic aesthetic is a recurrent theme in Gropius' speeches; I could have quoted similar pronouncements from his entire career. A very busy man and assiduous public speaker, Gropius often borrowed ideas and formulations from earlier drafts of essays and speeches.

51. The conditions for the competition, and all the contributions, are sumptuously reproduced in *The International Competition for a New Administration Building for the Chicago Tribune, MCMXXII; Containing All the Designs Submitted in Response to the Chicago Tribune's $100,000 Offer Commemorating Its Seventy-Fifth Anniversary, June 10, 1922* (1923).

118. Walter Gropius. *The Bauhaus,* Laboratory Workshop, Dessau, 1925–1926

119. Walter Gropius. *The Bauhaus,* Student Dormitories, Dessau, 1925–1926

120. Walter Gropius. *The Bauhaus,* Semidetached Houses for Professors, Dessau, 1925–1926

121. Walter Gropius. *The Bauhaus,* Directors House, Dessau, 1925–1926

122. Walter Gropius and Marcel Breuer. *Gropius Residence,* Lincoln, Massachusetts, 1937

123. Walter Gropius and Marcel Breuer. *Breuer Chair in Gropius Residence,* Lincoln, Massachusetts, 1937

124. Walter Gropius and Marcel Breuer. *Gropius Residence,* interior, Lincoln, Massachusetts, 1937

And the house that Gropius built in Massachusetts in 1937 for himself and his family remains inviting, pleasing, and practical [122]. It is palpably an architect's design; with its perspicuous geometric forms and its Bauhaus furnishings [123], it is a small museum of modernity. Yet it works as a house. By choosing regional materials in standard sizes Gropius emphasized the possibilities of the local style and the beauty implicit in mass production. The wide windows of the house welcome the open, slightly rolling New England landscape [124], but its separate staircases and shrewdly placed rooms respond to another human need: privacy. The Gropius house stands as a reminder that its architect fully recognized the principal danger facing the modern architect: he knew that while a sculpture may be a good place to visit, it is not a good place to live in.

3. The Informed Intuition

While the principles of functionalism permitted Gropius to realize his intentions, its language often did him a disservice. He sought to protect himself against misunderstandings by insisting that he knew functionalism to be more than "a rational process merely"; it included, he said, "psychological problems as well."[52] But in his speeches functionalism sometimes trapped him into offering engineer's reasons for aesthetic choices, or a simple explanation for a complex decision.

How much violence Gropius' rhetoric could do to his motives emerges instructively from the accounts he gave of his most revolutionary design, the Fagus shoe-last factory of 1911 [125, 126]. Its radically innovative "missing corner support—*die fehlende eckstütze,*" he said in 1933, had been prompted by economic calculation: his figures had shown that he could save money on construction by reducing the number of roof supports. Besides, by eliminating a heavy pillar he brought added light to the interior and facilitated the erection of movable partitions, both eminently practical for a factory. "Aesthetic motives," he argued, buttressing his invention with a resounding pronouncement, "have nothing to do with function."[53] Yet only a few years later, lecturing in London, Gropius offered a wholly different explanation of his "curtain-wall." He proudly showed slides of his "first attempt at making the walls almost entirely of glass," and called particular attention to "the fact that there are no front-supports at the corner of the building." Then he asserted, flatly: "this was done unconsciously." It was only "subsequently" that "it was seen that it was right in calculation as well."[54]

The two accounts contradict but do not cancel one another. It is easy to see what Gropius has done: in each of his reports he has isolated one strand from the complex of architectural creation and neglected all the others. The historian in search of causes cannot be satisfied with such simplifications. He needs the fully and accurately mapped hierarchy of motives. Certainly Gropius often acknowledged that more than one impulse entered into his work. His Pan-Am building was, in part, an aesthetic response to the long canyon produced on Park Avenue in the 1950s by the blank facades of newly built and largely anonymous sky-

52. See *Scope of Total Architecture,* 86.
53. February 16, 1933, "die schöpferischen grundlagen der modernen architektur," Geneva, Gropius Papers, Ordner 18/96–97; anticipated in earlier addresses like "Funktionelle Baukunst," December 1930, Gropius Papers, Ordner 18/191–212.
54. See Gropius Papers, Ordner 18/108.

125. Walter Gropius with Adolf Meyer.
Fagus Shoe Last Factory, Alfeld, 1911

126. Walter Gropius with Adolf Meyer.
Fagus Shoe Last Factory, interior, Alfeld,
1911

scrapers; and in part, a way of forestalling an even taller, even more looming structure [127]. And Gropius devised the hexagonal shape of his final design to express the realities of internal elevator traffic and, at the same time, to reduce its visual bulk by leading the observer's eye from its central mass toward its tapering sides. Whatever our verdict on Gropius' solution, the Pan-Am building candidly combines aesthetic and material considerations.

His earlier, much-published Sommerfeld house [128] is quite as diverse in its origins, if not more so. With its rustic appearance, its almost primitive deployment of wood, it has been read as an instance of Gropius' temporary deviation into Utopian romanticism, as a public acknowledgment of his debt to Frank Lloyd Wright, and as his contribution to the German passion for the *Gesamtkunstwerk*. In some measure, the Sommerfeld house is all of these things.[55] Yet there were still other causes at work. Sommerfeld, a building contractor who generously supported the Bauhaus in its neediest years, commissioned his *Blockhaus* in 1920, at a time when building materials were in desperately short supply. Resourcefully, he bought a scrapped German naval vessel and had the architects salvage its valuable teak and other lumber [129]. With Gropius, in the midst of romantic creativity, practicality kept breaking in.[56]

One of Gropius' last commissions, the Thomas Glass Works [130] of 1968, demonstrates the perils of monocausal and high-flown explanations. The lofty elevation of the central building, which houses the glass-blowing ovens, has seduced enthusiastic German critics into calling the factory a "glass cathedral," and into exclaiming that Gropius has "rediscovered the triangle."[57] The emphatic, stretched, flat wings, rhythmically interrupted by small triangular roofs that echo the great central structure, emphasize by their vigorous horizontality the stunning profile of the center roof [131]. They proclaim that art has gone into the making of the building. But in cool fact, the great triangle roof imposed itself on Gropius as the most rational enclosure for dissipating

55. Ise Gropius in conversation with Peter Gay, December 10, 1973. Efforts to realize the Wagnerian idea of the *Gesamtkunstwerk* have taken two very distinct forms: to van de Velde, it meant that he did all the designing himself. "For Gropius it meant, on the other hand, a collaboration with other artists, craftsmen, technicians, engineers, etc., who, though hopefully imbued with the same spirit, were supposed to make independent, complementary contributions to the whole." Ise Gropius, review of Franciscono, *Gropius and the Bauhaus*, in *Architectural Forum*, CXXXVI, 1 (January–February 1972), 16.

56. At the time that he was working on this house, on November 20, 1920, he wrote to his friend Behne ("Ekart"): "The more one is an artist the better—*je mehr Künstler, desto besser.*" Gropius Papers, Ordner 10/139.

57. Ise Gropius in conversation with Peter Gay, December 10, 1973. See "Giant Fume Hood," *Architectural Forum*, XCIV, 3 (April, 1971), 26–29. The anonymous author calls the factory "an impressive monument to the intelligence and humanity of its great architect." (p. 29).

127. Emery Roth, Walter Gropius and Pietro Belluschi. *Pan American World Airways Building*, 1958–1963

128. Walter Gropius and Adolf Meyer. *Sommerfeld House*, Berlin–Dahlem, 1920–1921

129. Walter Gropius and Adolf Meyer. *Sommerfeld House*, interior, Berlin–Dahlem, 1920–1921

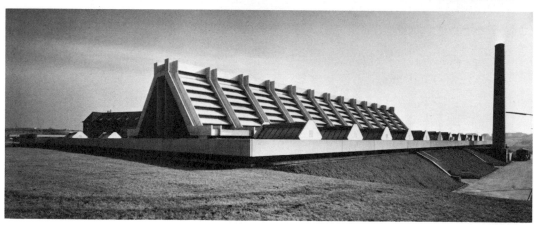

130. Walter Gropius and Alex Cvijanovic. *Thomas Glass Works*, Amberg, 1968

131. Walter Gropius and Alex Cvijanovic. *Thomas Glass Works*, Amberg, 1968

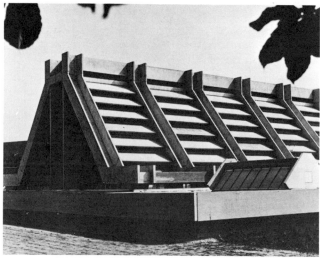

132. Walter Gropius with Adolf Meyer. *Fagus Shoe Last Factory*, Alfeld, 1911

the blasts of hot air generated by the ovens; he wanted to build a livable work space without resorting to the bulky and expensive device of air conditioning. With the Thomas works, we may for once justly apply that old cliché: form here follows function to perfection.

In his later years, Gropius came to recognize the multiplicity of motives that underlies every design, a multiplicity to which the designer himself has only limited access. In 1961, looking back at his Fagus works [132] from the distance of fifty years, he concluded that the design had "probably emerged first of all through intuition." He confessed his delight with creating the illusion of "floating lightness," which would stand in marked contrast to the earthbound, deliberate massiveness, the "seclusion from the hostile outside world," that typified the traditional design of his day. Then practical considerations, like cheapness and flexibility, soon imposed themselves to confirm his original intuition. At the moment of creation, Gropius thought, he had not grasped its complexity. "In retrospect today I see these insights clearly, but probably the genesis of the Fagus design was originally unconscious. The starting point was an intuitive new conception of space, its structural application an intellectual process." And he offered a causal schema for this process, not incongruent with my metaphor of the hourglass: "I know today that the mental process of design, if it is successful, must bring three components into simultaneous harmony: form, techniques, and economics. The first creative idea may be formal, constructive, or economic"; but whichever it is "it requires immediate application in the two other areas. Thus, design is a consistent, step-by-step process in which all functions are harmonized, the psychological as well as the practical ones."[58]

This is an important text. It supports the three-fold classification of causes—cultural, craft, and privacy—that I have been developing. And it offers a decisive clue to the causes that dominated the formation of Gropius, the architect. I have portrayed Gropius the political Utopian, Gropius the individualistic artist, Gropius the adroit collaborator. And he was all of these men, together and in turn. But the world that organized his impulses, conscious and unconscious, was the world of craft.

In appreciating craft, I am not deprecating intuition. Gropius' testimony on his creative processes is, I think, wholly persuasive. But the intuition that guided his pencil was of a particular kind. It was the craftsman's trained response to a stimulus—a tempting commission, an interesting site, a rewarding client, a promising material— that he has been schooled to recognize, to judge, and to use. This kind of intuition is exercise and experience internalized, practice become habitual and partly unconscious. It is the leap that spans problem and solution by incorporating all the intermediate steps almost instantaneously. But precisely because the workings of this informed intuition are so rapid, so deceptively easy, and so remote from the artist's conscious reach, its causal significance, though very great, is very elusive. It requires analysis to be seen for what it is: not a spontaneous, uncaused flash of genius but a finely tuned instrument brought to bear at the proper moment, sensitive enough to screen out the unworkable and, at the same time, supportive enough to let

58. "*Die stützenlose Ecklösung dieses Baues, die sich späterhin auch als ökonomisch erwies, entstand wohl zunächst aus der Intuition und weniger aus praktischen Erwägungen. Mich begeisterte der Gedanke mit den neuen konstruktiven Mitteln die Illusion schwebender Leichtigkeit der Baumasse zu erzielen im bewussten Gegensatz zu der Betonung der Erdenschwere und der Abgeschlossenheit gegen eine feindliche Aussenwelt, so kennzeichnend für die alten Bauweisen. . . . Im Rückblick sehe ich heute diese Erkenntnisse klar, aber die Entstehung des Entwurfs der Faguswerke war wohl ursprünglich unbewusst. Der Ausgangspunkt war eine intuitive neue Raumvorstellung, die strukturelle Durchführung ein intellektueller Vorgang. Heute weiss ich, dass der geistige Prozess des Entwerfens, wenn er erfolgreich ist, gleichzeitig drei Komponenten zum Gleichklang bringen muss—Form, Technik und Ökonomie. Der erste schöpferische Einfall mag entweder formal, konstruktiv oder wirtschaftlich sein, sogleich bedarf er der Ausrichtung innerhalb der beiden anderen Bedingungsgebiete. Entwurf ist also ein konsequenter Schritt-für-Schritt-Prozess der Harmonisierung aller Funktionen, nicht nur der praktischen, sondern auch der psychologischen.*" Gropius, May, 1961, in Helmut Weber, *Walter Gropius und das Faguswerk* (1961), 7. See also p. 51. Interestingly enough, the three illustrations that the 1913 *Jahrbuch* of the *Werkbund* gives to the Fagus factory leave that famous corner inconspicuous.

133. Martin Gropius and Heino Schmieden. *Museum of Arts and Crafts*, elevation, Berlin, 1875

the craftsman hold on to notions that somehow feel right—usually for good reason.[59]

By early 1911, when the Fagus commission came his way, Gropius' intuition was well stocked. He had *Kultur* in his bones: his father had been an architect, and so had his great uncle, Martin Gropius [133, 134, 135]; and his family was amply supplied with publishers, painters, and public servants. Berlin was a living, constantly changing parade of historic styles. Much like Manet before him, Gropius wandered through his native city with open eyes and, after 1907, with a professional guide, Peter Behrens. Much like Manet, Gropius witnessed a spectacular urban transformation during his youth. Yet unlike Manet, Gropius, the stroller in the city, found much to deplore. In 1888, when Wilhelm II ascended the German Imperial throne, Gropius was five. The new emperor, supremely self-assured and, in his own eyes, omnicompetent, promptly made himself a munificent and intrusive patron of those most public among the arts, sculpture and architecture. Much of what he commissioned in Berlin he intended as a celebration of his adored grandfather, Wilhelm I, the first emperor of modern Germany. One massive pile the young emperor inherited: Paul Wallot's Reichstag

59. On this type of professional intuition, see Peter Gay, *Style in History* (1974), 178–179. On Gropius, see Ise Gropius: "The clichés that are often printed about the working methods of Gropius and of those whom he introduced to the practice of architecture, namely, that they approached their tasks analytically and solved them to the exclusive dictate of a narrowly understood functionalism, are quite misleading. On the contrary, from my own observations I can say that as a rule Gropius started out on a new architectural task with one overriding, emotionally sustained idea in command, but he had early trained himself and others to bring such an idea immediately into context with such factors as would insure its relevance from the social, technical and aesthetic point of view." In *Concepts of the Bauhaus: The Busch-Reisinger Collection* (1971), 126–127. This is virtually a restatement of Gropius' own testimony, yet it strikes me, not as a bit of myth-making, but as a confirmation of Gropius' own insight.

134. Martin Gropius and Heino Schmieden. *Bank of the Cassen-Verein*, Berlin, 1870–1871

135. Martin Gropius and Heino Schmieden. *Gewandhaus*, Leipzig, 1881–1884

building, completed in 1894, had been started ten years before [136]. But the pointedly named and prominently placed Kaiser Wilhelm Gedächtniskirche went up in his own reign, between 1892 and 1895 [137]. And two years after its inauguration, in 1897, Berliners could make a new set of irreverent comments about still another, even more emphatic memorial to Wilhelm I [138], Reinhold Begas' vast, and vastly expensive National Monument to Emperor Wilhelm "the Great": "So," Berliners said, "that's how much bronze you can buy for four million marks!"[60]

The extravagant statuary dedicated to the memory of *"Wilhelm der Grosse"* had provided employment to a battalion of sculptors. The *Siegesallee* [139, 140], the most colossal artistic fantasy Wilhelm II realized in his reign, employed a small army. Vaguely patterned after classical models, the *Siegesallee* was an ostentatious three-dimensional family tree. It consisted of thirty-two statuary groupings, each with one of Wilhelm's predecessors in the center, flanked by two herms commemorating prominent figures of each reign. The long, wide vista was closed off at one end with a fountain crowned by a statue of Roland, the symbol of Berlin's freedom, and at the other by the *Siegessäule,* a column crowned by an angel of victory [136]. The avenue, completed with impressive dispatch between 1897 and 1900, was pretentious, irresistibly comical, and literally dazzling, for it was of pure white Carrara marble. As Gropius was growing up and committing himself to his vocation, his Berlin was a jumble, a veritable jungle, of styles—Romanesque, Gothic, Baroque, Neoclassical. It was—some of it—a chamber of horrors to study and to flee.

It was also, though less spectacularly, a museum of models to admire. However timidly, modernity was struggling to realize itself in the face of opulent and oppressive historicism. One building, Alfred Messel's Wertheim department store [141], embodied and dramatized this struggle within a single city block. Its first segment on the Leipziger Strasse, completed in 1896, seemed a triumphant adaptation of traditional means to modern ends. With its slender buttresses supporting a pseudo-Mansard roof, this cathedral of commerce discarded the customary forbidding facade and permitted the candid display of merchandise in generous windows. The building still cautiously clung to familiar decor but at the same time boldly ventured into a progressive functional eclecticism. But then, in 1904, Messel rounded off the complex with an adjacent building on the Leipziger Platz, in which com-

---

60. See Walther Kiaulehn, *Berlin: Schicksal einer Weltstadt* (1958), 303.

139. *Siegesallee*, Berlin, 1897–1901

BERLIN. KÖNIGSPLATZ MIT REICHSTAGSGEBÄUDE UND SIEGESALLEE.

136. Paul Wallot. *The Reichstag*, with the Siegessaüle on the right, Berlin, 1884–1894

140. *Siegesallee*, Berlin, 1897–1901

137. Franz Schwechten. *Kaiser–Wilhelm-Gedächtnis-Kirche*, Berlin, 1891–1895

138. Reinhold Begas. *National Monument to William "the Great,"* Berlin, 1897

141. Alfred Messel. *Wertheim Department Store*, Berlin, 1896–1904

plaisant grandeur won out over inventive adaptation; its aggressive mixture of Romanesque, Gothic, and French Renaissance added up to nothing more than Wilhelminian taste, if at its best.

Still, Messel made a beginning, and by the turn of the century Berlin's architectural landscape exhibited some refreshing departures from the ruling taste. There were some experimental railway terminals. There were some interesting stores by van de Velde. And there was always the work of Schinkel, the most famous architect that Berlin, and Germany, had produced in the early nineteenth century [142]. Schinkel's work was highly visible in Berlin and nearby Potsdam, and his reputation was enjoying something of a revival. In 1911, precisely while Gropius was grappling with the Fagus curtain-wall, the architectural writer Fritz Stahl hailed Schinkel as the "coming man" of German design who had been a century ahead of his age. Around the same time, the uncompromising modernist Adolf Loos exhorted the younger generation to study Schinkel's work and let its classicism purify their taste. And it was Schinkel's buildings that Gropius went to see with Behrens and in whom, he reports, "Behrens saw his artistic ancestor."[61]

Schinkel's influence on these twentieth-century architects, and on such severe, self-conscious modernists as Philip Johnson and Mies van

61. Fritz Stahl, *Schinkel* (1911), 3. See Gropius, "Peter Behrens," *Apollo,* 124–125. There is a typically vigorous and lucid appreciation of Schinkel's work by Nikolaus Pevsner, "Karl Friedrich Schinkel," in *Studies in Art, Architecture and Design,* Vol. I,

142. Karl Friedrich Schinkel. *Old Museum*, Berlin, 1823–1829

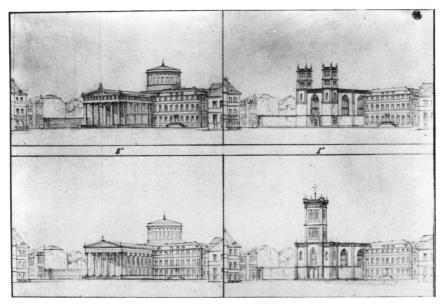

143. Karl Friedrich Schinkel. *Four Designs for the Friedrich–Werdersche Church*, Berlin, before 1828

144. Karl Friedrich Schinkel. *Guard House for the Royal Guards,* Berlin, 1816–1818

der Rohe is at first glance hard to understand, but only at first glance. It is true that Schinkel was the pliant instrument of his royal patrons, moving at will—their will—from sentimental medievalism to correct neoclassicism to romantic fancy [143a]. It is true too that, had he lived, he would have permanently disfigured the Acropolis by building an immense palace for the King of Greece in full view of the Parthenon. Yet, at the same time, Schinkel had an impressive gift for organizing spaces and translating his sense of form into ingenious visual equivalents [144]. The adroit compromises of his churches and the monumental revivalism of his museums half conceal, half reveal his originality, his prophetic spatial intuitions. A trained stroller in Berlin could feel a liberating architectural imagination at work in his buildings [145]. Mies van der Rohe, who confessed Schinkel's power over him, saw them as "an excellent example of classicism—the best I know." Schinkel, Mies adds, "had wonderful constructions, excellent proportions, and good detailing."[62] In some of his designs, like the Berlin Bauakademie, Schin-

From Mannerism to Romanticism (1968), 175–195. For Loos, see Hermann G. Pundt, *Schinkel's Berlin: A Study in Environmental Planning* (1972), 2. For the work of Messel, see Walter Curt Behrendt, *Alfred Messel* (1911) and M. Rapsilber, Fritz Stahl et al., *Alfred Messel,* 2 vols, (1911). Gropius' admiration for Schinkel's teacher Friedrich Gilly, which, according to Mrs. Gropius, was even greater than that for Schinkel himself, needs further documentation. Ise Gropius to Peter Gay, July 1, 1974.

62. Blake, "A Conversation with Mies," *Four Great Makers,* 94. See also Dearstyne, "Miesian Space," ibid., 130–132.

145. Karl Friedrich Schinkel. *Schauspielhaus*, Berlin, 1819–1821

146. Karl Friedrich Schinkel. *Bauakademie*, Berlin, 1831–1836

147. Ludwig Mies van der Rohe. *New National Gallery*, Berlin, 1968

148. Karl Friedrich Schinkel. *Old Museum*, Berlin, 1823–1829

kel departed from accepted models to invent a practically new solution to the traditional problem of the large public structure [146]. His functionalist rhetoric, which was beginning to be quoted once again in the early twentieth century and which would not have been out of place in a Bauhaus book, was the verbal counterpart of his impressive structure. Once Mies has drawn one's attention to it, his own Berlin National Gallery appears as a true, if distant, descendant of Schinkel's Old Museum [147, 148].

Among Schinkel's modern disciples, it was of course Peter Behrens who exercised the most pervasive influence on the shaping of Gropius' craft. The famous factories that Behrens built for the A.E.G. in Berlin were being completed, or on the drawing board, when Gropius was working in Behrens' atelier, and both the Turbine works of 1909 [149] and the small motors factory of 1911 [150] are in Schinkel's idiom, though handled with a masterly independence and impressively adapted to their twentieth-century function. Looking back in 1966, Gropius graciously acknowledged Behrens as his "teacher." With evident pleasure, he recalled Behrens' "comprehensive and thoroughgoing interest in the shaping of the whole environment, an interest that extended beyond architecture to painting, the stage, industrial products, and typography." This versatility had "a great attraction" for Gropius; being Gropius, he could not help being impressed by a designer who put his hand to factories and light bulbs, catalogues and electric heaters. I have called Behrens a one-man *Werkbund;* he was also, in anticipation, a one-man Bauhaus.

Behrens' words were as important for Gropius as his works. Characteristically (both for an educated German and a modern architect) Behrens greatly enjoyed explaining his convictions and fashioning theoretical justifications for his practice. This, too, Gropius later gratefully remembered: Behrens, he said, had taught him "the habit of thinking in principles."[63] Actually, Behrens had been compelled to struggle hard to clarify aesthetic principles for himself. He had begun as a painter and a designer of typefaces; around the turn of the century he had become enmeshed, with many others, in the sinuous tentacles of Art Nouveau [151]. But soon after 1900 its mechanical sensuality, its obligatory swooping curves and garlands, lost their interest for him. He began instead to experiment with a certain sobriety and to seek a style that would express, and at the same time purify, the values of modern industrial culture. The A.E.G. factories, which were to earn him a place in the history of architecture, are the realization of his style for the times. Whatever architectural historians might later say, for Behrens

---

63. "Behrens," *Apollo*, 124–125.

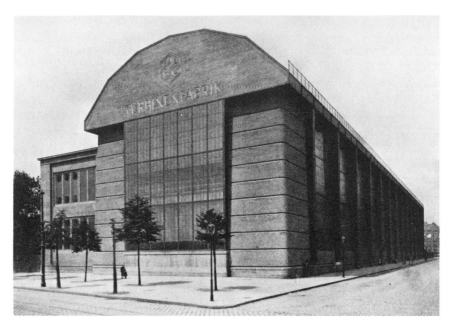

149. Peter Behrens. *AEG Turbine Factory,* Berlin, 1909

150. Peter Behrens. *AEG Small Motors
Factory,* Berlin, 1911

151. Peter Behrens. *The Kiss*, 1898

these factories were wholly modern. But especially in the much-published Turbine factory of 1909 [149], the massive monumentality of the corners veers into impressiveness for its own sake. The modernity of the building was stunning, its compromise with a certain romantic classicism rather more subtle. But a gifted and rebellious young architect like Gropius could take Behrens' most admired work as an invitation to admire and surpass the master.[64]

In the effort to see his way beyond his admirable and exasperating "teacher," Gropius drew on the constantly growing, by no means coherent, tradition of architectural modernism. The bold, imaginative functionalism of French engineers and the unapologetic, undecorated practicality of American silos gave him valuable points of departure. He sensed early, though he did not articulate it until much later, that revolutionary architecture must constantly return to the tradition; there are details in the Fagus design that go back to visual devices first employed by the ancient Greeks.[65] As Gropius saw it, the bad taste and dishonest revivalism of nineteenth-century "salon architecture" had sprung, not from obedience to, but disregard of, the great tradition of design.

For Gropius, in short, the architect's obligation never changed. It was in the twentieth century A.D. what it had been in the fifth century B.C. —to make buildings that one could live in. And that is why, for Gropius, with all his political passion and all his aesthetic individuality, the imperatives of craft imposed themselves on him. Speaking at the *Richtfest* of the Bauhaus in Dessau, Gropius put this primacy with happy concision: "The Bauhaus exists for the sake of building—*das bauhaus ist zum bauen da!*"[66] In characterizing his most personal creation, Walter Gropius also characterized himself [152].

64. On Behrens' "classicism," see Franciscono, *Gropius and the Bauhaus*, 30–33; on Gropius' differences with Behrens, and on Behrens' "monumentality," see Anderson, "Peter Behrens and the New Architecture of Germany, 1900–1917," 268–270, 287–290, 401–402, 411. In the 1920s, as is evident from his late designs, Behrens learned a good deal from Gropius' "cubism." See the issue devoted to Behrens, *Casabella*, No. 240 (June, 1960), and the illuminating catalogue *Peter Behrens (1868–1940)*, (1966). Gropius, of course, made his own compromises with the dominant tradition, as a walk around the exhibition factory of 1914 will demonstrate.

65. For "Greek" detailing, see Weber, *Gropius und das Faguswerk*, esp. 64–67. For the need for resuming the great tradition of architecture, see Gropius' lecture in Geneva, of February 16, 1933, Gropius Papers, 18/80–107, esp. 18/93. There are suggestive passages in Julius Posener, *From Schinkel to the Bauhaus* (1972).

66. Typescript in Gropius Papers, Ordner 18/35.

152. Walter Gropius in front of his home in Lincoln, Massachusetts, 1967

FOUR

Mondrian: The Claims of Privacy

1. In Solitary Company

Piet Mondrian was a solitary seeker, but he was alone in good company. The history of his artistic career is in large part a family history; significant tributaries to the current of his work rose from the world of craft, where painters value the judgment, invite the approbation, and borrow the techniques of congenial fellow-painters. Mondrian was prepared to recognize the fraternal dimension of his artistic achievement; he generously acknowledged his indebtedness and earnestly discussed his aesthetics. He even helped to found a polemical journal, *De Stijl*, to disseminate his "neoplastic" doctrine. At the same time he wore his cherished isolation like a badge of honor. Writing from Paris in 1914, at a decisive stage of his development, he noted that he was being strongly influenced by Picasso's work, "which I admire *very* much." And he added, immediately and a little defensively: "I am not ashamed to speak of this influence," since it is far better to keep improving one's art than to remain satisfied with one's imperfections, and "think oneself so original!" Yet, in the same letter, he took care to qualify his concession: "I am sure I am completely different from Picasso, as people are generally saying."[1] In his recollection the barrenness of the aesthetic landscape he had traversed loomed large. "I knew little of the modern art movement," he wrote late in life. "When I first saw the work of the Impressionists, van Gogh, van Dongen, and the Fauves, I admired it. But I had to seek the true way alone."[2] He was unalterably diffident, forever dissatisfied with the stage he had reached; but he was also at the end wholly certain that he had found his personal signature. That is why, in his autobiographical moments, he would stress his creative solitude at the expense of the comforting companionship he had known and valued: "I had to seek the true way alone."

1. Mondrian to H. P. Bremmer, January 29, 1914; in J. M. Joosten, ed., "Documentatie over Mondriaan (1)," Letter no. 5, *Museumjournaal*, **XIII,** 4 (1968), 213.
2. "Toward the True Vision of Reality," in Mondrian, *Plastic Art and Pure Plastic Art and Other Essays*, ed. Robert Motherwell (1951), 10.

It is too easy to dismiss such a claim as myth-making. It was, but Mondrian's private myth, like many such myths, contains a good measure of truth: a great artist's style is always bound to contain a powerful infusion of individual talent. Yet for the loneliest of artists his private history can never be his complete history. The other dimensions of his life, as I have reiterated from the beginning, have their psychological aspect and leave a psychological deposit. However much the artist himself may undervalue them, however deeply he represses them, what psychologists call the significant others are always there, and always significant.

It was only natural that the leap into abstraction should have been a collective enterprise. Avant-garde artists need approving society no less than safe academics, perhaps more: academics crave reassurance that they are indeed safe; the avant-garde, for their part, that their work is not simply eccentric or wholly arbitrary. It should therefore occasion no surprise that in the early days of Cubism there were times when it took a practiced eye to tell a Braque from a Picasso [153, 154];[2a] or that in the founding months of Neoplasticism, a van Doesburg was practically interchangeable with a Mondrian [155, 156]. These painters were pioneers crossing the frontier in a select caravan.

Unwittingly, historians of art have minimized the daring of this venture. To make order of the past is, of course, part of their professional obligation. But it also becomes at times a professional deformation: in mapping historic roads leading to, and from, Kandinsky, Delaunay, or Mondrian, historians have failed to acknowledge the strenuous travail of these artists' expedition, the breath-taking satisfaction of their arrival, and the intrinsic importance of their reports. One victim of such denigration has been Picasso, and his protest matters here not merely because he was Picasso but because one of those who victimized him was Mondrian. For Picasso nothing seemed more unjust, more uncomprehending, than to visualize past styles as though they were temporary halting places, lesser oases, on the road from one pure vision to another: "Many think that Cubism is an art of transition, an experiment which is to bring ulterior results. Those who think that way have not understood it. Cubism is not either a seed or a foetus, but an art dealing primarily with forms, and when a form is realized it is there to live its own life."[3] Picasso is right, and it is an important matter to be right about; to impose extraneous purposes on past art, to see it all bravely leading to the consummation of the present, is to misread its intentions, its meaning and often even its consequences. Few artists court the role

2a. I owe this illustration to John Golding, *Cubism: A History and an Analysis* (rev. ed., 1968), 91, Plates 26 and 27.

3. Statement published in 1923. Dore Ashton, ed., *Picasso on Art: A Selection of Views* (1972), 5–6.

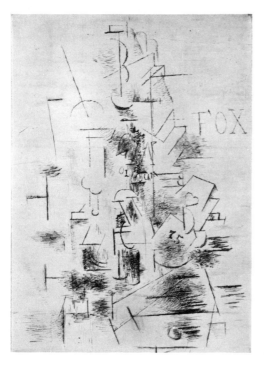

153. Georges Braque. *The Fox,* 1912

154. Pablo Picasso. *Still Life with Bottle,* 1912

155. Theo van Doesburg. *Composition II,* 1918

156. Piet Mondrian. *Composition with Color Planes No. 3,* 1917

of John the Baptist, humbly preparing the way for someone greater than they. When they think of posterity, they think of how much it will honor them for their own sake, for their own work. And they may be justified: it may be appropriate to construct a chain of historical continuity; it is quite inappropriate to despise the links that make it up.

Gratuitous, and even obtuse, as it seems for Mondrian to charge an artist as powerful and original as Picasso with cowardice or at least inconsequence, Mondrian read Picasso's place in the history of modern art in precisely that way. When he went to Paris in late 1911 he was, as he recalled, "immediately drawn to the Cubists, especially to Picasso and Leger." [See 154, 157] But "gradually," Mondrian adds, "I became aware that Cubism did not accept the logical consequences of its own discoveries; it was not developing abstraction toward its ultimate goal, the expression of pure reality."[4] This reminiscence says less about the history of art than about Mondrian's view of his own development as an artist, and thus deserves its place in history which, as I have argued, is largely about perceptions. Mondrian's evaluation of Picasso's Cubism fulfilled some complicated psychological requirements. Mondrian needed at the same time both a sense of his essential uniqueness and of comforting companions allied in a great enterprise: standing on Picasso's shoulders he had seen what Picasso had not been able to see, but then, after all, it was good to know that it was Picasso's shoulders on which he was standing. These feelings, apparently contradictory, actually complemented one another in Mondrian's psychic economy. Together they underscored the difficulty and facilitated the pursuit of Mondrian's exploration into an aesthetic no-man's-land.

If historians, with their unwarranted teleologies, have done less than justice to the intrepidity of such explorations, the vast quantities of abstract art crowding the galleries and museums of our own day further obstruct our perception of the imaginative energy that animated the first generation of abstract painters. I am not arguing that abstract art is somehow better, more advanced, than Fauvism or Cubism or Surrealism. It is not even much more difficult to read than these other styles: the words that many Cubist canvases incorporated into their design were no more than fragments of memory, illegible allusions to private experiences. And Magritte's famous little painting, *The Wind and the Song*, with its clearly lettered caption, *"Ceci n'est pas une Pipe,"* [158] should remind us that often modern figurative art, even when it pretends to offer an explanation, is actually engaged in mystification. The caption seems a deliberate false clue; after all, Magritte has painted a pipe. But on second thought, the caption is literally correct since what

4. "Toward the True Vision of Reality," 10.

157. Fernand Léger. *Smokers*, 1911

we are seeing is not a pipe but the painting of a pipe. The irrelevant title that Magritte has affixed to his canvas only compounds the confusion he has so willfully conjured up. Modern art, in short, has found many ways besides abstraction of saying nothing, and just as many ways of saying something that, without a commentary, must remain unintelligible.

Yet abstract art ventures beyond the planned unintelligibility, the

158. René Magritte. *The Wind and the Song*, 1928–1929

sheer mischievousness of Cubists and Surrealists. It cuts the last lifeline with the past and the last link with the outside world; it tosses aside all the obvious benefits that recognizable iconography provides and instead presents itself as an art demanding to be experienced and judged by reference to itself alone. With this demand, abstract art made a revolution in the history of man's aesthetic perception perhaps more far-reaching than the triumphant discovery of perspective in the early Renaissance. If Cubists and, later, Surrealists, were willing to be difficult, uninformative, and taciturn, abstract artists were willing to be silent. It was a resounding silence, deeply offensive and threatening to many art-lovers, especially in the early days, around 1910, before abstract forms had become familiar enough to be read as allusions to other forms in the same world. Some of the abstract painters, Mondrian among them, urgently wanted to communicate their sense of things, often the most portentous: their feelings about humanity, about the world, about God. They were often religious about their art in more ways than one. But they were prophets who could expect little honor, for their work sent out few explicit, and no easy, messages.

The relation of art to nature has always been problematic. Even when art was assigned the role of imitating nature, the precise character of that mimetic act was a matter of intense dispute. Those classic stories of naturalist still-lifes deceiving their viewers—of birds pecking at painted grapes—only underscore the severity of the problem by appearing, through a sleight of hand, to resolve it. "I would like to know," Picasso has asked in his blunt fashion, "if anyone has ever seen a natural work of art. Nature and art, being two different things, cannot be the same thing."[5] One quality that differentiates art from nature, little commented on but still uncanny, is that art has always enjoyed a factitious immortality. Before the advent of modernism, symbols and signs were common cultural property; everyone knew the meaning of a crucifix, remembered the attributes of saints, took pleasure in a landscape and found humor in a tavern scene. Yet even in those days art constituted a moment of frozen history, insolently refusing to age while generations who had stood before the same painting had grown old and disappeared from the world. Chardin's loaves, unlike the bread of every day, would never become stale; Canaletto's palazzi, miraculously perfect, would never need repair; Boucher's Venuses, defying the laws of nature, would never develop wrinkles. Even Landseer's *Monarch of the Glen* would never be unthroned. That is why *The Portrait of Dorian Gray,* with its reversal of the unshakable order, with that awful portrait subject to the vicissitudes of organic matter, remains such a shocking invention.

While the most realistic art intimated its distance from nature to all who would look, and while it opened, at least in principle, the way to decorative designs owing nothing to familiar shapes, the abstract art of which Mondrian's canvases is the supreme expression found more specific precursors in its past than this. There are passages in the German Romantics—texts that at least some modern painters, like Kandinsky, knew well—inviting artists to construct a new aesthetic in which color and composition would take precedence over recognizable subject matter; and Goethe, long before the writings of Rimbaud and Huysmans, discussed the possibilities of synaesthesia, which, playfully experimenting with the color and taste of sounds or the sound of colors and letters, served to emancipate art from anecdotes, from resemblances, from natural appearances. In the 1860s, as we know, Zola chose to analyze Manet's most scandalous paintings, the *Olympia* and the *Déjeuner sur l'Herbe* [20, 30], as colored patches.[6] And Walter Pater, with his much-quoted declaration that "all art constantly aspires towards the condition of music," wrote, as it were, the charter for abstract art.

But it is one thing to write the manifesto, another to go into battle; one thing to run away from home, another to cross the street. Gauguin professed to despise the earthbound realism of the Impressionists who, he said derisively, were "shackled by the need of probability," but his *The Yellow Christ* [159], though very yellow indeed, was still recogniz-

---

5. Statement published in 1923; Ashton, ed., *Picasso on Art,* 4. Mondrian often said the same thing, emphatically.
6. See pp. 78–79.

159. Paul Gauguin. *The Yellow Christ*, 1889

ably a Christ. Van Gogh assigned specific emotional significations to colors—in his system, blue stood for infinity, yellow for love. Yet his *The Night Café* of 1888 [2], explicitly designed to "express the terrible passions of humanity by means of red and green," remains, whatever else it may also be, a café at night.[7] Symbolists and Expressionists sought objective correlatives for inner states, but their artistic vocabulary, no matter how esoteric, retained at least tenuous ties with the language of tradition and with ordinary visual experience. The conquest of abstraction may have been a matter of many small steps, each facilitated by the artist's awareness of steps that others had taken before. It is instructive to find the most radical of Abstract Expressionists, Jackson Pollock, seeing himself as "part of a long tradition dating back with Cézanne, up through the Cubists, the post-Cubists, to the painting done today."[8] And Mondrian may have drawn decisive strength from this sequence of steps and this tradition. I am in fact claiming that he did. But at the same time he needed the support of his fellow-craftsmen, present and past, precisely because the last step he took sometime around 1917 was a step into the unknown.

The deliberate, hesitant pace of Mondrian's artistic revolution is a measure of the difficulty and the daring of abstraction. It was not until he was forty, in 1912 [160], that he undertook his really drastic deformations of nature—his earlier experiments, which date back only a year or two, no more [161], retain sufficient verisimilitude to permit the easy identification of their subject matter.[9] It was not until he was forty-two, in 1914, that his obsessive paintings of the ocean lost all but the most remote connection with nature [162]. And it was not until he was forty-five, in 1917, that he began to compose canvases consisting entirely of rectangles [156]. The grids which won immortality for him are the work of an even older man; they date from 1920 and after [163]. Like Manet, but for completely different reasons, Mondrian was the most reluctant of revolutionaries.

Had Mondrian stopped painting in 1911, before he went to Paris, he would have secured an approving, if modest, paragraph in the history of modern art as a gifted painter of landscapes [164, 165]. His art would

7. See Robert Goldwater, *Gauguin* (n.d.), 92; and Meyer Schapiro, *Van Gogh* (n.d.), 70.
8. Statement of 1950, quoted in Carter Ratcliffe, "Painterly vs. Painted," Thomas B. Hess and John Ashbery, eds., *Painterly Painting, Artnews Annual*, XXXVII (1971), 131.
9. The evolution of his various "trees" testifies to this change; they are conveniently grouped together in Michel Seuphor, *Piet Mondrian: Life and Work* (n.d.), catalogue illustrations nos. 169–200.

have been classified as enjoyable for its subtle color and its refined draftsmanship, and for a certain confidence of attack. But Mondrian's place would have remained modest because, however pleasing his canvases, they were derivative. Like most painters, Mondrian for many years painted like other painters.

There was little doubt from the earliest years, at least in his own mind, that he would become an artist. "Born in Holland 1872, at Amersfoort," so begins a draft of an autobiographical statement, "I early did painting, conducted by my father (amateur) and my uncle (painter) and became diplomes for school and high-school drawing teacher."[10] [166] These laconic sentences suppress a serious domestic conflict, and neglect to characterize its resolution for what it was: an ingenious compromise. Mondrian's father, evidently a talented draftsman, was a schoolteacher; in his authoritarian fashion, he dictated his son's choice of career—school teaching, thus validating his own profession. The elder Mondriaan[11] was, by all reports, a severe and orthodox Calvinist [167], and some biographers have professed to recognize the austere iconoclasm of early Calvinism in his son's late canvases—these paintings exemplifying what the psychoanalysts call the return of the repressed. But whatever the truth of this argument, the elder Mondriaan was no iconoclast: he put his artistic gifts to use in his teaching, doing biblical scenes on the blackboard for the edification of his pupils.[12] In any event, if the father would not do without art, neither would the son: Piet Mondriaan secured two diplomas, one in 1889, the other in 1892, that entitled him to teach drawing in elementary and in secondary schools.

10. From the ms. reproduced in Seuphor, *Mondrian*, 19; compare the final version in "Toward the True Vision of Reality," 10.

11. To avoid possible misunderstanding it may be useful to note that the family spelled its name Mondriaan, and that before 1910, the painter dropped an "a" though he was not wholly consistent about usage for some years.

12. See Seuphor, *Mondrian*, 44; Seuphor reports (p. 52) that around the age of nineteen, Mondrian briefly toyed with entering the clergy. Certainly his religious interests were lifelong.

160. Piet Mondrian. *Still Life with Ginger-pot II*, 1912

161. Piet Mondrian. *Windmill in Sunlight*, ca. 1908

162. Piet Mondrian. *Pier and Ocean*, 1914

163. Piet Mondrian. *Composition in Grey, Red, Yellow and Blue*, 1920

164. Piet Mondrian. *A Shallow Pond at Saasveld in Twente,* 1907–1908

165. Piet Mondrian, *By the Sea,* 1908–1909

This was the ingenuity of the compromise: the younger Mondriaan would match his own impulsion with his father's desire—he would teach but he would teach art.

The compromise soon proved unstable, though it later provided Mondrian with some unexpected gratification: his friend and biographer Michel Seuphor recalls seeing the two Dutch diplomas, "yellow with age and carefully folded," in New York; Mondrian had preserved them "to prove that he also knew how to draw academically."[13] This is to anticipate the familiar philistine objection to abstract art that it requires no skill, an anticipation as unnecessary as it is touching: even after Mondrian had his way and secured his father's permission to devote himself to the study of art, he continued his academic training for several years. And his early landscapes and drawings of flowers amply demonstrate his technical competence in line and color.

They also demonstrate his dependence. For years Mondrian was little more than a satellite, though a brilliant one. He made choices among available styles. From the beginning he rejected what he considered the sentiment of romanticism: "I prefered to paint landscaps, houses, etc. by gray dampy weather or by very strong sunlight when the atmosphere by its dencity the particularitys of things and the great lines accentue them selves. I sketched by moonlight—cows lying down or staying immovable on Dutch's flat meadows & houses with their dead windows then. But not as romantist: I saw with realist eyes."[14] But he did not yet see the world wholly with his own eyes; his canvases bear the imprint of the Hague Realist school, and, later, that of the Amsterdam Impressionists, notably of George Hendrik Breitner [168]. Even when he began to move beyond these mildly modern schools by adopting pure colors and laying on his paint in broad flat strokes [169, 170], he took his inspiration from the work of other painters, from the Fauves and from late Neo-Impressionism. Mondrian discarded his old masters by appealing to new masters [171]. In retrospect, we recognize the steady, if glacial, movement of his art in a single direction: toward simplification. But it was a long time before he found his own simplicity. Z3The five years of his liberation from nature—between 1912 and 1917 —continue to show the same openness to other painters but with a significant difference: his work suggests, and his letters confirm, that he was increasingly using the art of others to clarify his own mind. He was searching for purity in art and for universal principles of beauty, and in this search he confronted his fellow-painters as an equal. While he was in Paris he appreciatively studied the Futurists but thought them too closely tied to mere sensations; he thought even better of the Cu-

13. Seuphor, *Mondrian*, 45.
14. From the ms. in Seuphor, *Mondrian*, 19.

166. *Mondrian's Uncle, Frits Mondriaan, at the Easel*

167. Pieter Cornelis Mondriaan, Mondrian's Father, *The World is the Truth*

168. George Hendrik Breitner. *The Damrak in Amsterdam*

169. Piet Mondrian. *Lighthouse at Westkapelle*, ca. 1909

170. Piet Mondrian. *Dune II*, 1908–1909

171. Jan Theodoor Toorop. *Middelburg Canal*, 1907

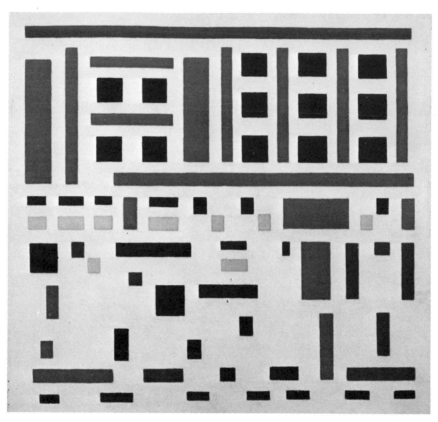

172. Bart van der Leck. *Geometric Composition, II,* 1917

bists for "taking the great step toward abstraction."[15] And after he returned to the Netherlands in 1914 he came to know Bart van der Leck [172] and Theo van Doesburg [155], two painters who were battling their own way into abstraction and whose energetic, self-confident manifestos greatly impressed him. The result was the journal *De Stijl,* founded in 1917, inspired, edited and, in the main, financed by van Doesburg. It was through his collaboration with the De Stijl group that Mondrian finally found his way to himself, to his unmistakable grids. In 1931, in an obituary tribute to van Doesburg, Mondrian reviewed these debts. He had learned from the divisionists and the pointillists, he wrote, to do without the "natural aspect of color"; and in Paris, "the Cubists had made me see that there is also a possibility of doing without the natural aspect of form." He had continued to experiment, using only straight lines placed in "rectangular opposition;" [156, 162] and it

15. Mondrian to Bremmer, in Joosten, "Documentatie over Mondriaan," 213 (see note 1 above). For these crucial years, see J. M. Joosten, "Mondrian: Between Cubism and Abstraction," in *Piet Mondrian, 1872–1944,* Centennial Exhibition (1971), 53–66.

was in that period that he had "met artists of a mind fairly close to my own," first of all van der Leck, who was still a figurative painter but painted in uniform planes and pure colors. "My technique, more or less Cubist, hence more or less pictorial, underwent the influence of his precise technique. Shortly afterward I had the pleasure of making the acquaintance of Van Doesburg." Full of vitality, full of zeal for abstract art, sincerely valuing Mondrian's work, van Doesburg "came to ask me to collaborate on a review he intended to publish and which he wanted to call Stijl. I was happy to be able to publish my ideas about art that I was then in process of committing to paper," and to work with congenial artists.[16] Mondrian was writing in an elegiac mood, for a special audience, at a time of mourning. "In lapidary inscriptions," Samuel Johnson has said, "a man is not upon oath." But while the occasion induced Mondrian to minimize his share in the creation of Neoplasticism, his survey states his obligations with fair precision. This is what I meant when I said at the beginning that Mondrian, the solitary seeker, was alone in good company.

2. The Assault on Nature

Yet, Mondrian's conquest of abstraction was more than an aesthetic venture. Even his early work occasionally sounds notes different from the chamber harmonies of likeminded craftsmen. There are some rather mysterious drawings of dying flowers [173] and ambitious paintings of women who are emblems rather than models [174], works hinting at a mental world larger than art—or, better, a larger world disclosed and expressed by art—to which an inquiry into art alone cannot secure access. For many years Mondrian did not publish his commitments to that wider world; he confined his speculative flights to conversations with a favorite brother and an intimate friend, canvassing the large themes that the young normally feel obliged to canvass. Then, in the early issues of De Stijl, Mondrian made it plain that his program for modern art was also a program for modern man. The style he had so slowly evolved was more than a style: it was a diagnosis, a manifesto, perhaps a cure.

16. De Stijl, last number (1932), 49.

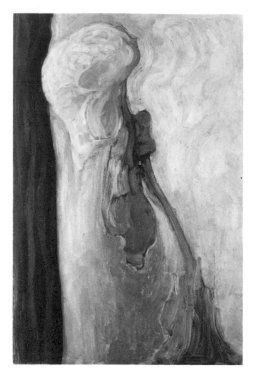

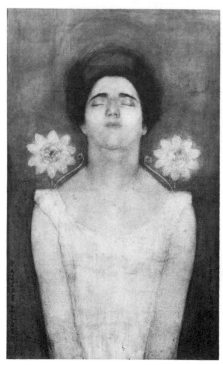

173. Piet Mondrian. *Dying Chrysanthe-mum,* 1908

174. Piet Mondrian. *Passion Flower,* ca. 1903–1904

To describe the art of Mondrian's maturity as a commentary on industrial civilization is to walk through an open door. The sophisticated connoisseur, the casual tourist, the baffled philistine all share a sense that these implacable grids say something about a world dominated by machines and by time tables, a world in which rationalism is king. Those rhythmic and relentless rectangles, objective, cool, and impenetrable, may speak of a desperate search for order and clarity amidst the chaos of modernity, or, quite the contrary, celebrate the century that has at last expelled mystery from its ancient hiding places. The proliferation of Mondrian's characteristic patterns—on book jackets [175], shopping bags, even on dresses—is of more than incidental interest, but it does nothing to specify the meaning, and the causes, of Mondrian's art; it only demonstrates the smooth pliancy of commercial culture.[17] Mondrian's art is quintessentially modern, certainly, but its eloquence is only apparent; his art is, in effect, wholly unreadable.

There is something appropriate about this illegibility. Mondrian, after all, was not a political cartoonist. Yet the conviction will not down that the striking resemblance of his work to the blank faces of skyscrapers

17. This, in any event, takes us into the realm of the *effect of* Mondrian rather than the *causes working on* him.

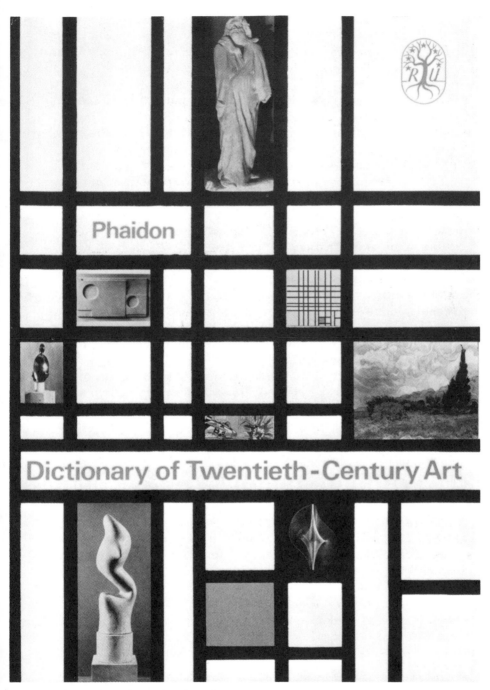

175. Book Jacket (after Mondrian)

or the angular compositions of modern design is not fortuitous. Mondrian's vision and the most modern manifestations of the modern world seem somehow, and intimately, involved with one another.

His pronouncements on art lend color to the portrait of Mondrian, the emphatically public artist, who draws his inspiration from the most pervasive concerns of his century and who intends to express the spirit of the modern. "The artist," he wrote in the first volume of *De Stijl*, "is simply the more or less appropriate *instrument* through which a culture . . . expresses itself aesthetically." All mature persons form "part of the spirit of the age" and all in some measure "represent it." But the modern artist—and Mondrian meant, of course, himself and his associates—represents it most completely. The first, most important, quality of Neoplasticism is its *"reasonableness—redelijkheid."* It is above all about reasonableness that modern man asks. That is why Neoplasticism, wholly rational, is supremely *"an art for this time."*[18] It is so even more because, in addition to being rational, it is abstract, a quality that twentieth-century culture finds increasingly congenial: "The life of cultivated modern man," Mondrian wrote in the opening number of *De Stijl*, "is gradually turning away from the natural: it is growing more and more to be an *abstract* life."[19]

It is tempting to ascribe the confident tone of such assertions to the heady experience of translating a private sensibility into something of an institution. They date, after all, from 1917 and 1918, when the De Stijl group, a coterie of likeminded painters, sculptors, and architects, had just been formed. But in fact Mondrian continued to take the same generous view of his art, its sources, its meaning, and its consequences for the rest of his life. At once the product of society and its spokesman, he said art must assist the modern forces struggling for supremacy. "What a beautiful task lies in prospect before art," he exclaimed in 1931: "to prepare the future."[20] And he did not scale down these claims in his last years; as late as 1942 he reiterated them on the occasion of his first exhibition in the United States. Sketching his artistic development, Mondrian insisted that he had always worked "in accord with the spirit of modern times"; his experiments, like those of his friends, had been attempts to "make the public aware of the possibilities of pure plastic art" and "to demonstrate its relationship to and its effect on modern life." The task of plastic art was to bring clarity into the world, a task in Mondrian's eyes of "great importance for humanity." Mankind,

18. *De Stijl*, I, 5 (1918), 50–51. The series of essays that Mondrian published in the early numbers of the first volume of this journal bore the collective title "De nieuwe beelding in de schilderkunst." I will refer to this series by volume, number, and pages only.

19. *De Stijl*, I, 1 (1917), 4.

20. Quoted from *Cahiers d'art*, VI, 1 (1931), 43, in Hans L. C. Jaffé, *Piet Mondrian* (n.d.), 59.

"after centuries of culture, can accelerate its progress" by gaining "a truer vision of reality." And it is art that will serve as the engine of acceleration: "Even in this chaotic moment," he triumphantly concludes, "we can near equilibrium through the realization of a true vision of reality. Modern life and culture helps us in this. Science and technics are abolishing the oppression of time. But these advances used in a wrong way still cause great dislocations. Our way leads toward a search for the equivalence of life's unequal oppositions. Because it is free of all utilitarian limitations, plastic art must move not only parallel with human progress but must advance ahead of it. It is the task of art to express a clear vision of reality."[21] In this exalted self-appraisal the artist appears as a liberator, a worthy companion to the physicist and the philosopher, all together freeing mankind from subjectivity, from confusion, from the oppression of time.

Such pretensions, and such prose, cry out for criticism. They beg all the questions they purport to settle, and offend against the very lucidity they promise to provide; they are as abstract and opaque as the art they celebrate. Mondrian sees the world caught in a struggle between antagonistic forces: chaos, disequilibrium, confusion battling order, balance, clarity. And as he opposes the former, so he supports the latter. Such preferences are hardly startling and, until we know what Mondrian means by chaos or by order, in no way informative. There are times when the historian must regret the modern artist's irresistible urge to explain himself.

Yet there are passages when Mondrian lapses into specificity. He is far from hostile to science and technology. For Mondrian the city, especially the metropolitan capital, constitutes the vital center for the new, rational, abstract society that he wants "plastic art" to help bring into being. The city corrects the essential disorderliness of raw nature: "The truly modern artist," he wrote in 1918, "sees the metropolis as the supreme form of abstract life; it stands closer to him than nature" and is more likely to give him a sense of beauty. "In the metropolis, nature has already been set right, reduced to order by the human spirit."[22] Rural nature is capricious, but its "caprice" is "quickly set right in the metropolis—*wereldstad.*"[23] *Broadway Boogie Woogie* [176] is a spirited homage to New York; and his writings, his conversation, and the titles of some of his paintings contain touching tributes to Paris and London. The distance that separates Manet the *flâneur* and Mondrian the hermit is great; so is the distance between Gropius, who utilized technology, from Mondrian, who merely exclaimed over it. But the urban

21. "Toward the True Vision of Reality," 13–15.
22. *De Stijl*, **I**, 11 (1918), 194.
23. *De Stijl*, **V**, 3 (1922), 45.

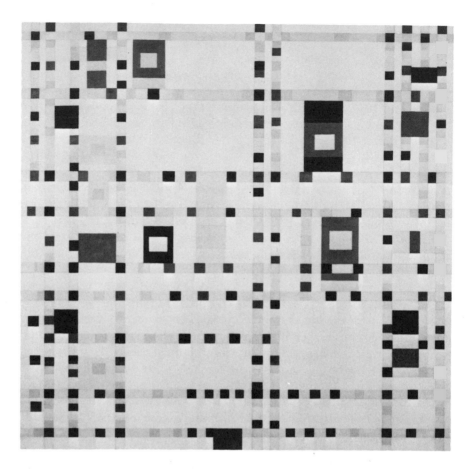

176. Piet Mondrian. *Broadway Boogie Woogie,* 1942–43

impulses, so palpable in Manet and Gropius, were also at work in Mondrian, though in a more subterranean fashion.

Art, then, was for Mondrian a cultural product and a cultural weapon, a privileged instrument for the construction of an urban and, in the best sense of that word, artificial order. Yet Mondrian's perception of his world, no matter how persistent his call for reality, suffers from a curious remoteness. His feelings seem, like his paintings, abstract, even abstracted. The word "oppression" is much under Mondrian's pen; he sees it as man's principal adversary: "Humanity, as well as art, needs freedom." Yet in 1941, when he wrote this ringing sentence, it did not have the meaning that the current headlines would seem to make imperative. Mondrian had left Paris for London in 1938, fearful of the coming war; he had left London for New York in 1940, fearful of the Blitz. The daily news from Europe was catastrophic—his Dutch homeland occupied, Belgium overrun, France conquered, Britain besieged.

A celebration of freedom would seem only logical, almost mandatory. But at the same time, in the same essay, Mondrian blandly noted that he saw a universal law of progress at work in history: "Humanity is constantly developing toward freedom. . . . Time proves that humanity, despite its deviations, is always moving in the right direction."[24] And since all modern art is "a *liberation from the oppression of the past,*"[25] even the destructiveness of modern warfare has a function in the historical drama: "In war many relics of the past are destroyed, among them many beautiful specimens of art. Obviously it is hard to see beautiful things disappear. But life, as continuous progress, is always right."[26] One begins to wonder: if Mondrian is in tune with the world which world is it that he is in tune with? His much-reiterated realism, it would seem, is a form of mysticism.

Mondrian was indeed a mystic, and his mysticism amounts to more than an irresponsible use of abstract nouns or the spouting of metaphysical generalities. Much of his life he was committed to theosophy, and even after he left the movement in the 1920s his sympathies with its teachings did not diminish. This long-standing and much-discussed infatuation in no way compromises the claim that Mondrian drew his inspiration from culture, for the theosophical cult to which he subscribed was a response to modern industrial civilization.[27] To embrace theosophy was to enact a ceremony of rejection. In 1888 Madame Blavatsky, the founder of the faith, somberly warned her Western readers in her most famous book, *The Secret Doctrine,* that "all is doubt, negation, iconoclasm and brutal indifference, in our age of the hundred 'isms' and no religion. Every idol is broken save the Golden Calf."[28]

In what they diagnosed as this desperate plight, Blavatsky and her devoted, if sometimes rebellious followers—Annie Besant, Edouard Schuré, Rudolf Steiner—sought light from an occult and antique tradition of Western mysticism, from mythical figures like Orpheus and Hermes, and from Eastern mystics whose message provided the answers that Western seekers could not find in official Christianity or modern atheism: "Never," Edouard Schuré wrote in 1889, "has the aspiration after spiritual life, the invisible world, rejected by the materialistic theories of scientists and by worldly opinion, been more serious and more real. We find this aspiration in the regrets, in the doubts, in

---

24. "Plastic Art and Pure Plastic Art," in *Plastic Art and Pure Plastic Art,* 43.
25. "Plastic Art and Pure Plastic Art," 42.
26. "Plastic Art and Pure Plastic Art," 41.
27. Considering the stupefying mediocrity of its theology, it might be better to call theosophy not a response but a symptom.
28. Helena Petrovna Blavatsky, *The Secret Doctrine: The Synthesis of Science, Religion and Philosophy* (1888), 2 vols. in one, I, 675.

the dark melancholy and even the blasphemies of our naturalist novel-
ists and our decadent poets."[29] In delightful contrast, theosophy promised to still doubts and dispel melancholy.

Theosophy seems a rather paradoxical choice for those, like Mondrian, who professed themselves moderns: its roots were ancient and its
ideas alien, its living Asian gurus faced Western culture with blank
incomprehension, and its doctrines offered Western man no remedy
other than escape. But human nature thrives on paradoxes: it is simply
a fact that in the late nineteenth and early twentieth century many
apostles of modernism, though admirers of some aspects of modernity,
in general loathed the modern world. And many of them—Vasily Kandinsky and Franz Marc, Victor Hugo and William Butler Yeats—embraced esoteric doctrines and practiced spiritualistic rituals that were
as hostile to existing Christian sects as they were to contemporary
positivism. In the Middle Ages, number mysticism had been the superstition of the learned; now, in the time of Mondrian, theosophy became
the superstition of the avant-garde.

Theosophy provided entertainment, reassurance, the excitement
normally associated with the uncanny and the secret, and, above all,
relief from what many sensitive spirits found to be the unbearable
tedium and invincible vulgarity of commercial bourgeois culture. It
offered an alternative to materialism. There was a conviction abroad
that science and its ubiquitous companion, technology, had ruthlessly
truncated human possibilities, sheering off man's deepest probes and
highest flights to make life flat, two-dimensional. Science had succeeded
in exposing Christianity as false, even absurd; this had made official
religion intellectually as well as emotionally unavailable. But science,
while performing this necessary act of destruction, had constructed no
satisfying substitute: positivism, the religion of the scientist, was aridity
itself, a very desert of thought that offered no shelter from the blazing
sun of fact and the icy blast of scientific theory. Science, so this argument went, gave man technical information that few could grasp, crea-
ture comforts that only the philistine could enjoy, and a view of a
universe vastly indifferent to the happiness, the lot, the very existence
of man—a cosmic yawn. Amidst ennui and despair, theosophy restored
hope, a sense of mystery, of adventure, and of intimacy among the
adept.

What made theosophy so peculiarly seductive was that it committed
its devotees to nothing decisive. It would be inaccurate to say that it
ended philosophical and theological confusion. Being itself the most
confused of eclectic compilations, theosophy legitimated confusion; it

29. Schuré, *Les grands initiés: Esquisse de l'histoire secrète des religions* (1889; 100th
printing, 1927), xxiii.

licensed the faithful to hold beliefs that a more demanding theology or more rigorous metaphysics would have exposed as, quite simply, inconsistent. Theosophy had something for everyone, almost as though Madame Blavatsky had put her doctrines together after consulting public opinion polls. She advertised *The Secret Doctrine* in its subtitle as "the synthesis of science, religion, and philosophy," and the self-confidence of the definite article is as notable as the comprehensiveness of her claim. With its veiled, intentionally imprecise notion of the unknowable God, theosophy could attract even some followers of the agnostic Herbert Spencer. Theosophists professed to credit spiritual evidences which a scientist could, at best, regard with skepticism, but Madame Blavatsky diplomatically asserted that, at least on the level of observable realities, "the teachings of occult and so-called exact Science" could not possibly conflict.[30] It is instructive that Annie Besant, the most spectacular convert the theosophists could boast in the late nineteenth century, came to the faith from atheism and Socialism; it is equally instructive that one reason for her conversion was her conviction that theosophy could explain more phenomena than atheist science ever could. And theosophy offered even more pleasures to its initiates than colorful Eastern mysteries, the gratifying sense of belonging among a few select spirits, and the tantalizing hope that beyond the limited revelations Madame Blavatsky had seen fit to reveal there were other, yet greater illuminations: it drew freely on magical numbers— three, four, and seven. These numbers were rich with sacred resonance and responsive to deep psychological rhythms; they gave a welcome stable structure to what amounted in essence to a bland, even impudent syncretism of Christian and oriental doctrines, ancient and modern superstitions, familiar and esoteric ritual, unscientific claims and scientific certainty, and irreconcilable philosophical ideas.

Theosophy is so instructive a symptom of civilization at the turn of the century because it was in no way an isolated phenomenon. Though partially independent of one another, often incompatible and sometimes downright antagonistic, the concurrent streams of aestheticism, symbolism, and Romantic Catholicism shared with theosophy a deeply value-impregnated dualism.[31] All sharply differentiated between the world of business, science, mundane styles like Realism and Impressionism on one side, and the world behind the mask, lofty contemplation, disdainful distance from philistine pleasure-seekers on the other. Pater's aristocratic Epicureanism, Wilde's paradoxical tributes to artifice,

30. *Secret Doctrine*, I, 477.
31. For one of these strands, particularly interesting since it remained largely embedded in official religion, see Richard Griffiths, *The Reactionary Revolution: The Catholic Revival in French Literature, 1870–1914* (1966).

Mallarmé's commitment to difficult diction, Gauguin's symbolist canvases, Stefan George's slavish and aristocratic coterie—all, like theosophy, dramatized a widespread need for escape from everyday experience, from the visible, the vulgar, the material, to some thinner, purer air. And, different as they were, all these movements offered the same sort of ladder from the lower to the higher world: allusion, symbol, legend, mystical correspondences, esoteric rites.

The appeal of such notions to the artist is obvious enough: to exalt the spirit is to exalt him, its guardian; to make religion into an art is to invite the heady reversal of making art into a religion. "Art," wrote Mondrian in 1917, "—however much it is an end in itself—is, just like religion, a means by which the universal is known."[32] Theosophy, with its inconstant and incongruous allies in painting, poetry, and theology, offered hope that an ambitious artist might realize Shelley's proud fantasy and become the unacknowledged legislator to a world desperately in need of laws.

Mondrian's official association with theosophy dates from May, 1909, when he joined the Dutch Theosophical Society; his most intense preoccupation with its doctrines came around 1916, when he held long, earnest conversations with the Dutch "Christosoph" M. H. J. Schoenmaekers. It is significant that Mondrian, who bought few books and kept fewer, had Schoenmaekers' theosophical writings in his studio.[33] At the same time Mondrian's religious ruminations, his search for purity, as yet only fleetingly visible in his paintings, precede his commitment to theosophy by several years. Its doctrines did not provide him with a sudden flood of illumination; rather, they fitted and confirmed his own hard-won beliefs. A long letter he wrote to the sympathetic Dutch critic Israel Querido in the Summer of 1909, a few months after he had joined the Theosophical Society, sounds so calm in its parade of generalities that it must reflect views long held, not recently acquired. The letter, a very credo of the artist as a young thinker, is a significant document. It speaks of Mondrian's passionate drive toward the spiritual and the

32. *De Stijl*, **I**, 5 (1918), 52. "For me the whole artistic problem," Mondrian noted late in life, in his somewhat uncertain English, "is to make empty space living in an universal way." Slip of paper exhibited in a biographical show at the Sidney Janis Gallery, February 7–March 9, 1974.

33. On Mondrian's engagement with Schoenmaekers and with theosophy in general, see the informative and well-documented essay by R. P. Welsh, "Mondrian and Theosophy," in *Piet Mondrian, 1872–1944*, 35–51. See also Martin S. James, "Mondrian and the Dutch Symbolists," *The Art Journal*, **XXIII**, 2 (Winter 1963–64), 103–111; Sixten Ringbom, "Art in the 'Epoch of the Great Spiritual,'" *Journal of the Warburg and Courtauld Institutes*, **XXIX** (1966), 386–418 (which, though it is mainly about Kandinsky, throws much light on the involvement of modernists with theosophic doctrines); and a few brilliant interpretative pages in Richard Ellmann, *Yeats: The Man and the Masks* (1948), ch. V, "Combatting the 'Materialists.'"

abstract, and displays, once again, the link he saw between the progress of art and the progress of culture. He was aware that his painting was in transition, that there were hills beyond hills he was not yet able to see, let alone climb. "For the present at least," he wrote, presciently and modestly, "I shall restrict my work to the customary world of the senses, since that is the world in which we still live. But nevertheless art already can provide a transition to the finer regions, which I call the spiritual realm." Art is "the path of ascension; away from matter." To take this path in art makes it necessary for the artist to eschew the portrayal of motion and activity. Querido had described Mondrian's painting of 1908, *Devotion* [177], as showing a "prayerful act," and, a little differently, as "a praying girl without action." Mondrian found neither of these characterizations satisfactory. In what is only apparently a quibble he insisted that he had intended to show a "girl conceived devotedly, or viewed devotedly." He did not despise the great tradition; the old masters had depicted actions beautifully. But, as a principled modern, Mondrian laid down the rule that "everything done

177. Piet Mondrian. *Devotion*, ca. 1908

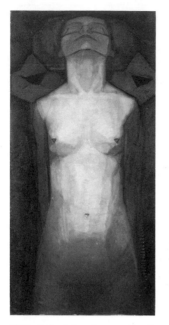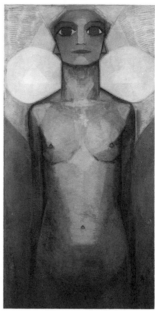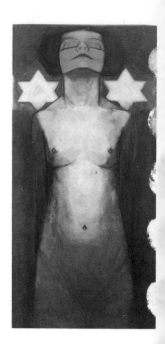

178. Piet Mondrian. *Evolution* (triptych), ca. 1911

in our own time must be expressed very differently." Specifically this
meant an art that was static and abstract. That is why he had given the
girl's hair "that sort of red, to tone down the material side of things, to
suppress any thoughts about 'hair,' 'costume,' etc., and to stress the
spiritual." It is an illuminating confession, in which, as we can now see,
Mondrian's ultimate reliance on pure line and pure color is already
implicit. And he was to conceive his late work, as he conceived his more
tentative work of 1909, in contemplative terms. It was the result, and
the expression, of devout, deeply felt thought. Even though most artists
deny it, he told Querido, there is an "important relationship between
philosophy and art."[34]

The strange triptych he painted about 1911, *Evolution* [178], demonstrates that for Mondrian, at least, philosophy meant theosophy: the
magical number three which dominates the work, the aseptic asexuality
of the three women, the occult emblems that accompany them, the
spiritual progression marked by the figure in the center whose eyes
have been opened, the very theme of illumination and spiritual growth
underscored by the theosophical title—all these are unthinkable without the writings of Madame Blavatsky and Rudolf Steiner. And Mondrian's experiments with straight lines and austere crosses [179] that
mark his work in the years just before his adoption of Neoplasticism in
1917 show the same unmistakable traces.

34. See Joop Joosten, ed., *Two Mondrian Sketchbooks, 1912–1914*, tr. Robert Welsh
(1969), 9–10.

179. Piet Mondrian. *Composition in Black and White*, 1917

Yet while it is proper, and has proved profitable, to cull the writings of the leading theosophists for passages invoking "philosophical crosses" or the esoteric meaning of flowers, Mondrian was not an illustrator to anyone's book, not even Rudolf Steiner's or Madame Blavatsky's. He valued theosophy highly for being, as he said in 1914, a "spiritual science"; it had done much for him, he thought, leading him toward clarity in the realm of spiritual evolution.[35] But he knew himself well enough to know that he was not at home in organizations and that he had little in common with most of those who called themselves theosophists. His friend Charmion von Wiegand has testified that, to him, organizations "represented limitations, a division in the total unity he sought to achieve, and a restriction in the context of his universal philosophy."[36] Therefore that famous series of rectangles to which he

35. *Sketchbooks,* 13 *n.*
36. See Margit Rowell, "Interview with Charmion von Wiegand, June 20, 1971," in *Piet Mondrian, 1872–1944,* 77.

confined his experiments in the last quarter century of his life, subtly but distinctly revising their shapes, their colors, their compositions are not direct transcriptions of ideas, not even of ideas he fervently embraced.

It is true enough that Mondrian consistently viewed himself as an artist of ideas, with deep roots and an exalted mission in society. It was characteristic of him to dedicate his little book of 1920, *Le Néo-Plasticisme,* to the new men yet to come—*"aux hommes futurs."* It was equally characteristic of him to say, nine years later: "To be concerned exclusively with relations, while creating them and seeking their equilibrium in art and in life, that is the good work of today, that is to prepare the future."[37] But for all his political protestations, all his expressed conviction that theosophy was blessed with specific and clear doctrines, it was rather its general ladder of spiritual ascent that attracted him most. Even his social program was only a series of optimistic and shapeless commonplaces. It was the drift of its doctrine, rather than individual tenets, that made him feel at home in theosophy and infused his art: his philosophy was vagueness piled upon vagueness—fortunately, I am tempted to comment, for his painting.

Yet it is possible to be concrete about the abstract and clear about the vague. We can specify the appeal of theosophy for Mondrian and, with that, its causal power for his art. His own testimony is explicit enough: it was spirituality he sought and cherished. For Steiner, as for his fellow-prophets, man is threefold in essence: in ascending purity, he lives through his body, his soul, and his spirit. His first environment, as Rudolf Steiner graphically put it, includes "the objects, intelligence of which flows into him through the gates of his senses, which he touches, smells, tastes, hears, and sees." The second consists of the impressions these objects make on him, his pleasures and pains, his desires and aversions. The third is on a far higher level; here, in the dazzling light of knowledge and insight, where the secrets of body and soul are laid bare, man's godlike essence emerges. "Man," Steiner sums it up, "is citizen of three worlds. Through his body he belongs to the world which he also perceives through his body; through his soul he constructs his own world; through his spirit a world is revealed to him that is elevated above the two others."[38] The spirituality of Steiner—and of Mondrian—thus has a critical as well as a constructive aspect, a negative as well as a positive definition. It is an achievement, but a flight as well; it is a search that follows a rejection. "Everything changes by growth," he wrote in an important dialogue of 1920. "Man, by growing, transcends and goes beyond nature." This is what Mondrian had meant when he said about

37. See Seuphor, *Mondrian,* 168.
38. Steiner, *Theosophie: Einführung in übersinnliche Welterkenntnis und Menschenbestimmung* (5th ed., 1910), 9, 11.

art—his art—that it is "the path of ascension; away from matter."[39]

At this critical point, Mondrian's polemical vocabulary raises an inconvenient paradox. If, as he said, he admired the art that is an escape from matter, how could he, at the same time, admire the modern metropolis—the greatest concentration, the very triumph, of matter? In reconciling this apparent contradiction the historian finds himself propelled from the worlds of craft and of culture into Mondrian's intimate private world. The matter that Mondrian found hateful, and therefore rejected, was by no means coextensive with all manifestations of materiality. His anxiety and aversion rather came to fasten on the organic, the living—on the out-of-doors, and even more on the human body, with its curves, its smells, its unpredictability, its disorderly passions. There are authenticated anecdotes reporting Mondrian sitting in cafés with friends, asking to change places with them so that he would not have to look at trees or at the moving shapes of passers-by. And one powerful reason why he preferred New York to Paris was that Paris with its tree-lined boulevards was still "so romantic." New York, it seemed, had happily shed this form of slavery to the senses.[40] What enabled Mondrian to be a devotee of theosophy and at the same time of the metropolis—what made it, in fact, perfectly consistent—was that he experienced both as a concentrated, systematic assault on nature.

3. Shapes of Reticence

The recognition of Mondrian's pervasive and overpowering hostility toward nature propels us toward the core of his character, the purest, most deeply buried springs of his art. Mondrian himself had some awareness of just how thoroughly this visceral aversion was enmeshed with his efforts at achieving pure plasticity: "Abstract art," he wrote in 1943, "is in opposition to the natural vision of nature."[41] But he made the connection on a philosophical, not on the psychological level; much

39. Mondrian, "Natural Reality and Abstract Reality," included in Seuphor, *Mondrian*, 352.

40. See Seuphor, *Mondrian*, 74; *Sketchbooks*, passim; Nelly van Doesburg, "Some Memories of Mondrian," in *Piet Mondrian, 1872–1944*, 71–72.

41. "A New Realism," in *Plastic Art and Pure Plastic Art*, 26.

as he prized "pure intuition," he insisted that it was "a mistake to suppose that a non-figurative work comes out of the unconscious."[42] At this critical point I refuse to follow Mondrian—or rather, feel compelled to go beyond him: I want to argue that it was precisely out of the unconscious that his nonfigurative work came.

As we might expect, Mondrian offers his interpreter little assistance here; he can never resist elevating psychological traits into metaphysical questions—in itself an instructive form of denial. Mondrian regards intuition as a prominent quality in the artist but sees both its origins and its significance as objective. They lead the observer from the individual to his civilization. "Intuition," he writes, "enlightens and so links up with pure thought." The authentic—that is, the intuitive—artist is the spokesman for cultural tendencies far more consequential than he can ever be by himself. "How many errors have been and are being committed through vague and confused intuition?" he asks rhetorically, and responds: "Art certainly shows this clearly. But art shows also that in the course of progress, intuition becomes more and more conscious and instinct more and more purified. Art and life illuminate each other more and more; they reveal more and more their laws according to which a real and living balance is created."[43] Neoplastic intuition is the humble instrument of history, the Neoplastic artist a soldier in the great army moving irresistibly toward clarity and purity.

Mondrian would thus have rejected the analytical distinction I have drawn between the worlds of culture and of craft: he envisioned his work neither as pure aesthetic play nor as direct social criticism. It was not other than aesthetic, nor would it be precise to say that it was more than aesthetic: to Mondrian, plastic expression was in itself a cultural act, born of a cultural hunger and designed for its satisfaction. But intuition, no matter how cosmic in its reach, manifested itself in specific moments, even in Mondrian. Intent as he was on evoking the social and metaphysical resonances of his paintings, he recognized the working of a shaping aesthetic impulse within him. When Charmion von Wiegand protested that the colored squares he had introduced into his *Broadway Boogie Woogie* [176] violated his theory, Mondrian promptly and disarmingly rejoined: "But it works. You must remember, Charmion, that the paintings come first and the theory comes from the paintings." Those privileged to watch him at work saw him revise his canvases again and again. In his American years he used colored tapes to find his

42. Note Mondrian's definition of the unconscious as "a collection of individual and pre-natal memories." "Plastic Art and Pure Plastic Art," 62.
43. "Plastic Art and Pure Plastic Art," 54. I have called elevating psychological traits into metaphysical questions a "form of denial." It is only fair to add that it is a denial that may become typical of more than individuals; whole strata of society, like German academic historians, have engaged in it.

180. Piet Mondrian. *New York*, 1942

design: as Charmion von Wiegand recalls, he would push the tapes "across the canvas until the intervals and the relation of the planes were 'right.' " Using the magical word "intuition" somewhat less grandly than was Mondrian's way, she noted that his procedure was entirely intuitive: "He did everything by eye."[44] For all the mathematical and rational appearance of his mature work, Mondrian made no calculations and used only the simplest tools—a ruler, strips of paper, and, in his last years, tapes [180]. "He often repeated," Michel Seuphor reports, "that the rightness of proportions and relations depended on intuition alone."[45] Mondrian, in short, had a certain awareness that what he called "pure intuition" contained a psychological component: he

44. "Interview with Charmion von Wiegand," *Piet Mondrian, 1872–1944*, 82, 79.
45. Seuphor, *Mondrian*, 207.

aimed, as he was working, at a certain sense of repose, the resolution, however temporary, of the tension that drove him on.

But this feeling of satisfaction is still far from the center of his individuality. It does not differentiate him from other painters or poets, for the tensions and resolutions here at play are the common property of all serious artists. It is characteristic of Mondrian *as* artist that no single solution should have provided him with that sense of rightness for long: it may be that his grids, on which he so fanatically concentrated from 1921 on, appear less like a debate with other painters than with himself, but it is with himself as a painter that he is conducting this internal colloquy. It is the private counterpart to the companionship that other avant-garde artists gave him in the years of his break with nature—a continuing aesthetic exploration. Only the hasty viewer will judge an array of his canvases to be monotonous. In fact, Mondrian exploited the possibilities inherent in his austere, self-imposed vocabulary to the utmost: he uses thick lines and thin [181], playing in the early 1920s with stubby black bands that do not quite reach the edge of his canvas [182]; he uses a small palette of primary colors, sometimes in combination, sometimes singly [183]; he varies his designs, sometimes crowding his picture space with repeated parallels like so many prison bars [184], sometimes emptying it of all but a white ground barely cut by pairs of black bands [185]; he pivots his canvas to convert squares into lozenges [180, 185]; even the possible shape of his canvases—perfect squares [186], near squares [181] and, rarely, tall elongated rectangles [187]—is open to his restless investigations. It was in the late 1920s that Mondrian's simplifications reached their logical limit, but the development of his art does not follow a single course; sometimes he would venture into drastically different modes of expression in the space of one year. Whatever the answers to his peremptory call for pure plastic art, he found none of them to be definitive.

But to see Mondrian simply as the devout craftsman who acts, through his craft, as a commentator and critic of culture is to accept him at his own evaluation. It is to stop at the boundary that Mondrian himself has drawn, and to stop there is to stop short. Behind his serious, thoughtful, deeply felt play with lines and planes, behind his manifest philosophical purposes, there stands a latent central animus. It is part of the historian's conventional wisdom that he must respect intentions. This is a useful injunction. But respectfulness must not cripple skepticism; the second quality is as essential, and as professional, as the first. George Bernard Shaw made this point long ago: "The existence of a discoverable and perfectly definite thesis in a poet's work," he wrote in 1891 about Ibsen, "by no means depends on the completeness of his

181. Piet Mondrian. *Fox Trot A,*
1927

183. Piet Mondrian. *Composition*

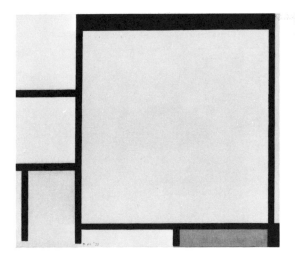

182. Piet Mondrian. *Composition
with Red, Yellow and Blue,* 1922

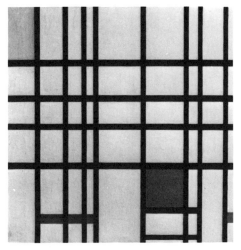

184. Piet Mondrian. *Composition
with Red, Yellow and Blue,* 1939–
1942

185. Piet Mondrian. *Composition à la Diagonal*, 1930

186. Piet Mondrian. *Fox Trot B,* 1930

187. Piet Mondrian. *Composition,* 1935–1942

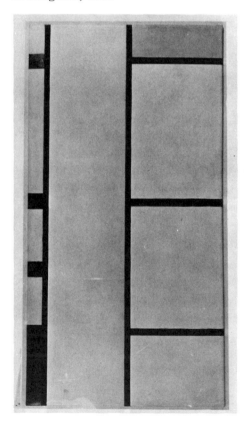

intellectual consciousness of it."[46] What holds for a thesis holds even more emphatically for causes, especially with an artist like Mondrian, whose iconographical messages are so illegible and whose explanations, precisely because they are so single-minded and so doctrinaire, explain so little. His conscious intentions concealed what I would call his unconscious intentions—impulses and purposes inaccessible to his awareness and therefore inaudible, or only faintly audible, in his correspondence, his manifestos, and his autobiographical statements. By and large the conflicts that determined the direction, even the nature, of his art play themselves out on a darkened stage.

Inarticulate as they are, yielding up their secrets with the utmost reluctance, Mondrian's paintings speak of a heroic effort at discipline. They speak of patience and of self-denial. The knife-edge sharpness of his lines, the even tone and texture of his planes reflect Mondrian's distaste for chance. Mondrian's announced ideal, "dynamic equilibrium," reveals more than he intended it to reveal: it evokes, not quietude, serenity, or indifference but an intense self-conquest in which passion is compelled to order. Mondrian resolutely rejected spontaneity and turned his back on the creative potentialities of the accidental. In his work, deliberation is master.

This deliberation is an indispensable weapon in Mondrian's strategy of concealment. His art is an art of exclusion, an elaborate ritual to evade invasions of privacy. Even the bland neutrality of his customary title, *Composition,* offers as little information to the interpreter as possible; the hints that occasional titles like *Fox Trot A* or *Trafalgar Square* ungraciously provide are rare, curt and inexplicit.

The inexpressiveness of Mondrian's art has its own eloquence; it is expressive of Mondrian's character. A silent witness says much by his silence. Fortunately, what we know of the man fits his reticent paintings to perfection. When Charmion von Wiegand met him, she was forcibly struck by his "sharp ascetic features," which she likened to those of "a Catholic priest or a scientist."[47] It is a perceptive assessment; it characterizes a man who has given up much for the sake of utter concentration. As we know, for man, that unruly animal, asceticism is a triumph, often dearly bought, over raging inner turmoil, the firm restraining hand of Plato's charioteer checking his willful, spirited horses of passion.

In Mondrian (to move from Plato to Freud) this restraint manifested itself in deep inhibitions and a marked obsessiveness. We do not know enough—at all events, I do not know enough—about his fantasies or the details of his daily routine to venture a conclusive diagnosis. But his habits, his philosophy, and his art convincingly reinforce one another;

46. "Preface," *The Quintessence of Ibsenism* (1891; ed. 1912), vi–vii.
47. Quoted by Seuphor, *Mondrian,* 60.

they suggest an overriding fear, the fear of what he called "primitive animal instinct."[48] He was sensitive, remote, self-protective. Nelly van Doesburg, who knew him well in the 1920s and 1930s, recalled the "personal fetish" he made of adopting French customs, a venture in mimicry he repeated after he went to London: "When I later visited him in England," she writes, "Mondrian had adopted the English cigarette and other national habits with the same dedication previously shown toward France."[49] Adaptability here reads like a flight into invisibility.

I do not know whether Mondrian's symptoms amount to a full-fledged obsessional neurosis but his obsessive rigidity was plain to all who knew him. It manifests itself in his perfectionism, his compulsive need to rework his paintings as long as they remained in his studio: the dates assigned to some of them, stretching sometimes between six or seven years [see 187], make Mondrian kin to Cézanne in habits and, possibly, in character. It manifests itself also in his notable neatness. "There was something of the preacher in him," writes Frank Elgar, summing up the impressions of those who knew Mondrian best, "a quality emphasized by his physical appearance. His dress was always scrupulously correct, always meticulously neat, even though his garments were threadbare. His demeanour was that of a rather buttoned-up *petit bourgeois*"—and the adjective, buttoned-up, carries a great deal more weight than Elgar seems to suspect. Mondrian was, Elgar concludes, reticent, solitary, retiring, and taciturn.[50] Photographs of his studios, candid rather than posed, confirm his austerity: the rooms where he worked were bare, spare, clean, as empty as possible, decorated with rectangles as though Mondrian were living in one of his own paintings [188, 189]. It is poignant to see his studio in Paris about 1926, its starkness relieved by a single tulip in a vase, and that tulip artificial, painted white [190].

The obstinate rigidity of his domestic arrangements was striking enough to haunt the memories of his friends. "Within the artificial surroundings of his studio," Nelly van Doesburg recalled many years later, "the placement of ashtrays, table settings, etc., could not be altered for fear of disturbing the 'equilibrium' of the total decor which he sought."[51] Clearly, Mondrian's equilibrium was precarious, tenuous in the extreme; his ceremonies of neatness, of cleanliness, of persistence were defenses against passions bubbling just beneath the surface [191].

As usual, Mondrian made a philosophy of necessity; his style of life

48. "Plastic Art and Pure Plastic Art," 54.
49. "Some Memories of Mondrian," 69–70.
50. Frank Elgar, *Mondrian*, tr. Thomas Walton (1968), 100.
51. "Some Memories of Mondrian," 71.

188. *Mondrian's Last Studio in New York, 1944*

189. *Mondrian's Studio in Paris, mid-1920s*

190. *Mondrian's White Tulip*, Paris, ca. 1926

191. *Mondrian in Amsterdam, before 1910*

was self-conscious, even programmatic. In a series of dialogues dating from 1919 and 1920, he has one of his interlocutors exclaim: "Your studio doesn't really surprise me. Everything here breathes your ideas. Other studios are not at all like this." The speaker who is Mondrian's voice readily accepts this assessment: "Most of the other painters are not like me, either. These things go together. Most painters show a preference for unmodern things." He is convinced, he adds, that "the present-day artist should show preference for the trend of his age in all matters. This studio expresses to some extent the idea of Neo-Plasticism,"[52] an expressiveness all the easier to achieve since the style of painting appropriate to the modern world transcends painting for its own sake, and reaches out to other arts. All painting, Mondrian could have paraphrased Pater, aspires to the condition of architecture.

I have no wish to reduce Mondrian's aesthetic thought to its unconscious sources, but I am certain that the sources existed and significantly shaped his work. His assault on nature, so critical for his religion and his admiration of the city, reemerges in his style of life—and in his style of painting. That assault was a counterattack, a way of managing anxieties

52. "Natural Reality and Abstract Reality," 335.

192. Piet Mondrian. *Self Portrait,* ca. 1900

193. Piet Mondrian. *Self Portrait,* ca. 1908

that would otherwise be intolerable. But, then, what was Mondrian afraid of? We are all afraid, but, more desperately than most, the obsessive personality needs to escape fears and deny conflicts with his endless rituals, his compulsive cleanliness, his stubborn refusal to change the most trivial arrangement. There is one curious, immensely instructive clue to Mondrian's fears: his brother Carel reports that Mondrian had "an almost maniacal fear of injuring his eyes"; he would close them "at the slightest danger" or, more dramatically, cover them with his hands.[53] Indeed, in his early self-portraits, Mondrian's eyes stare meaningfully and directly; they seem emphatic, sad, and vulnerable [192, 193]. Castration is punishment for illicit desires; and so vivid a fear of castration recalls to mind Charcot's famous exclamation: *"C'est toujours la chose génitale . . . toujours, toujours, toujours."*

In fact, the course of Mondrian's relations with women followed a single significant pattern all his life, and amplifies the tantalizing glimpse into his unconscious that his brother Carel unwittingly provided: he would fall in love, and then, in Nelly van Doesburg's words, "something always seemed to 'happen' which prevented the creation of more lasting bonds."[54] While he seemed to regret the invariable reverses that kept him a life-long bachelor, Mondrian's overwhelming response to this fate was surely one of relief. When acquaintances would playfully suggest he get married, he would reply, "I am too poor" or, even more transparently, "I am too busy," replies that constitute "good" reasons which barely conceal the real reasons.[55]

Mondrian seems to have talked about women incessantly, with the theoretical exuberance of a prurient teen-ager. His very enthusiasm is suspect; it committed him to nothing. "Although he was in his fifties when I knew him in Paris," Nelly van Doesburg writes, "the subject of women was ever on his lips. He would interrupt any type of conversation in order to comment with boyish enthusiasm upon the physical attractiveness of some admired example of the opposite sex. His taste was catholic in this respect, ranging from the refined beauty of a number of female acquaintances to the more direct appeal of pin-up posters. He was completely captivated by the charms of Mae West, who at the time was quite young but nonetheless used artificial make-up in a way that Mondrian found attractive."[56] There is deep pathos in this account, especially in his fascination with Mae West, that ambiguous sex object whom Parker Tyler in a perceptive remark once called a woman impersonating a male female impersonator.

53. It is recorded in Seuphor, *Mondrian,* 46.
54. "Some Memories of Mondrian," 71.
55. I owe one authoritative version of this anecdote to Robert Motherwell. Conversation of January 19, 1973.
56. "Some Memories of Mondrian," 70–71.

Mondrian's manner of social dancing, the single physical contact with women that he unequivocally enjoyed, reveals the same corrosive ambivalence. He went dancing as often as he could and repeatedly took lessons. Often he chose as his partners the wife or mistress of one of his friends—one means of securing safety. Another means, even more instructive, was his posture, rigid, graceless, distant, in short, desexualized: "He would pick out the prettiest girl" one of his acquaintances reports, "and would dance stiff as a ramrod, his head in the air, and without saying a word to his partner."[57] In view of the fame that his exuberant *Broadway Boogie Woogie* [176] enjoys, it is important to recognize that to Mondrian the meaning of the dance it celebrates strikingly differs from its customary connotations: "True Boogie-Woogie," he told J. J. Sweeney shortly before his death, "is homogeneous in intention with mine in painting: destruction of melody which is the equivalent of destruction of natural appearance; and construction through the continuous opposition of pure means—dynamic rhythm." And he added, "I think the destructive element is too much neglected in art."[58] Certainly Mondrian did not neglect the destructive —or, better, the repressive—element. It has been suggested that his suppression of black lines in his last paintings represents a return toward the world of the senses from the stark asceticism of the early 1930s. Certainly these paintings testify to his continued aesthetic vigor, his capacity for pushing his self-imposed frontiers ever further. But being in his seventies Mondrian could scarcely have experienced a revival of the erotic, or at best he experienced it as he did when he danced with women not available to him—as the safest of self-indulgences.

As with other feelings, Mondrian clothed his sexual feelings in philosophical garb. He found even the dance to be pregnant with profound meaning, seeing it as part of the great assault on nature that modern culture had undertaken: "The *machine*," he wrote in *De Stijl*, "is more and more taking the place of natural forces. In fashion we see a characteristic tightening of form and an internalization of color, both of them signs of a withdrawal from nature. In *modern dance* (two-step, boston, tango, etc.) we see the same tightening up: the round line of the old dances (waltz, etc.) has given way to the straight line, while every movement is immediately neutralized—*opgeheven*—by a countermovement—a sign of the search for equilibrium."[59] And he generalized

57. See Seuphor, *Mondrian*, 170.
58. Sweeney, "Piet Mondrian," *The Museum of Modern Art Bulletin*, **XII**, 4 (1945), 12; **XIII**, 4–5 (1946), 36.
59. *De Stijl*, **I**, 5 (1918), 53. Mondrian's interest in jazz was strong and persistent. He published an article on "De jazz en de Neo-Plastik," in the *International Journal* in 1927, and collected Boogie-Woogie records.

194. Theo van Doesburg. *Counter-composition of Dissonants XVI*, 1925

the essence of the dance, that close confrontation of man and woman, into the essence of the human world. Here, once again, theosophical doctrine proved helpful: it supplied theoretical justification for feelings Mondrian had already experienced on his own. For theosophists, the female principle expresses the low order of the body, while the male principle aspires to the higher realm of the spiritual. It was the Futurists' conviction of man's superior place in the world scheme that made them sympathetic to Mondrian, much as he disliked their lyrical materialism. Their "hatred of *woman* (the feminine)," he wrote, "is entirely justified," for it is "the *woman* in *man*" that is the "direct cause of the domination of the tragic in art"—the sentimental, the emotional, the irregular, the curved, all "tragic" qualities that Mondrian hoped to overcome with his Neoplastic art.[60] In his unceasing search for the equilibrium that would end the reign of the tragic over modern culture Mondrian found even the diagonal line an intolerable betrayal: when van Doesburg, after several years of close collaboration with Mondrian, introduced diagonals into his paintings, Mondrian broke with him and withdrew from the De Stijl group [194].

In the late nineteenth century, and in the early twentieth, philoso-

60. *Le Néo-plasticisme* (1920). I am citing from the soon-to-be-published collection of Mondrian's writings, ed. Harry Holtzman, tr. Harry Holtzman and Martin James. The Futurists' presumed assault on sensuality took forms very similar to those that Mondrian chose. In his "Technical Manifesto of Futurist Sculpture," dated April 11, 1912, Umberto Boccioni concludes that "the straight line is the only means that can lead to the primitive virginity of a new architectural construction of sculptural masses or zones." In Joshua C. Taylor, *Futurism*, Exhibition Catalogue, Museum of Modern Art (1961), 132.

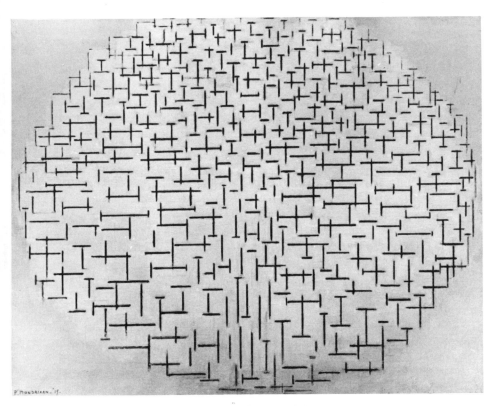

195. Piet Mondrian. *Composition No. 10,* 1915

phers and playwrights, sociologists and artists talked a good deal about the confrontation of the male and female principles; it appears in the novels of Zola, the plays of Shaw, the speculations of Weininger, the theorizing of Freud. Mondrian's contribution to this interminable debate was as imprecise and portentous as all his philosophizing. The entry he made into a sketchbook he kept around 1913 achieves a clarity that is quite exceptional: *"Female:* static, preserving, obstructing element," he noted. *"Male:* kinetic, creative, expressive, progressing element." In the same note he contrasted woman, the "matter-element," with man, the "spirit-element," and gave this opposition visual correlatives: "Woman: horizontal line/ Man: vertical line," a pairing that has as its logical consequence: "Male artist: spiritual joy/ Female artist: material joy."[61] The famous "plus-and-minus" experiments he began to do shortly after he wrote this note represent the encounter of the two principles in the simplest, starkest terms. Whatever sensuality may lurk in Mondrian's explanations—or, rather, anticipations—of these paintings, that sensuality is thoroughly repressed, both in his sketchbooks and in his art [195].

61. *Sketchbook,* 16.

It did not become more explicit later. In 1917 and 1918, in a much-quoted series of articles he published in *De Stijl*, he returned to the two principles with a gain in emphasis but a certain loss of lucidity. He made enormous claims, arguing that as "extreme opposites" the male and the female embody the most fundamental relationship in nature. His long, tortuous discussion of "male inwardness" and "female outwardness," of growing purification, of the clarification of opposites and other esoteric matters is exceedingly obscure. But this much is clear: the female principle stands in Mondrian's scheme for all that is representative and concrete; in art, it embraces the portrayal of nature, including landscape, still-life, and interior as well as the figure. In sharp contrast, the male principle, especially in its Neoplastic purified form, is abstract and universal. This is nothing more than a reiteration of the familiar theosophist identification of the female with body and the male with spirit. But Mondrian's resplendent parade of abstract nouns and vague verbs barely conceals a fundamental attitude that has been too little noticed. Like many other artists of his time—like Beardsley and Munch and Strindberg—Mondrian was convinced that throughout the past the female principle had been more powerful than the male. The rise of Neoplasticism, therefore, with its pressure toward determinate, abstract clarity was nothing less, and nothing more, than a blow in the long battle for male liberation—a blow struck not for the sake of superiority, by any means, but for equality, for what Mondrian envisioned as the ideal of the future: "female-male equilibrium." Politically and socially this seems a reasonable and decent ideal; but what matters in our search for Mondrian is that it represents an ideal far less than a symptom—the symptom of a man who was afraid.

In the course of his exposition Mondrian insisted that the confrontation of the male and female principles clearly displayed the *"unity of life and art.*"[62] We are entitled, I think, to take this implicit invitation seriously. The steps from Mondrian's life to Mondrian's art are few; once we have perceived the contours of his inner life, they need little boldness. Had he been anyone else he would have been just another fussy bachelor, starting affairs he could not consummate, driven back into himself by his awe of female superiority, staring at the provocative nudes in magazines that cater to such tastes, a bank clerk, perhaps, in reality as he was in appearance. But fortunately for himself and for art he was Mondrian, an artist who could transform his neurosis into painting. In 1926, when he heard that the Dutch government had outlawed the Charleston as obscene, Mondrian exploded into an eloquent and revealing protest: "How could they ban that sporting dance! The danc-

62. *De Stijl*, I, 12 (1918), 140–145.

ers keep at a certain distance from each other, and spend so much energy in doing the steps that they hardly have time for thoughts of sex."[63] Here in this exclamation we have the prototype of Mondrian's psychological strategies: sensuality disarmed by distance, energy borrowed from the erotic translated into aesthetic activity, an activity so vigorous that one hardly has time for thoughts of sex. As he danced, so he painted. Is there in modern art an instance of sublimation more splendid than this?

To speak of Mondrian's art as a form of sublimation is to say less than would appear at first glance. Sublimation is not the monopoly of the neurotic or of the artist; it is a universal, perfectly reasonable defense mechanism by which an individual diverts sexual energies from forbidden into permissible channels, or gives these energies an altogether new form. It provides gratification for repressed impulses in ways that are privately acceptable and socially useful. I said at the beginning of this book that there is sublimation in all aesthetic effort; I should add that there is a piece of sublimation in all adult activity—in the pursuit of politics, in the conduct of business, in the practice of religion, even in explicitly erotic activity. The artist, as Freud noted long ago, is peculiarly well equipped to sublimate; it may be this gift that directs him toward art in the first place. To diagnose sublimation in art is therefore, by itself, scarcely significant. This is true all the more in that the results of sublimation often bear little resemblance to its origins; to identify its work therefore requires some ingenuity. The textbook model for artistic sublimation is the sculptor who translates his infantile wish to play with his feces into the game of making mud pies and then, as an adult, finds his vocation modeling in clay;[64] but the model is too straightforward to be very helpful—the life of the psyche is never that simple.

Certainly Mondrian's sublimation was highly elaborate. Yet at the same time it was peculiarly expressive. It therefore takes a privileged rank among the causes that made his art. Mondrian's aesthetic choices emerged from his unconscious conflicts; as he translated these choices into his paintings, wielding his ruler and applying his brush, these conflicts guided his hand. He found sensuality so frightening that it was his dread of desire, rather than the desires themselves, that ultimately shaped his abstract designs. No sentiment, no curves, no touching—that is how he lived and that is what his paintings proclaim. He, like his art, was full of emotions; the equilibrium for which he groped with such patience, such inventiveness, and such needy anxiety was anything but static. It was, as he himself insisted, dynamic, even if that dynamism had

63. See Seuphor, *Mondrian,* 170.
64. Charles Brenner, *An Elementary Textbook of Psychoanalysis* (ed. 1957), 106–107.

origins of which he was unaware. His paintings offer impressive evidence just how much beauty the talented can wrest from fear. Of course—I need hardly say it—Mondrian's paintings were not rooted in fear alone, but in hard work, thoughtful experimentation, wide acquaintance, and a discriminating eye. They are, at their best, modern masterpieces. But if we ask *why* they are rather than *what* they are, psychology must take precedence over stylistics and over sociology. They embody Mondrian's urge to ward off, to omit, to do without, to silence the imperious demands of passions which, allowed to rise to consciousness, would have been too dangerous to manage, too fearful to face. Painting was, for Mondrian, the aesthetic correlative for his repressions, his way of coming to terms with himself—at once an expression of his problem and an embodiment of his solution. If his famous grids symbolize the sad truth that his only way of life was an ascetic denial of sensuality, they also symbolize, to our lasting delight, his own private salvation.

Postscript

It is a commonplace to say about a great work of art that it carries an
air of inevitability about it; we say that we cannot conceive it to be other
than it is, as though its maker had held a Platonic model of the completed work in his mind from the beginning and carried it through to
its predestined form. The psychological origins of this feeling are easy
to explain. The successful work, by definition, carries its own validation.
It is precisely because we find it masterly that it imposes its lines, its
rhythms, its colors on the public. Intrepid restorers and editors have
sometimes interfered with original intentions, painting loin cloths on
Michelangelo's nudes or "improving" the end of *King Lear*. But in
general, the great painting or sonnet is sacred, and forecloses, with its
sheer authority, any possibility of alternatives.

This sense of inevitability is not confined to great art. Indeed, it is
more general than all art. It forms part of a general attitude toward the
past, of the feeling that since things happened in a certain way they
could not have happened differently. The "counterfactual" speculations in which some historians have engaged have never won wide
support. Again, this is understandable. Like all historical research, the
causal analysis of the past is, after all, retrospective. The event has
happened; its causes have done their work, and the historian moves
from the accomplished fact to the forces that accomplished it. History-
as-event is the incarnation of possibilities; history-as-writing is their
record.

But while this authority of the actual is perfectly understandable it
leads historians to misjudge the real situation. Historical events are
contingent. They might have happened in some other way, or perhaps
not have happened at all. The vastly complicated intersection of potentialities pressing toward the actuality of the historical event is so richly
textured that it seems almost impossible to disentangle, even with hindsight. International tensions may make a war likely, but when, where,
or even whether the first shot is fired depends on more than looming

possibilities. The deadly monotony of academic art may make an avant-garde rebellion likely, but who will paint what to signalize the emergence of a new style cannot be predicted by the most perceptive observer. Of course, statesmen and speculators attempt to measure the chances of future events happening in a certain way and at a certain time; they are engaged in a kind of prospective causal analysis. And by taking a hand in the historical process they may increase the probability of the event they desire. Their prophecies may be self-fulfilling. But experienced and shrewd as they may be, even they cannot be sure of the future. If they could be sure, and right, all the time, they would all be millionaires, or immortal foreign ministers. But they cannot be, if only because the clash of their wills, interests, and calculations in itself lends an inescapable uncertainty to the outcome. I am here, of course, dealing with the central distinction between necessary and sufficient causes, a distinction generally implicit but rarely explicit in these pages. Necessary causes supply the context of preconditions—the causes without which an event *could* not have happened. Sufficient causes are the triggers that convert possibilities into actuality—the causes without which an event *would* not have happened. For art historians, sufficient causes are a particularly delicate matter and I respect their sensitivity to them. Like artists, art historians are extremely reluctant to reduce works of art to a set of causes. They do not like to "establish" why Manet painted his *Olympia* precisely as he did; to do so seems to diminish Manet's stature as an artist, to dissolve his indefinable genius into mere social or psychological pressures, and to leave no room for aesthetic decisions. I can only say that, however confident these chapters may sound, I, too, am baffled by the mysteries of the creative process. What I have done has been to suggest ways of thinking about cause, to develop a possible structure of explanation that suggests hierarchies of necessary, and at times sets of sufficient, causes. Beyond that, I find myself in company with the art historian, and seek refuge in Freud's celebrated disclaimer: "Before the problem of the creative artist analysis must, alas, lay down its arms." So, I want to add, must history.

List of Illustrations

Measurements are given in inches, width preceeds height.

Introduction

1. Hals, *The Meàger Company,* begun 1633. Oil. Rijksmuseum, Amsterdam.
2. Van Gogh, *The Night Café,* 1888. Oil, 36 1/4 × 28 1/2. Yale University Art Gallery, New Haven. Bequest of Stephen Carlton Clark, BA, 1903, photograph Joseph Szaszfai.
3. Picasso, *Guernica,* 1937. Oil on canvas, 305 3/4 × 137 1/2. On extended loan to The Museum of Modern Art, New York, from the artist.
4. Picasso, *Colombe Volant,* 1952. Color lithograph, 28 × 22. Courtesy, Museum of Fine Arts, Boston, George Peabody Gardner Fund.
5. Verrocchio, *Baptism of Christ,* ca. 1472. Oil. Uffizi, Florence, photograph, Alinari.
6. Cézanne, *L'Enlèvement,* 1867. Oil, 45 × 34 1/4. Fitzwilliam Museum, Cambridge. By permission of the Trustees of the late Lord Keynes.
7. Boltin, *Untitled 2000,* 1970. Photograph, Lee Boltin.
8. *The Hourglass of Time*
9. Picasso, Study for *Horse's Head,* 1937. Pencil on blue paper, 8 1/4 × 10 1/2. On extended loan to The Museum of Modern Art, New York, from the artist.
10. Picasso, *Hand with Broken Sword,* 1937. Pencil on white paper, 17 7/8 × 9 1/2. On extended loan to The Museum of Modern Art, New York, from the artist.
11. Munch, *Vampire,* 1894. Drypoint. Courtesy, Museum of Fine Arts, Boston, William Francis Warden Fund.
12. Munch, *Madonna,* detail, 1895–1902. Color lithograph. Courtesy, Museum of Fine Arts, Boston, William Francis Warden Fund.
13. Pissarro, *Place du Theátre Français* (Pluie), 1898. Oil on linen, 36 × 29. The Minneapolis Institute of Arts, The William Hood Dunwoody Fund.
14. Daumier, *Les Paysagistes,* 1865. Lithograph, hand colored. Courtesy Museum of Fine Arts, Boston, Babcock Bequest.

Manet

15. Fantin-Latour, *Portrait of Edouard Manet,* 1867. Oil on canvas, 35 1/2 × 46. Courtesy of The Art Institute of Chicago, Stickney Fund.
16. Degas, Study for a *Portrait of Edouard Manet at the Races,* ca. 1864. Graphite pencil on buff paper, 9 5/8 × 12 5/8. The Metropolitan Museum of Art, New York, Rogers Fund, 1918.

17. Manet, *Self-Portrait with Palette*, 1879. Oil, 26 1/4 × 32 3/4. Collection of Mr. and Mrs. John L. Loeb.
18. Manet, *The Absinthe Drinker*, 1858–1859. Oil, 42 1/2 × 72 1/2. The N.Y. Carlsberg Glyptothek, Copenhagen.
19. Manet, *Portrait of Antonin Proust*, 1880. Oil on canvas, 37 3/4 × 51. The Toledo Museum of Art, Edward Drummond Libbey, 1925.
20. Manet, *Olympia*, 1863. Oil, 76 1/2 × 52 1/5. Louvre, Paris.
21. Manet, *Sortie du Port de Boulogne*, 1864. Oil on canvas, 35 1/2 × 28. Courtesy of The Art Institute of Chicago, Potter Palmer Collection.
22. Manet, *The Spanish Singer*, 1860. Oil on canvas, 45 × 58. The Metropolitan Museum of Art, New York, Gift of William Church Osborn, 1949.
23. Manet, *Mademoiselle Victorine in the Costume of an Espada*, 1862. Oil on canvas, 50 1/4 × 65. The Metropolitan Museum of Art, New York, The H. O. Havemeyer Collection, Bequest of 1929.
24. Goya, *Tauromaquia*, No. 5, ca. 1815. Etching, aquatint and drypoint. The New York Public Library, Prints Division, Astor, Lenox and Tilden Foundations.
25. Ingres, *Le Bain Turque*, 1862–1863. Oil, 42 1/2 diameter. Louvre, Paris.
26. Cézanne, *The Basket of Apples*, 1890–1894. Oil on canvas, 32 × 25 3/4. Courtesy of The Art Institute of Chicago, Collection Helen Birch Bartlett.
27. Manet, *The Old Musician*, 1862. Oil on canvas, 97 3/4 × 73 3/4. National Gallery of Art, Washington, D.C., Chester Dale Collection, 1962.
28. Watteau, *Gilles*, ca. 1717–1719. Oil, Louvre, Paris.
29. Manet, *The Absinthe Drinker*, 1861–1862. Etching, third state, 5 3/4 × 9 3/4. Courtesy of The Art Institute of Chicago.
30. Manet, *Déjeuner sur L'Herbe*, 1863. Oil, 105 4/5 × 83 1/5. Louvre, Paris.
31. Manet, *Woman with a Parrot*, 1866. Oil on canvas, 50 5/8 × 72 7/8. The Metropolitan Museum of Art, New York, Gift of Erwin Davis, 1889.
32. Manet, *Bar at the Folies-Bèrgeres*, 1881. Oil, 52 × 38 2/5. Courtauld Institute Galleries, London.
33. Manet, *Madame Manet au Canape Bleu*, ca. 1878. Oil, 24 2/5 × 20. Louvre, Paris.
34. Manet, *Olympia*, 1863. Oil, 76 1/2 × 52 1/5. Louvre, Paris.
35. Manet, *The Dead Toreador*, 1864. Oil on canvas, 60 3/8 × 29 7/8. National Gallery of Art, Washington, D.C., Widener Collection, 1942.
36. Gérôme, *The Death of Caesar*, 1867. Oil, 57 1/4 × 33 5/8. Walters Art Gallery, Baltimore.
37. Manet, *Guerre Civile*, 1871. Lithograph, 20 × 15 3/4. Yale University Art Gallery, New Haven.
38. Jean Chanfreau of France, after slipping in a match against Mark Cox at Cleveland, April 12, 1973. United Press International.
39. Manet, *Copy of Self-Portrait of Tintoretto*, ca. 1854. Oil, 19 5/8 × 24. Musée de Dijon.
40. Tintoretto, *Self-Portrait.* Oil, Louvre, Paris.
41. Manet, Sketch after *The Barque of Dante* (after Delacroix), ca. 1854. Oil on canvas, 16 1/8 × 13. The Metropolitan Museum of Art, New York, Bequest of Mrs. H. O. Havemeyer, 1929. The H. O. Havemeyer Collection.
42. Delacroix, *The Barque of Dante*, 1822. Oil, 98 2/5 × 75 3/5. Louvre, Paris.
43. Manet, *Dead Christ with Two Angels*, 1864. Oil on canvas, 59 × 70 5/8. The Metropolitan Museum of Art, New York, Bequest of H. O. Havemeyer, 1929. The H. O. Havemeyer Collection.
44. Magritte, *The Human Condition, I*, 1934. Oil, 31 1/2 × 39 3/8. Collection of Claude Spaak.

75. Garnier, *Opera House, Paris,* 1861–1875. Photograph. Yale University Library, Todd Family Papers.
76. Manet, *Ballet Espagñol,* 1862. Oil on canvas, 36 × 24. The Phillips Collection, Washington, D.C.
77. Manet, *Le Ballon,* 1862. Lithograph, 20 1/8 × 15 7/8. The New York Public Library, Prints Division, Astor, Lenox and Tilden Foundations.
78. Manet, *Battle between the "Kearsarge" and the "Alabama,"* 1864. Oil, 50 4/5 × 53 3/5. John G. Johnson Collection, Philadelphia.
79. Manet, *Bar at the Folies-Bergères,* 1881. Oil, 52 × 38 2/5. Courtauld Institute Galleries, London.
80. Manet, *At the Café,* 1878. Oil, 15 3/5 × 19. Walters Art Gallery, Baltimore.
81. Manet, *Portrait of Mallarmé,* 1876. Oil, 14 2/5 × 11. Louvre, Paris.
82. Manet, *Portrait of Glemenceau,* 1879. Oil, 29 3/5 × 37 4/5. Louvre, Paris.
83. Manet, *Le Repos* (Portrait of Berthe Morisot), 1870–1871. Oil on canvas, 43 3/4 × 58 1/4. Museum of Art, Rhode Island School of Design, Providence, Bequest of Mrs. Edith Stuyvesant Vanderbilt Gerry.
84. Manet, *George Moore (au Café),* ca. 1879. Oil on canvas, 32 × 25 3/4. The Metropolitan Museum of Art, New York, Gift of Mrs. Ralph J. Hines, 1955.
85. Manet, *La Musique aux Tuileries,* 1860. Oil, 47 3/5 × 30 2/5. National Gallery, London.
86. Attributed to Velazquez, *The Little Cavaliers.* Louvre, Paris.
87. Manet, *Rue Mosnier, Paris, Decorated with Flags on June 30, 1878,* 1878. Oil on canvas, 31 1/2 × 25 1/2. Collection of Mr. and Mrs. Paul Mellon.
88. Manet, *Blonde Nude,* 1878. Oil, 20 4/5 × 25. Louvre, Paris.
89. Manet, *Chez le Père Lathuille,* 1879. Oil, 44 4/5 × 37 1/5. Musée des Beaux-Arts de Tournai, Belgium.
90. Manet, *Nana,* 1877. Oil, 46 4/5 × 60. Hamburger Kunsthalle.
91. Manet, *The Railroad,* 1873. Oil, 45 1/8 × 36 3/4. National Gallery of Art, Washington, D.C., Gift of Horace Havemeyer in memory of his mother Louisine W. Havemeyer.

Gropius

92. Gropius, *The Bauhaus,* Dessau, 1925–1926. Photograph, Courtesy of The Museum of Modern Art, New York.
93. Muthesius, *Hans Freudenberg,* Berlin–Nikolassee, 1907–1908. Photograph, Dr. Franz Stoedtner, Dusseldorf.
94. Scott, *St. Pancras Hotel,* London, 1865. Photograph, Yale University Art Gallery, New Haven.
95. Voysey, *"Broadleys" on Lake Windemere,* 1898. Photograph, Courtesy of The Museum of Modern Art, New York.
96. Gropius with Meyer, *Deutscher Werkbund Exposition,* Cologne, 1914. Photograph, Courtesy of The Museum of Modern Art, New York.
97. Van de Velde, *Werkbundtheater,* Cologne, 1914. Photograph, Dr. Franz Stoedtner, Dusseldorf.
98. Gropius, *The Bauhaus,* plan, Dessau, 1925–1926. Photograph, Courtesy of The Museum of Modern Art, New York.
99. Kandinsky, *Abstraction,* ca. 1925. Lithograph, 9 × 11 1/2. From the Collection of the Author.
100. Klee, *Red-Green Steps,* 1921. Watercolor on paper, 8 13/16 × 12 3/4. Yale Univer-

126. Gropius with Meyer, *Fagus Shoe Last Factory*, interior, Alfeld, 1911. Photograph, Dr. Franz Stoedtner, Dusseldorf.
127. Roth, Gropius and Belluschi, *Pan American World Airways Building*, New York, 1958–1963. Photograph, Joseph W. Molitor.
128. Gropius and Meyer, *Sommerfeld House*, Berlin–Dahlem, 1920–1921. Courtesy of The Architects Collaborative.
129. Gropius and Meyer, *Sommerfeld House*, interior, Berlin-Dahlem, 1920–1921. Courtesy of The Architects Collaborative.
130. Gropius and Cvijanovic, *Thomas Glass Works*, Amberg, 1968. Courtesy of The Architects Collaborative, Photograph, Louis Reens.
131. Gropius and Cvijanovic, *Thomas Glass Works*, Amberg, 1968. Courtesy of The Architects Collaborative.
132. Gropius and Meyer, *Fagus Shoe Last Factory*, Alfeld, 1911. Photograph Collection, Yale University Art Library, New Haven.
133. Gropius and Schmieden, *Museum of Arts and Crafts*, elevation, Berlin, 1875.
134. Gropius and Schmieden, *Bank of the Cassen-Verein*, Berlin, 1870–1871.
135. Gropius and Schmieden, *Gewandhaus*, Leipzig, 1881–1884. Photograph, Dr. Franz Stoedtner, Dusseldorf.
136. Wallot, *The Reichstag*, with the Siegessäule on the right, Berlin, 1884–1894. Yale University Library, Todd Family Papers.
137. Schwechten, *Kaiser Wilhelm Gedächtnis-Kirche*, Berlin, 1891–1895. Yale University Library, Todd Family Papers.
138. Begas, *National Monument to William "the Great,"* Berlin, 1897. Photograph Collection, Yale University Art Library, New Haven.
139. *Siegesallee*, Berlin, 1897–1901. Yale University Library, Todd Family Papers.
140. *Siegesallee*, Berlin, 1897–1901. Yale University Library, Todd Family Papers.
141. Messel, *Wertheim Department Store*, Berlin, 1896–1904. Photograph Collection, Yale University Art Library, New Haven.
142. Schinkel, *Old Museum*, Berlin, 1823–1829. After Max Ring, "Die Kaiserstadt Berlin und ihre Umgebung."
143. Schinkel, *Four designs for the Friedrich-Werdersche Church*, Berlin, before 1828. Staatliche Museen zu Berlin.
144. Schinkel, *Guard House for the Royal Guards*, Berlin, 1816–1818. Yale University Library, Todd Family Papers.
145. Schinkel, *Schauspielhaus*, Berlin, 1819–1821. Yale University Library, Todd Family Papers.
146. Schinkel, *Bauakademie*, Berlin, 1831–1836. After Max Ring, "Die deutsche Kaiserstadt Berlin und ihre Umgebung."
147. Mies van der Rohe, *New National Gallery*, Berlin, 1968. Photograph, Reinhard Friedrich.
148. Schinkel, *Old Museum*, Berlin, 1823–1829. Yale University Library, Todd Family Papers.
149. Behrens, *AEG Turbine Factory*, Berlin, 1909. Photograph, Courtesy of The Museum of Modern Art, New York.
150. Behrens, *AEG Factory for Small Motors*, Berlin, 1911. Photograph, Dr. Franz Stoedtner, Dusseldorf.
151. Behrens, *The Kiss*, 1898. Colored Woodcut, 8 1/2 × 10 5/8. Busch-Reisinger Museum, Harvard University, Cambridge.
152. Walter Gropius in front of his house in Lincoln, Massachusetts, 1967. Courtesy of The Architects Collaborative.

176. Mondrian, *Broadway Boogie Woogie,* 1942–1943. Oil on canvas, 50 × 50. Collection, The Museum of Modern Art, New York. Given anonymously.
177. Mondrian, *Devotion,* ca. 1908. Oil, 23 5/8 × 36 5/8. Collection, Haags Gemeentemuseum, The Hague.
178. Mondrian, *Evolution,* (triptych), ca. 1911. Oil, each ca. 34 × 71. Collection, Haags Gemeentemuseum, The Hague.
179. Mondrian, *Composition in Black and White,* 1917. Oil, 43 1/5 × 43 1/5. Rijksmuseum Kröller-Müller, Otterlo.
180. Mondrian, *New York,* 1942. Oil, 38 3/8 × 44 3/4. Courtesy, Harry Holtzman.
181. Mondrian, *Fox Trot A,* 1930. Oil, 43 1/4 diagonal. Yale University Art Gallery, New Haven, Gift of the Artist for the Collection Société Anonyme.
182. Mondrian, *Composition with Red, Yellow and Blue,* 1922. Oil, 19 1/8 × 16 3/8. The Minneapolis Institute of Arts, Gift 1965: Mr. and Mrs. Bruce B. Dayton.
183. Mondrian, *Composition.* Oil on canvas, 19 3/4 × 19 7/8. Yale University Art Gallery, New Haven, Gift of Collection Société Anonyme.
184. Mondrian, *Composition with Red, Yellow and Blue,* 1939–1942. Oil, 23 3/16 × 28 3/8. The Tate Gallery, London.
185. Mondrian, *Composition à la Diagonal,* 1930. Oil, 29 1/2 diagonal. The Solomon R. Guggenheim Museum, New York.
186. Mondrian, *Fox Trot B,* 1929. Oil, 17 3/4 × 17 3/4. Yale University Art Gallery, New Haven, Gift of The Société Anonyme. Photograph, Joseph Szaszfai.
187. Mondrian, *Composition,* 1935–1942. Oil on canvas, 20 1/16 × 40 3/16. Collection of Mr. and Mrs. Burton Tremaine, Meriden, Connecticut.
188. Mondrian's Last Studio in New York, 1944. Photograph, Courtesy Harry Holtzman.
189. Mondrian's Studio in Paris, mid-1920s. Photograph, Courtesy Harry Holtzman.
190. Mondrian's White Tulip, Paris, ca. 1926. Photograph, Courtesy Harry Holtzman.
191. Mondrian in Amsterdam, before 1910. Photograph, Courtesy Harry Holtzman.
192. Mondrian, *Self-Portrait,* ca. 1900. Oil on canvas mounted on masonite, 15 1/2 × 19 7/8. The Phillips Collection, Washington, D.C.
193. Mondrian, *Self-Portrait,* ca. 1908. Charcoal, 21 11/16 × 31 1/2. Collection, Haags Gemeentemuseum, The Hague.
194. Van Doesburg, *Counter-composition of Dissonants XVI,* 1925. Oil, 70 7/8 × 39 3/8.
195. Mondrian, *Composition No. 10,* 1915. Oil on canvas, 33 1/2 × 42 1/2. Rijksmuseum Kröller-Müller, Otterlo.

Bibliography

This bibliography is necessarily highly selective; I have listed mainly those books and articles I cite in the text, and those that have been in some sense important to me. I have sometimes ordered the entries alphabetically, sometimes chronologically, depending on which seemed to me most logical.

Introduction

1. Causes in History and Philosophy

Braithwaite, R. B., *Scientific Explanation: A Study of the Function of Theory, Probability and Law in Science* (1953). An advanced but clear analysis.

Collingwood, R. G., *The Idea of History* (1946). A very special use of "cause" in history, arguing that all history is the history of thought.

Dray, William H., *Philosophy of History* (1964). An economical introduction to technical problems of historiography.

————, ed., *Philosophical Analysis and History* (1966). A modern anthology.

Gallie, W. B., *Philosophy and the Historical Understanding* (1964). Takes the view that history is in principle not like science, and treats history as essentially narrative.

Gay, Peter, *Style in History* (1974). See especially both the Introduction and the Conclusion.

Gillispie, Charles Coulston, *The Edge of Objectivity: An Essay in the History of Scientific Ideas* (1960). Far larger than its title, this book is a powerful contribution to the clarifying of what science—and hence causal inquiry—amount to.

Hampshire, Stuart, *Thought and Action* (1959).

————, *Freedom of the Individual* (1965). Both brilliant, lucid contributions to the philosophy of action; both subtle vindications of free will.

Hart, H. L. A., *Punishment and Responsibility: Essays in the Philosophy of Law* (1968).

———— and A. M. Honoré, *Causation in the Law* (1959). Powerful analyses of determinism, responsibility, and the nature of cause.

Hexter, J. H., *The History Primer* (1971). History as rhetoric; amusing, interesting, but not, I think, persuasive.

Hempel, Carl G., *Aspects of Scientific Explanation and Other Essays in the Philosophy of Science* (1965). This collection contains the much-debated classic "The Function of General Laws in History"; I accept Hempel's argument that in principle causal explanation in history is like causal explanation in other sciences.

————, *Philosophy of Natural Science* (1966). Lucid introduction by a master.

MacIntyre, Alasdair, "The Antecedents of Action," and "The Idea of a Social Science," in MacIntyre, *Against the Self-Images of the Age: Essays on Ideology and Philosophy* (1971), 191–210, 211–229. Reasoned defenses of causal analysis, and of the coexistence of determinism and free will (directed against Melden, Peters, Winch, cited below).

Melden, A. I., *Free Action* (1961). A volume in the series of Wittgensteinian books on "philosophical psychology." See Peters and Winch below.

Michotte, Albert, *The Perception of Causality* (1946; tr. 1963). An important psychological analysis of a logical act.

Mink, Louis O., *Mind, History, and Dialectic: The Philosophy of R. G. Collingwood* (1969). A perceptive exposition.

Nagel, Ernest, *The Structure of Science: Problems in the Logic of Scientific Explanation* (1961). A systematic statement of the view that history belongs to the same cognitive family as the other sciences.

Peters, P. S., *The Concept of Motivation* (1960). (See Melden above.)

Piaget, Jean, and Bärbel Inhelder, *The Psychology of the Child* (1966; tr. Helen Weaver, 1969). One of several books in which Piaget deals with the perception of causation. (See also Michotte cited above.)

Social Science Research Council, Bulletin 54, *Theory and Practice in Historical Study* (1946).

————, Bulletin 64, *The Social Sciences in Historical Study* (1954). While the earlier of these collections counseled historians to abandon the very notion of cause, the later collection tentatively returns to it—rightly so.

Winch, Peter, *The Idea of a Social Science and Its Relation to Philosophy* (1958). Perhaps the best known among the writings in philosophical psychology. While I do not accept it, I have learned from this book.

2. Psychology and Psychohistory

Arnheim, Rudolf, *Towards a Psychology of Art* (1966). A gathering of often significant essays.

————, *Picasso's Guernica: The Genesis of a Painting* (1962). Psychological analysis of a single work.

Barbu, Zevedei, *Problems of Historical Psychology* (1960). A venturesome, not wholly successful, essay seeking to link history and psychology—though not psychoanalysis.

Brenner, Charles, *An Elementary Textbook of Psychoanalysis* (1955; ed. 1957). Fulfills the promise of its title.

Cochran, Thomas C., "Economic History, Old and New," *American Historical Review*, **LXIV**, 5 (June, 1969), 1561–1572. A lucid argument for going beyond economic motivation in economic history.

Cominos, Peter T., "Late-Victorian Sexual Respectability and the Social System," *International Review of Social History*, **VIII**, 1, 2 (1963), 18–48, 216–250. A significant attempt to give a psychological account of a normal and pervasive cultural trait: gentility. If the essays fail (largely because of an excessive reliance on Fromm) they are still something of a model of what needs to be done.

Eissler, K. R., *Leonardo da Vinci: Psycho-analytic Notes on the Enigma* (1961). A voluble, spirited, and not too-good-tempered defense of Freud's essay on Leonardo against Meyer Schapiro. (See the Schapiro essay cited below.)

Elias, Norbert, *Über den Prozess der Zivilisation: Soziogenetische und Psychogenetische Untersuchungen*, 2 vols. (2nd enlarged ed., 1969). A path-breaking and profound study of man's progressive repression in behalf of civilization; far too little known.

Ellenberger, Henri F., *The Discovery of the Unconscious: The History and Evolution of Dynamic Psychiatry* (1970). Though excessively bulky and often irritating, this full history pays close attention to psychologists other than Freud.

Erikson, Erik H., *Childhood and Society* (2nd ed., 1963). Probably Erikson's most important book; still close to Freud.

————, *Young Man Luther: A Study in Psychoanalysis and History* (1958). One of the first, still the most cited of psychobiographies. Moving as a piece of wisdom literature, it scarcely succeeds on the level of psychohistory but its seminal importance in the literature remains undisputed. (For other recent psychobiographies, see Rudolph Binion, *Frau Lou: Nietzsche's Wayward Disciple* [1968]—relentless, and a stranger to the idea of overdetermination; Frank Manuel, *A Portrait of Isaac Newton* [1968]—not wholly convincing but reasonably tentative; Arthur Mitzman, *The Iron Cage: An Historical Interpretation of Max Weber* [1970]—not tentative enough, though suggestive; all too quick to generalize about the German character.)

————, *Insight and Responsibility: Lectures on the Ethical Implications of Psychoanalytic Insight* (1964). Humane essays, though not as tough-minded as Erikson's earlier collection, *Identity and the Life Cycle, Psychological Issues*, **I**, 1 (1959), a splendid array of papers on ego psychology.

————, "On the Nature of Psycho-Historical Evidence: In Search of Gandhi," in *Philosophers and Kings: Studies in Leadership, Daedalus* **IIIC**, 3 (Summer, 1968), 695–730. Adumbration of what was to become the somewhat disappointing *Gandhi's Truth: On the Origins of Militant Nonviolence* (1969), but valuable for its skeptical comments on psycho-history.

Freud, Anna, *The Ego and the Mechanisms of Defence* (1936; tr. Cecil Baines, 1937). Among the first elaborations of Freudian ego psychology. A classic.

————, *Normality and Pathology in Childhood: Assessments of Development* (1965). An important later work.

Freud, Sigmund, *The Standard Edition of the Complete Psychological Works,* (tr. and ed., James Strachey et al., 24 vols 1953–1975). The lazy, but not inaccurate way to deal with Freud's voluminous work is to refer to this soundly translated and intelligently annotated edition as a whole. But I will single out the writings I have cited, as well as others most relevant to history and to art.

————, "A Reply to Criticisms of My Paper on Anxiety Neurosis" (1895), *S. E.*, **III** (1962), 121–139.

————, *The Psychopathology of Everyday Life* (1901), *S. E.*, **VI** (1960).

————, *Three Essays on the Theory of Sexuality* (1905), *S. E.*, **VII** (1953), 125–243.

————, "Psychopathic Characters on the Stage" [1905–1906] (1942), *S. E.*, **VII**, 305–310.

————, "Delusions and Dreams in Jensen's *Gradiva*" (1907), *S. E.*, **IX** (1959), 3–95.

————, "Creative Writers and Day-Dreaming" (1908), *S. E.*, **IX**, 141–153.

————, "Character and Anal Eroticism" (1908), *S. E.*, **IX**, 167–175.

————, " 'Civilized' Sexual Morality and Modern Nervous Illness" (1908), *S. E.*, **IX**, 177–204.

————, "Leonardo da Vinci and a Memory of His Childhood" (1910), *S. E.*, **XI** (1957), 59–137.

————, "The Dynamics of Transference" (1912), *S. E.*, **XII** (1958); 97–108.

————, "The Occurrence in Dreams of Material from Fairy Tales" (1913), *S. E.*, **XII**, 279–287.

————, "The Theme of the Three Caskets" (1913), *S. E.*, **XII**, 289–301.

————, *Totem and Taboo: Some Points of Agreement Between the Mental Life of Savages and Neurotics* (1913), *S. E.*, **XIII** (1955), 1–161.

————, "The Claim of Psycho-Analysis to Scientific Interest" (1913), *S. E.*, **XIII**, 165–190.

————, "The Moses of Michelangelo" (1914), *S. E.*, **XIII**, 211–238.

————, "Thoughts for the Times on War and Death" (1915), *S. E.*, **XIV** (1957), 273–302.

————, "From the History of an Infantile Neurosis" [1914] (1918), *S. E.*, **XVII** (1955), 3–122.

————, "A Childhood Recollection from *Dichtung und Wahrheit*" (1971), *S. E.*, **XVII**, 145–156.

————, *Beyond the Pleasure Principle* (1920), *S. E.*, **XVIII** (1955), 3–64.

————, *Group Psychology and the Analysis of the Ego* (1921), *S. E.*, **XVIII**, 67–143.

————, *The Ego and the Id* (1923), *S. E.*, **XIX** (1961), 3–66.

————, *The Future of an Illusion* (1927), *S. E.*, **XXI** (1961), 3–56.

————, *Civilization and Its Discontents* (1930), *S. E.*, **XXI**, 59–145.

————, "Humour," (1927), *S. E.*, **XXI**, 159–166.

————, "Dostoevsky and Parricide" (1928), *S. E.*, **XXI**, 175–196.

————, "The Goethe Prize," (1930), *S. E.*, **XXI**, 207–214.

————, "New Introductory Lectures on Psychoanalysis," esp. Lecture **XXXV**, "The Question of a *Weltanschauung*" (1933), *S. E.*, **XXII** (1964), 158–182.

————, "Why War?" (1933), *S. E.*, **XXII**, 197–215.

————, *The Origins of Psychoanalysis: Letters to Wilhelm Fliess, Drafts and Notes, 1887–1902* (eds. Maria Bonaparte, Anna Freud, Ernst Kris; tr. Eric Mosbacher and James Strachey, 1954).

Geertz, Clifford, *The Interpretation of Cultures* (1973). A wide-ranging collection of essays by a brilliant anthropologist, rethinking such worn topics as the notion of ideology and man's place in culture. See especially, "The Impact of the Concept of Culture on the Concept of Man," 33–54; and "Ideology as a Cultural System," 193–233.

Gibson, James J., *The Senses Considered as Perceptual Systems* (1966). An authoritative account by a psychologist ready to argue in behalf of objectivism.

Gombrich, E. H., *Art and Illusion: A Study in the Psychology of Pictorial Representation* (2nd ed., 1961). A persuasive account of the varieties of perception and its limited reliability.

Hartmann, Heinz, *Ego Psychology and the Problem of Adaptation* (1937; tr. David Rapaport, 1958).

————, *Psychoanalysis and Moral Values* (1960).

————, *Essays on Ego Psychology: Selected Problems in Psychoanalytic Theory* (1964).

————, Ernst Kris, Rudolph M. Loewenstein, *Papers on Psychoanalytic Psychology, Psychological Issues,* **IV**, 2 (1964). Indispensable essays in psychoanalytic ego psychology, the bridge between history and psychology. The first is Hartmann's classic early formulation.

Hughes, H. Stuart, "History and Psychoanalysis: The Explanation of Motive," in Hughes, *History as Art and as Science* (1964). A clearheaded and sympathetic essay.

Klein, George S., *Perception, Motives, and Personality* (1970). A brilliant collection of essays by a psychologist equally at home in psychoanalytic theory and experimental psychology; a powerful brief for the potential dependability of perception.

Kris, Ernst, *Psychoanalytic Explorations in Art* (1952). Brave and suggestive attempts by a Freudian to rush in where Freud himself feared to tread.

La Barre, Weston, *The Ghost Dance: The Origins of Religion* (1970). An impressive tour de force by a distinguished psychoanalytically oriented anthropologist; of great interest to the historian.

Langer, William L., "The Next Assignment," *American Historical Review,* **LIII**, 2 (January, 1958), 283–304. The celebrated presidential address calling on historians to avail themselves of psychology.

Loewenberg, Peter, "The Psychohistorical Origins of the Nazi Youth Cohort," *American Historical Review,* **CXXVI**, 5 (December, 1971), 1457–1502. One of the first attempts by a historian-psychoanalyst to apply psychoanalysis to groups.

Loewenstein, Rudolph M., Lottie M. Newman, Max Schur, and Albert J. Solnit, eds., *Psychoanalysis—A General Psychology: Essays in Honor of Heinz Hartmann* (1966). A volume interesting not merely for its content but for its very title.

Mazlish, Bruce, ed., *Psychoanalysis and History* (1963). A small introductory anthology.

Muensterberger, Warner, ed., *Man and His Culture: Psychoanalytic Anthropology After 'Totem and Taboo'* (1969). A collection of interest to historians; note especially Géza Róheim, "The Psychoanalytic Interpretation of Culture," 31–51; and the seminal, much anthologized essay by Anne Parsons, "Is the Oedipus Complex Universal? The Jones-Malinowski Debate Revisited and a South Italian 'Nuclear Complex,' " 331–384.

Namier, Sir Lewis, "History," in Namier, *Avenues of History* (1952), 1–10.

————, "Human Nature in Politics," in Namier, *Personalities and Powers* (1955), 1–7. Brief, witty essays by a masterly practitioner much influenced by psychoanalysis.

Neumann, Franz L., "Anxiety and Politics," tr. Peter Gay, in Neumann, *The Democratic and the Authoritarian State* (1957), 270–300. A pioneering effort by an independent left-wing political theorist to apply Freudian ideas to history and politics.

Parsons, Talcott, *Social Structure and Personality* (1964). A collection of essays by a sociologist acknowledging the influence of Freud on his own thinking, and seeking to find convergences between psychoanalysis and sociology.

Philosophers and Kings: Studies in Leadership, Daedalus, **IIIC,** 3 (Summer, 1968). An anthology of essays on psychohistory, already cited for Erikson's contribution; mainly on psychobiography—William James, Isaac Newton, James Mill, Charles De Gaulle and others. Interesting though necessarily of unequal merit.

Róheim, Géza, *The Origin and Function of Culture* (1943).

————, *Psychoanalysis and Anthropology: Culture, Personality and the Unconscious* (1950). Both interesting contributions to the psychological interpretation of history.

Runciman, W. G., "Sociology in Its Place," in Runciman, *Sociology in Its Place and Other Essays* (1970), 1–44. Persuasive attack (by a sociologist) on sociologists' claims to autonomy.

Schafer, Roy, *Aspects of Internalization* (1968). A technical psychoanalytic account of how culture invades the individual.

Schapiro, Meyer, "Leonardo and Freud: An Art-Historical Study," *Journal of the History of Ideas,* **XVII** (1956), 147–178. A brilliant and respectful critique, not of Freud, but of one essay by Freud. (See the defensive counterattack by Eissler cited above.)

Spector, Jack J., *The Aesthetics of Freud: A Study of Psychoanalysis and Art* (1972). A useful survey.

Wallace, A. F. C., *Culture and Personality* (1961). Psychoanalysis and cultural anthropology harmonized.

Weinstein, Fred, and Gerald M. Platt, *Psychoanalytic Sociology: An Essay on the Interpretation of Historical Data and the Phenomena of Collective Behavior* (1973). An intriguing provisional effort well described in its subtitle.

Wilbur, G. B., and Warner Muensterberger, *Psychoanalysis and Culture: Es-*

says in Honor of Géza Róheim (1951). An interesting anthology of studies in convergence.

Wittkower, Rudolf and Margot, *Born Under Saturn: The Character and Conduct of Artists, a Documented History from Antiquity to the French Revolution* (1963). A mine of cultural history, the book is extremely (excessively) skeptical of Freud's contribution to the analysis of art and history.

Wolman, Benjamin B., ed., *The Psychoanalytic Interpretation of History* (1971). Includes some rather feeble contributions and some interesting efforts; the latter includes Peter Loewenberg, "Theodor Herzl: A Psychoanalytic Study in Charismatic Political Leadership," 150–191.

3. History and Philosophy of Art

Ackerman, James S., "Western Art History," in Ackerman and Rhys Carpenter, *Art and Archeology* (1963), 123–229. An impressive survey of styles of art history in America today, learned and attractively argumentative.

Antal, Frederick, "Remarks on the Method of Art History," *The Burlington Magazine*, XCI (1949), 49–52, 73–75. A sophisticated Marxist view.

Baxandall, Michael, *Painting and Experience in Fifteenth Century Italy: A Primer in the Social History of Pictorial Style* (1972). A brief, to my mind exciting, essay, relating art to its economic background (without vulgarizing it) and seeking to discover what contemporaries *saw* in the pictures they looked at. A model for other researchers.

Berenson, Bernard, *Aesthetics and History in the Visual Arts* (1948). Conservative, even stodgy view by a connoisseur who rejected modernist art.

Collingwood, R. G., *The Principles of Art* (1938). One of Collingwood's most uncompromisingly Idealist (and most interesting) books.

Focillon, Henri, *The Life of Forms in Art* (tr. Charles Beecher Hogan, George Kubler, and S. Lane Faison, Jr.; 2nd English ed., 1948). The difficult but justly famous analysis of the role of form in art; enlarged in this edition by Focillon's moving essay on the shaping hand.

Frankl, Paul, *Das System der Kunstwissenschaft* (1938). Technical analysis by a fine art historian of the Gothic.

Friedländer, Max J., *On Art and Connoisseurship* (tr. Tancred Borenilus; 1942). Informal, unsystematic, suggestive essays in the art of seeing.

Gombrich, E. H., *Meditations on a Hobby Horse and Other Essays on the Theory of Art* (1963). A collection of Gombrich's beautifully written, beautifully argued essays in aesthetics, including such important pieces as "Meditations on a Hobby Horse or the Roots of Artistic Form" (1951), 1–11; "Psycho-Analysis and the History of Art" (1953), 30–44; the review of Arnold Hauser's famous book "The Social History of Art" (1953), 86–94; "Art and Scholarship," 106–111; and other skirmishes for good sense.

————, *Aby Warburg: An Intellectual Biography* (1970). A substantial life, drawing heavily on Warburg's own writings, of the seminal German art historian and founder of the Warburg Library.

Haskell, Francis, *Patrons and Painters: A Study in the Relations Between Ital-*

ian Art and Society in the Age of the Baroque (1963). Sound, convincing; the very model of a monograph.

Hauser, Arnold, *The Social History of Art*, 2 vols. (tr. Stanley Godman, 1951). Erudite, controversial, excessively schematic but sometimes remarkably perceptive. (See Gombrich's review cited above.)

————, *The Philosophy of Art History* (1958). Less dogmatic and hence more successful, than the better known *Social History of Art;* strikingly sympathetic to psychoanalysis.

Kahler, Erich, *The Disintegration of Form in the Arts* (1968). Intelligent, despairing lectures.

Kubler, George, *The Shape of Time* (1962). A learned and difficult brief essay, developing possible convergences between anthropology and art.

Kuhns, Richard, *Structures of Experience: Essays on the Affinity Between Philosophy and Literature* (1970). Civilized essays exploring the truthfulness of art, and the artistic mode of truth.

Langer, Susanne K., *Feeling and Form: A Theory of Art* (1953). Aesthetic theory based on Cassirer's philosophy of symbolic forms.

————, ed., *Reflections on Art* (1958). One of many, and one of the best modern anthologies. (See also Philipson below.)

Panofsky, Erwin, "Über das Verhältnis der Kunstgeschichte zur Kunsttheorie," *Zeitschrift für Aesthetik und allgemeine Kunstwissenschaft*, **XVIII** (1925), 129–142. A brilliant attempt to find the boundaries between art history and art theory.

————, "The History of Art as a Humanistic Discipline," in T. M. Greene, ed., *The Meaning of the Humanities* (1940), 89–118. An exhilarating essay by one of the world's great art historians.

————, *Studies in Iconology: Humanistic Themes in the Art of the Renaissance* (1939). A stunning series of lectures on iconographical puzzles; the theoretical introductory chapter is a model of lucidity.

————, "The History of Art," in W. R. Crawford, ed., *The Cultural Migration: The European Scholar in America* (1953), 82–111. Moving and informative comparison between German and American art history.

Philipson, Morris, ed., *Aesthetics Today* (1961). A valuable collection which contains, among other things, Meyer Schapiro's fine long essay, "Style," 81–113.

Venturi, Lionello, *History of Art Criticism* (tr. Charles Marriott, 1936). Still useful, though a larger, fuller history is much to be desired.

[For other titles on the history of art, see below: Manet, Section 4; Mondrian, Section 4.]

Manet

1. Biographies, Reminiscences, Documents, Illustrated Volumes

Bataille, Georges, *Manet* (1955). A characteristic illustrated volume published by Skira; reliable critical text.

Bazire, Edmond, *Manet* (1884). The first biography, by a friend; well illustrated, alive with reminiscences, but critically seriously deficient.

Courthion, Pierre, *Manet* (1962). An intelligent introductory essay followed by a selection of large color plates.

_____, and Pierre Cailler, *Portrait of Manet by Himself and His Contemporaries* (tr. Michael Ross, 1960). Collection of letters and documents by Manet, eye-witness reports, critical estimates by friends and critics; the first edition of this handy compendium was by Courthion, *Manet raconté par lui-même et par ses amis* (1945), but the English version is drawn from the enlarged, two-volume edition of 1953.

Duret, Théodore, *Histoire d'Edouard Manet et de son œuvre* (1902). Both extensive biography and catalogue, this book has been reprinted a number of times, including in an incomplete English translation, *Manet and the French Impressionists* (1910). A valuable source.

Jedlicka, Gotthard, *Edouard Manet* (1941). Good critical biography.

Florisoone, Michel, *Manet* (1947). An anthology of statements by and about Manet, useful reproductions, informative introduction.

Guiffrey, Jean, *Lettres illustrées d'Edouard Manet* (1929). There is an English version of this collection of twenty-two late letters, beautifully illustrated with Manet's water colors: *Letters with Aquarelles* (1944).

Manet, Edouard, *Lettres de jeunesse* (1929). Charming but not very revealing letters from the seventeen-year-old Manet.

_____, scattered correspondence, partly unpublished, in the Fondation Doucet in the Bibliothèque d'Art et d'Archéologie, Paris, cartons 21 and 59. The juice has been squeezed out of these letters, however; see Courthion and Cailler above, Moreau-Nélaton and Tabarant below.

Moreau-Nélaton, Etienne, *Manet raconté par lui-même*, 2 vols. (1926). A full, beautifully illustrated biographical study using Manet's own words, or those of his closest associates, as much as possible. Though almost half a century old, still a gold mine.

Moore, George, *Confessions of a Young Man* (1888).

_____, *Modern Painting* (1898)

_____, *Memoirs of My Dead Life* (1906). Vigorous, often fascinating glimpses into the life and working habits of Manet, whom Moore knew well and who painted Moore twice.

Perruchot, Henri, *La vie de Manet* (1959). Somewhat jazzed up biography.

Proust, Antonin, "Souvenirs de Manet," *Revue Blanche*, **XII** (February, March,

April 1897). Vivid recollections by a life-long and intimate friend.

————, *Edouard Manet, Souvenirs* (1913). This affectionate account, interspersed with Manet's sayings, is an expansion of the articles in the *Revue Blanche;* much criticized for incoherence and occasional incomprehension, it remains an irreplaceable source of information.

Richardson, John, *Edouard Manet, Paintings and Drawings* (1958). Good collection of reproductions with lucid commentary and introduction.

Tabarant, Adolphe, *Une Correspondance inédite d'Edouard Manet, Lettres du siège de Paris* (1935). Letters from Manet to his wife, from besieged Paris in the Winter of 1870.

Zola, Emile, *Edouard Manet: Etude biographique et critique* (1867). First informal, fascinating account of Manet the young artist. Often reprinted. I have used Antoinette Ehrard, ed., Zola, *Mon Salon, Manet, Ecrits sur l'art* (1970).

2. Exhibition catalogues, Catalogues raisonnés

De Leiris, Alain, *The Drawings of Edouard Manet* (1969). Not quite complete, yet a valuable survey.

Duret, Théodore, see entry in first section above.

Guérin, Marcel, *L'Oeuvre gravé du Manet* (1944). A fine catalogue, incorporating the work of Moreau-Nélaton (see below).

Hanson, Anne Coffin, *Edouard Manet, 1832–1883* (1966). A catalogue of an exhibition shown first in Philadelphia, then in Chicago; filled with insights and important suggestions.

Harris, Jean Collins, *Edouard Manet: Graphic Works* (1970). Announced as a definitive catalogue, it is practically that. For almost all purposes, exhaustive.

———— and J. Isaacson, *Manet and Spain, Prints and Drawings* (1969). Exhibition catalogue for a show at Ann Arbor, dealing with the important and controverted question of Manet's Spanish debts.

Jamot, Paul, Georges Wildenstein, with the assistance of Georges Bataille, *Manet*, 2 vols. (1932). An excellent work of reference that includes all the paintings and pastels, gives chronological accounts, reprints comments on Manet, and is generally immensely useful to the student of Manet.

Moreau-Nélaton, Etienne, *Manet: Graveur et lithographe* (1906). Though still interesting, now superseded by Guérin, cited above.

Orienti, Sandra, ed., *The Complete Paintings of Manet* (1971). A handy survey for those who have no access to the other critical catalogues.

Tabarant, Adolphe, *Manet: Histoire catalographique* (1931). Somewhat like Duret's work, part catalogue, part biography.

————, *Manet et ses œuvres* (1947). An immensely detailed history of Manet and his works; very fully illustrated, though with tiny illustrations. A brave attempt but in many ways an ugly book.

Zola, Emile, "Preface" to *Exposition des œuvres d'Édouard Manet* (1884). The posthumous exposition at the Ecole Nationale des Beaux-Arts.

3. Special Studies

Ackerman, Gerald M., "Gérôme and Manet," *Gazette des Beaux-Arts,* **LXX** (1967), 163–176. An interesting juxtaposition of two apparently very different painters; should be read in conjunction with Ackerman's catalogue, *Jean-Léon Gérôme (1824–1904)* (1972), a brave but to my mind not wholly successful effort to rehabilitate Gérôme.

Bowness, Alan, "Manet and Mallarmé," *Bulletin, Philadelphia Museum of Art,* **LXII,** 293 (1967), 213–221. Analysis of a friendship; may be read in conjunction with Mallarmé's neglected essay, "The Impressionists and Edouard Manet," *Art Monthly Review,* **I,** 9 (1876), 117–121. (See Harris below.)

————, "A Note on Manet's Compositional Difficulties," *Burlington Magazine,* **CIII** (1961), 276–277. A vigorous, wholly justified, defense of Manet's ability to draw.

Busch, Günter, *Edouard Manet, Un Bar aux Folies-Bergère* (n.d., 1956). Good brief study.

Dorival, Bernard, "Meissonier et Manet," *Art de France,* **II** (1962), 223–226. Another of those confrontations between academic and rebel.

Faison, S. Lane, "Manet's Portrait of Zola," *Magazine of Art,* **XLII** (1949), 162–168. A detailed analysis.

Fried, Michael, "Manet's Sources, Aspects of His Art, 1859–1865," *Artforum,* **VII,** 7 (March, 1969), 28–82. Enormously learned and vehemently revisionist, this essay raises important questions about Manet's sources, but its thesis, that Manet was essentially a "French" painter, seems to me untenable. (See Reff's refutation cited below.)

Gurevich, V., "Observations on the Wound in Christ's Side," *Journal of the Warburg and Courtauld Institutes,* **XX** (1957), 358–362. A typical Warburg essay: a careful iconographical study, with special attention to Manet, of the history of Christ's wound in art; it draws useful inferences about the cultural meaning of Manet's *Dead Christ.*

Hamilton, George Heard, *Manet and His Critics* (1954, 2nd ed. 1969). Learned, informative, amusing survey of the responses to Manet—including some appreciative ones.

————, "Is Manet Still 'Modern'?" *Artnews Annual* **XXXI** (1966), 104–131, 159–163. He is.

Hanson, Anne Coffin, "A Group of Marine Paintings by Manet," *Art Bulletin,* **XLIV** (1962), 332–336. A valuable analysis.

————, "Notes on Manet Literature," *Art Bulletin,* **XLVIII** (1966), 432–438. Surveys recent work.

————, "Manet's Subject Matter and a Source of Popular Imagery," *Museum Studies,* No. 3, Art Institute of Chicago (1968).

————, "Popular Imagery and the Work of Edouard Manet," in Ulrich Finke, ed., *French 19th Century Painting and Literature* (1972), 133–163. Both valuable revaluations of Manet's relation to popular French illustrators.

Harris, Jean Collins, "A Little-known Essay on Manet by Stéphane Mallarmé," *Art Bulletin*, **XLVI** (1964), 559–563.

————, "Manet's Race-Track Paintings," *Art Bulletin*, **XLVIII** (1966), 78–82.

————, "Edouard Manet as an Illustrator," *Bulletin, Philadelphia Museum of Art* (April–June, 1967). All three informative articles.

Jamot, Paul, "Manet and the Olympia," *Burlington Magazine*, **L** (1927), 27–35. (See also Reff's article below.)

————, "Etudes de Manet," *Gazette des Beaux-Arts*, **XV** (1927), 27–50, 381–390. Both draw on Jamot's immense learning, given fuller expression in the catalogue I cited above.

Martin, Kurt, *Edouard Manet, Die Erschiessung Kaiser Maximiliens von Mexico* (1948). Specialized monograph.

Meier-Graefe, Julius, *Edouard Manet* (1912). Pioneering essay by a perceptive German critic and historian of art.

Reff, Theodore, "The Symbolism of Manet's Frontispiece Etching," *Burlington Magazine*, **CIV** (1962), 182–186. A suggestive essay.

————, "Copyists in the Louvre, 1850–1870," *Art Bulletin*, **XLVI** (1964), 552–559. A significant survey and analysis.

————, "The Meaning of Manet's Olympia," *Gazette des Beaux-Arts*, **LXIII** (1964), 111–122. A penetrating reading.

————, " 'Manet's Sources,' A Critical Evaluation," *Artforum*, **VIII**, 1 (September, 1969), 40–48. A refutation, to my mind devastating, of Fried's article cited above.

Rewald, John, *Manet Pastels* (1947). Intelligent, well informed.

Rosenthal, Léon, *Manet aquafortiste et lithographe* (1925). See now the studies of Harris and Guérin.

Sandblad, Nils Gösta, *Manet: Three Studies in Artistic Conception* (1954). An attractive set of essays, sensitive to Manet's artistic debts and urban environment, concentrating on the *Olympia*, the *Musique aux Tuileries*, and the *Execution of Emperor Maximilian*.

4. *The Wider World: Art and Culture*

Baudelaire, Charles, *Curiosités esthétiques* in *Œuvres complètes* (ed. Crépet, 1923).

————, *L'Art romantique*, in *Œuvres* (ed. Crépet, 1925). These two volumes contain Baudelaire's perceptive salons, studies of Delacroix, occasional essays on laughter, "l'art philosophique," and the essay on Guys, "Le peintre de la vie moderne." Indispensable for an understanding of modernism in general and Manet in particular.

Bénédite, L., *Théodore Chassériau, sa vie et son œuvre*, 2 vols. (1931). Outstanding among many useful biographies of nineteenth-century French artists.

Boas, George, ed., *Courbet and the Naturalistic Movement* (1938). Good collection of essays.

————, "Il faut être de son temps," *Journal of Aesthetics and Art Criticism*, **I** (1941), 52–65. Pioneering study of a pervasive nineteenth-century cliché. (See also Nochlin below.)

Boime, Albert, *The Academy and French Painting in the Nineteenth Century* (1971). A recent monograph that shows the untenability of the old dichotomy between avant-garde and academic art; especially interesting on Manet's teacher, Couture.

Charlton, D. G., *Secular Religions in France, 1815–1870* (1963). A useful study of substitutes for Christianity in the lifetime of Manet.

Claretie, Jules, *Peintres et sculpteurs contemporains*, 2 vols. (1882). Comments by an alert *flâneur*.

Couture, Thomas, *Méthode et entretiens d'atelier* (1867). Valuable (though partly unintentional) testimony to contemporary tastes by a traditional if unacademic painter.

Duranty, Edmond, *La Nouvelle peinture. A propos du groupe d'artistes qui expose dans les Galeries Durand-Ruel* (1876), recent ed. Marcel Guérin, 1946. Pioneering contemporary discussion and appreciation of "new painting."

Finke, Ulrich, ed., *French 19th Century Painting and Literature* (1972). An interesting collection; I have already cited the Hanson article in it. I should add that there are informative essays by Francis Haskell, "The Sad Clown: Some Notes on a 19th Century Myth," Alan Bowness, "Courbet's Early Subject Matter," Theodore Reff, "Degas and the Literature of His Time," as well as others.

Gauss, Charles Edward, *The Aesthetic Theories of French Artists from Realism to Surrealism* (1949; ed. 1966). A brief survey.

Gilman, Margaret, *Baudelaire the Critic* (1943). An important monograph on an important subject.

Graña, Cesar, *Modernity and Its Discontents: French Society and the French Man of Letters in the Nineteenth Century* (1967). Originally published in 1964 under the title *Bohemian Versus Bourgeois*, this is an interesting analysis of the anti-bourgeois ideology current among French avant-garde writers.

———, *Fact and Symbol: Essays in the Sociology of Art and Literature* (1971). Has some useful exploratory essays.

Hemmings, F. W. J., ed. (with R. J. Niess), Zola, *Salons* (1959). A fine critical edition of Zola's art criticism.

———, *Emile Zola* (2nd ed., 1966). A judicious, fairly economical life.

———, *Culture and Society in France, 1848–1898: Dissidents and Philistines* (1971). An introductory, well-informed survey.

Lethève, Jacques, *La vie quotidienne des artistes français au XIXe siècle* (1968). Chatty, based on secondary materials, but useful.

Marguery, H., "Un pionnier de l'histoire de l'art: Thoré-Bürger," *Gazette des Beaux-Arts*, 5th series, **XI** (1925), 229–245; **XII** (1926), 295–311, 367–380. Though still inadequate, the only treatment we have of this important critic.

Nochlin, Linda, *Realism* (1971). Suggestive survey of realism in art as well as literature. Hardly definitive but interesting.

Pinkney, David H., *Napoleon III and the Rebuilding of Paris* (1958). Authoritative.

Rewald, John, *The History of Impressionism* (4th ed., 1973). First published in 1946 and continuously revised, this is an indispensable history; judicious, accurate, informative.

Rouart, D., ed., *Correspondance de Berthe Morisot* (1950). Handsome edition connecting letters and other documents with informative narrative; important for Manet.

Schapiro, Meyer, "Courbet and Popular Imagery," *Journal of the Warburg and Courtauld Institutes,* **IV** (1941), 164–191. A pioneering exploration of the relation between high and popular culture; much later work is indebted to it.

H. Shickman Gallery, *The Neglected 19th Century: An Exhibition of French Paintings* (1970).

————, *The Neglected 19th Century: An Exhibition of French Paintings,* Part II (1971). Two illustrated catalogues containing, among others, several Coutures.

Sloane, Joseph C., *French Painting Between the Past and the Present: Artists, Critics & Traditions from 1848 to 1870* (1951). A fascinating survey of artistic views and critical opinion in the formative years of Manet's art; two chapters are specifically devoted to Manet.

Tabarant, Adolphe, *La vie artistique au temps de Baudelaire* (1942). An informative, crowded collective portrait; unfortunately not indexed.

Thompson, J. M., *Louis Napoleon and the Second Empire* (1955). Among a large literature, perhaps the most accessible biography.

Venturi, Lionello, ed., *Les Archives de l'Impressionisme,* 2 vols. (1939). A valuable collection of correspondence between the Impressionists' dealer, Paul Durand-Ruel, and all the leading Impressionists.

White, Harrison C., and Cynthia A. White, *Canvases and Careers: Institutional Change in the French Painting World* (1965). Pedestrian but informative; on numbers and income of French painters.

Zeldin, Theodore, ed., *Conflicts in French Society: Anticlericalism, Education and Morals in the 19th Century* (1970). An interesting quartet of essays on French society in the time of Manet, including a fine piece by the editor on "The Conflicts of Moralities: Confession, Sin and Pleasure in the Nineteenth Century."

————, *France 1848–1945:* vol. I, *Ambition, Love and Politics* (1973). First of a proposed two-volume history, highly unorthodox in approach, with chapters on morals and marriage, professions, classes, and political activity.

Gropius

1. Writings by Gropius

Gropius was an active polemicist, and most of his unpublished lectures (along with much interesting correspondence) can be found in the Gropius Papers, Bauhaus Archiv, Berlin; with photocopies in the Houghton Library, Harvard

University. For a full listing of Gropius' writings, see the exhaustive listing down
to 1961 in *Hans M. Wingler, Das Bauhaus: 1919–1933, Weimar, Dessau, Berlin*
(1962) 540–542, listing 120 items; there is an English version (somewhat enlarged) of Wingler's vast documentary compendium (1968).

"Programm zur Gründung einer allgemeinen Hausbaugesellschaft auf künst-
     lerisch einheitlicher Grundlage mbH. Ziel: Industrialisierung des Haus-
     baues" (1910). Reprinted in substantial part in Wingler, *Bauhaus,* 26–27.
     A prescient memorandum.
"Die Entwicklung moderner Industriebaukunst," *Die Kunst in Industrie und
     Handel, Jahrbuch des Deutschen Werkbundes 1913* (1913), 17–22. Part of
     the ongoing polemic about modernity in the *Werkbund.*
"Der stilbildende Wert industrieller Bauformen," *Der Verkehr, Jahrbuch des
     Deutschen Werkbundes 1914* (1914), 29–32. See just above.
"Vorwort," *Programm des Staatlichen Bauhauses in Weimar* (1919). Reprinted
     in several publications; see Wingler, *Bauhaus,* 38–42. The famous mani-
     festo.
Idee und Aufbau des Staatlichen Bauhauses Weimar (1923). A defensive and
     explanatory pamphlet.
Internationale Architektur, Bauhausbücher 1 (1925; 2nd ed., 1927). Appropri-
     ately enough, it was its director who inaugurated the series of books ema-
     nating from the Bauhaus with an illustrated statement.
(ed.), *Neue Arbeiten der Bauhauswerkstätten,* Bauhausbücher 7 (1925). An in-
     formative collection.
"Das flache Dach," *Bauwelt,* **XVII** (1926), 162–168, 223–227, 361. Widely read
     and influential results of an "Umfrage" concerning the aesthetic and eco-
     nomic possibilities of the flat roof. Gropius published several articles on this
     burning question in other journals, notably *Stein, Holz, Eisen,* in this pe-
     riod. (See Wingler, *Bauhaus,* 540.)
"Der Architekt als Organisator der modernen Bauwirtschaft und seine For-
     derungen an die Industrie," in F. Block, *Probleme des Bauens,* vol. I,
     Wohnbau (1928), 202–214. On a favorite theme: the architect as organizer.
bauhausbauten dessau, Bauhausbücher 12 (1930). An account of the achieve-
     ment of the Dessau Bauhaus, in the new typography avoiding all capitals.
The New Architecture and the Bauhaus (tr. P. Morton Shand, 1935). The first
     important statement of Gropius' architectural vision in English. Reissued
     in 1965.
(ed.), with Ise Gropius and Herbert Bayer, *Bauhaus 1919–1928* (1938). Copi-
     ously illustrated catalogue for a famous exhibition at the Museum of Mod-
     ern Art, New York.
Scope of Total Architecture (1955). A small but important collection of essays,
     talks, reviews on architectural education, modern architects and their
     craft, and on planning.
Letter to Helmut Weber, May, 1961, in Weber, *Walter Gropius und das Fagus-
     werk* (1961). A revealing statement on the inspiration for the celebrated
     "curtain wall" of 1911.
"Unity in Diversity," in *Four Great Makers of Modern Architecture: Gropius,*

Le Corbusier, Mies van der Rohe, Wright, Record of a symposium at the Columbia School of Architecture, May, 1961 (1963), 216–229. A useful restatement of Gropius' lifelong convictions.

Apollo in der Demokratie (1967); *Apollo in the Democracy* (1968). A late collection of speeches and papers, some originally in German, others in English, selected by Ise Gropius. It contains such articles as "The Curse of Conformity" (1958), a long essay on Japan, reports of "encounters" with other architects including Peter Behrens, Le Corbusier, and Frank Lloyd Wright.

2. On Gropius and His World

Waentig, Heinrich, *Wirtschaft und Kunst* (1909). A sensitive early survey on the relation of design to culture and economic life.

Stahl, Fritz, *Schinkel* (1911). An enthusiastic book that helped to rediscover Schinkel at a time that Behrens and Gropius were rediscovering him for themselves.

Behrendt, Walter Kurt, *Alfred Messel* (1911).

Rapsilber, M., Fritz Stahl, et al., *Alfred Messel,* 2 vols. (1911). Two fully illustrated and excessively enthusiastic books on a cautiously experimental Berlin architect.

Hoeber, Fritz, *Peter Behrens* (1913). A preliminary report, in mid-career.

Tessenow, Heinrich, *Handwerk und Kleinstadt* (1919). A passionate appeal for the return to small-town intimacy; of importance to Gropius at the end of World War I.

Wasmuth, Ernst, *Walter Gropius und Adolf Meyer, Bauten* (1923). A progress report.

The International Competition for a New Administration Building for The Chicago Tribune, MCMXXII; Containing All the Designs Submitted in Response to the Chicago Tribune's $100,000 Offer Commemorating Its Seventy-Fifth Anniversary, June 10, 1922 (1923). A document as lavish and expansive as it title; an unconscious bit of valuable social history.

Cremers, Paul Joseph, *Peter Behrens, sein Werk von 1909 bis zur Gegenwart* (1928). A useful monograph. (For the early work see Hoeber cited above.)

Hegemann, Werner, *Das Steinerne Berlin: Geschichte der grössten Mietskasernenstadt der Welt* (1930). A highly charged, but also highly informative, assault on the tragedy of Berlin's urbanization, by a writer with a good eye and a sharp pen.

Hitchcock, Henry-Russell, and Philip Johnson, *The International Style: Architecture Since 1922* (1932; with new foreword and appendix by Hitchcock, 1966). A pioneering appreciation, upon its first appearance, of the new architecture, including Mies van der Rohe, Oud, Gropius and others.

Pevsner, Nikolaus, *Pioneers of the Modern Movement* (1936; 3rd rev. ed., *Pioneers of Modern Design from William Morris to Walter Gropius,* 1960). A vigorous, vastly popular history which appreciates the "rationalists" (like Gropius) and has grave reservations about the "anti-rationalists" (like the proponents of Art Nouveau and the Expressionists in architecture).

Giedion, Sigfried, *Space, Time and Architecture* (1941). A pioneering work, very bulky but very influential, treating modern architecture as part of modern culture; highly admiring of Gropius. Several later editions.

Moholy-Nagy, Sibyl, *Moholy-Nagy: Experiment in Totality* (1950; 2nd ed., 1969, with Introduction by Walter Gropius). A lyrical but revealing portrait of the brilliant designer who was very close to Gropius during the Bauhaus years.

Grote, Ludwig, ed., *Die Maler am Bauhaus* (1950). A catalogue of paintings done in the Bauhaus.

Argan, Giulio Carlo, *Walter Gropius e la Bauhaus* (1951; German tr. 1962). An Italian appraisal.

Hildebrandt, Hans, *Oskar Schlemmer* (1952). An informative study of this central Bauhaus figure.

Giedion, Sigfried, *Walter Gropius: Work and Teamwork* (1954). The first full account by an influential admirer.

Jaffé, H. L. C., *De Stijl 1917–1931: The Dutch Contribution to Modern Art* (1956). Ventures into the architectural work of this influential experimental group.

Schlemmer, Tut, ed., *Oskar Schlemmer: Briefe und Tagebücher* (1958). Significantly supplements the Hildebrandt study cited above.

Kiaulehn, Walther, *Berlin: Schicksal einer Weltstadt* (1958). A chatty, journalistic but informative history of modern Berlin.

Hitchcock, Henry-Russell, *Architecture: Nineteenth and Twentieth Centuries* (1958; 2nd ed., 1963). Among many histories of modern architecture perhaps the most judicious.

Herbert, Gilbert, *The Synthetic Vision of Walter Gropius* (1959). An attempt at comprehensive understanding.

Banham, Reyner, *Theory and Design in the First Machine Age* (1960; 2nd ed., 1967). An important essay. *Casabella*, No. 240 (June, 1960). A special issue devoted to Peter Behrens, with many articles on him and some material by him; fully illustrated.

Drexler, Arthur, *Ludwig Mies van der Rohe* (1960). An illustrated short account.

Fitch, James Marston, *Walter Gropius* (1960). Helpful brief appreciation; a good introduction.

Jones, Cranston, *Architecture Today and Tomorrow* (1961). A general survey.

Hess, Hans, *Lyonel Feininger* (1961). A full biography of one of the most interesting (and independent) artists to be associated with the Bauhaus.

Weber, Helmut, *Walter Gropius und das Faguswerk* (1961). A very important monograph on Gropius' architectural revolution.

van de Velde, Henry, *Geschichte meines Lebens* (ed. and tr. Hans Curjel, 1962). A somewhat synthetic product, it remains the best account of van de Velde's productive life we have.

Wingler, Hans M., *Das Bauhaus* (cited in the first section); *the* documentary collection.

Four Great Makers of Modern Architecture: Gropius, Le Corbusier, Mies van der Rohe, Wright, Record of a Symposium at the Columbia School of Architecture, 1961 (1963). Among the articles I found most useful were Peter Blake, "A Conversation with Mies," 93–104; Howard Dearstyne, "Miesian Space Concept in Domestic Architecture," 129–140; James Marston Fitch, "Mies van der Rohe and the Platonic Verities," 154–163; Esmond Shaw, "The Influence of the Bauhaus," 244–246; Thomas H. Creighton, "Walter Gropius and the Arts," 247–258.

Summerson, John, *Heavenly Mansions and Other Essays on Architecture* (ed. 1963). A delightful series of essays; particularly relevant here was "Architecture, Painting and Le Corbusier," 177–194.

Adler, Bruno, *Das Weimarer Bauhaus* (1963). A series of lectures devoted to "Ideengeschichte."

Arbeiten aus der graphischen Druckerei des Staatlichen Bauhauses in Weimar 1919–1925 (1963). Catalogue of an exhibition of the important graphic work of the Weimar period.

Bauhaus. Idee—Form—Zweck—Zeit (1964). Catalogue of an exhibition in Frankfurt am Main.

Posener, Julius, ed., *Anfänge des Funktionalismus. Von Arts and Crafts zum Deutschen Werkbund* (1964). A valuable anthology of writings (including much from Muthesius) with an informative introduction.

Sharp, Dennis, *Modern Architecture and Expressionism* (1966). An intelligent appraisal.

Metz, Don, *New Architecture in New Haven* (1966; 2nd ed., 1973). An album, with pictures and sections, publishing Don Metz's Gay residence.

Scheidig, Walther, *Crafts of the Weimar Bauhaus 1919–1924: An Early Experiment in Industrial Design* (tr. Ruth Michaelis and Patrick Murray, 1967). Useful survey.

Herzfeld, Hans, ed., *Berlin und die Provinz Brandenburg im 19. und 20. Jahrhundert* (1968). A bulky collective history of modern Berlin, stronger on demography and economics than on art and architecture. Paul Ortwin Rave's chapter, "Die bildende Kunst" is, however, not useless.

Gay, Peter, *Weimar Culture: The Outsider as Insider* (1968). An attempt to offer a comprehensive interpretation of the Weimar Republic, and place the Bauhaus' "hunger for wholeness."

Lane, Barbara Miller, *Architecture and Politics in Germany, 1918–1945* (1968). The first serious attempt to link buildings with politicians, hence of interest. But misreads, to my mind, the central apolitical animus of the Bauhaus and exaggerates the connections of Weimar and the 1930s.

Naylor, Gillian, *The Bauhaus* (1968). A thoroughly illustrated introduction.

Pevsner, Nikolaus, *The Sources of Modern Architecture and Design* (1968). Essentially a reworking of *Pioneers of the Modern Movement* (cited above); written with Pevsner's customary learning and vigor.

————, "Karl Friedrich Schinkel," in Pevsner, *Studies in Art, Architecture and Design,* Vol. I, *From Mannerism to Romanticism* (1968), 175–195. A valuable brief survey of Schinkel's work, stressing the modernity of his writings and in the Bauakademie without gushing over his "genius."

Anderson, Stanford Owen, "Peter Behrens and the New Architecture of Germany, 1900–1917," Columbia dissertation (1968). A comprehensive analysis.

Rickey, George, *Constructivism: Origins and Evolution* (1968). A useful study; contains an important letter from Gropius to the author.

Roters, Eberhard, *Painters of the Bauhaus* (tr. Anna Rose Cooper, 1969). See also Grote cited above.

Fifty Years Bauhaus (1969). An exhibition at the Illinois Institute of Technology in collaboration with the Bauhaus Archive.

Neumann, Eckhard, ed., *Bauhaus und Bauhäusler: Bekenntnisse und Erinnerungen* (1971). An attractive anthology of reminiscences, refuting any notions of Gropius as cultural commissar.

Franciscono, Marcel, *Walter Gropius and the Creation of the Bauhaus in Weimar: The Ideals and Artistic Theories of Its Founding Years* (1971). A highly specialized and highly informative monograph, drawing on much unpublished material. It is bound to correct many errors about crucial years in Gropius' career.

Concepts of the Bauhaus: The Busch-Reisinger Museum Collection (1971). A most informative catalogue, with significant essays by Ise Gropius, Herbert Bayer, T. Lux Feininger and others, and excellent illustrations.

Pehnt, Wolfgang, "Gropius the Romantic," *The Art Bulletin* (1971), 379–392. An important reappraisal, to be read in conjunction with Franciscono, cited above; uses interesting unpublished materials.

Gropius, Ise, Review of Franciscono, *Walter Gropius* (cited above), *Architectural Forum*, **CXXXVI**, 1 (January–February, 1972), 16–28. A revealing essay.

————, *Walter Gropius: Buildings, Plans, Projects 1906–1969* (1972). An excellent handy catalogue, with useful annotations and good photographs.

Posener, Julius, *From Schinkel to the Bauhaus* (1972). Publication of a brilliant series of lectures given some years before; important in establishing the link between the nineteenth and twentieth centuries.

Wirth, Irmgard, *Die Familie Gropius: Carl Wilhelm und Martin Gropius in Berlin* (n.d., 1972). Small but valuable pamphlet for an exhibition at the Berlin Museum.

Pundt, Hermann G., *Schinkel's Berlin: A Study in Environmental Planning* (1972). An informative monograph on Behrens' (and in a sense, Gropius') "master."

Jencks, Charles, *Modern Movements in Architecture* (1973). Polemical, aggressive, perverse, independent, hence interesting, though often, to my mind, wrong-headed.

Cook, John W., and Heinrich Klotz, eds., *Conversations with Architects* (1973). Extremely revealing, though by no means always pleasing, interviews with Paul Rudolph, Bertrand Goldberg, and seven other modern architects. It includes such gems as Philip Johnson saying, "Whoever commissions buildings buys me [including Hitler]. I'm for sale. I'm a whore. I'm an artist." (p. 37.)

Mondrian

1. Writings by Mondrian

Mondrian wrote a good deal, mainly but not solely in *De Stijl;* for the specialist, the best bibliography is in Hans L. C. Jaffé, *Piet Mondrian* (1970), 161–162. In the following list, I shall concentrate on Mondrian's main writings and on collections that conveniently bring together sets of his essays.

"De Nieuwe Beelding in de Schilderkunst," *De Stijl,* **I,** 1–6, 8–12 (1917–1918). A continuous argument in eleven installments.

"Natuurlijke en Abstracte Realiteit," *De Stijl,* **II–III** (1919–1920). A series of dialogues, in thirteen installments; a translation, *Natural Reality and Abstract Reality,* appears in Michel Seuphor, *Piet Mondrian: Life and Work* (1956), 301–352. A central document for the understanding of Mondrian.

"De Jazz en de Neo-Plastiek," *Internationale Revue,* **I,** 12 (1927), 421–427. Adumbrates ideas about the modern dance that he will develop later in his writings and some of his paintings.

Neue Gestaltung, Neoplastizismus, Nieuwe Beelding, Bauhausbücher 5 (1925). A collection of five essays published between 1920 and 1923, translated into German.

Plastic Art and Pure Plastic Art, and Other Essays (ed. Robert Motherwell, 1945; 3rd unchanged ed., 1951). Collects six significant late essays into one convenient volume. They are: "Plastic Art and Pure Plastic Art," in *Circle,* ed. J. L. Martin, Ben Nicholson, Naum Gabo (1937); *Toward the True Vision of Reality* (1942); "Pure Plastic Art," in *Masters of Abstract Art,* eds. Stephan C. Lion and Charmion von Wiegand (1942); "Abstract Art," preface for *Art of This Century,* ed. Peggy Guggenheim (1942); "Liberation from Oppression in Art and Life" (1945); "A New Realism" (written but not published in 1943).

De Stijl (ed. Hans L. C. Jaffé, tr. from the French by R. R. Symonds and the German by Mary Whitall, 1971). A very well-selected anthology that includes a number of Mondrian's writings for this journal in excerpt, including six sections of his "De Nieuwe Beelding in de Schilderkunst," and half a dozen other pieces.

"Documentatie over Mondrian, 1–3," *Museumjournaal voor Moderne Kunst,* **XIII,** (1968), 4–6, 208–215, 267–270, 321–326. Revealing early Mondrian letters edited by Joop Joosten.

Two Mondrian Sketchbooks, 1912–14 (tr. Robert Welsh, ed. Joop Joosten, 1969). As revealing as, perhaps more than, the letters.

Note: Harry Holtzman is preparing a complete collection of Mondrian's writings, translated by Martin James and Harry Holtzman, to be entitled, *The New Art, the New Life: The Collected Writings of Piet Mondrian.* Its appearance will make earlier anthologies obsolete.

2. Biographies, Interviews, Reminiscences, Illustrated Volumes

van Doesburg, Nelly, "Some Memories of Mondrian," in *Piet Mondrian, 1872–1944,* Centennial Exhibition, Guggenheim Museum (1971), 67–73. Frank and penetrating.

Elgar, Frank, *Mondrian* (tr. Thomas Walton, 1968). Dependent on Seuphor and others, but sensible summary, thoroughly illustrated.

Holtzman, Harry, "Piet Mondrian's Personality," Preface to *Mondrian: Paintings, Drawings, Constructions, Documents,* Catalogue of Sidney Janis Gallery Exhibition (February 7, 1974–March 9, 1974). A foretaste of what Holtzman will put into the preface of his collected writings of Mondrian.

Hunter, Sam, *Mondrian* (1958).

Jaffé, Hans L. C., *Piet Mondrian* (n.d.). A collection of color reproductions from all parts of Mondrian's career, with an appreciative and well-informed introduction.

Seuphor, Michel, *Piet Mondrian: Life and Work* (1956). A triple threat of a book, indeed a quadruple threat: a full biography, a set of intimate recollections, a gathering of inaccessible documents, and a widely used *catalogue raisonné.* Obviously indispensable.

Sweeney, James J., "Piet Mondrian," *Museum of Modern Art Bulletin,* **XII** (1945), 4; **XIII** (1946), 4–5. Interesting late interview.

Charmion von Wiegand, "The Meaning of Mondrian," *Journal of Aesthetics and Art Criticism,* **II,** 8 (Fall, 1943), 62–70.

————, "Interview" by Margit Rowell, in *Piet Mondrian, 1872–1944,* Centennial Exhibition (1971), 77–86. Though perhaps rather too admiring, a most revealing set of comments from a painter who knew Mondrian well in his last years.

Wijsenbeek, L. J. F., and J. J. P. Oud, *Mondriaan* (1962). An interesting collection.

Wijsenbeek, L. J. F., *Piet Mondrian* (1968). Extensively reproduces Mondrian's work, with significant introductory comments and a full bibliography to 1967.

3. Special Studies

Blok, Cornelis, "Mondriaan's Vroege Werk," *Museumjournaal voor Moderne Kunst,* **VIII,** 2 (August, 1962), 33–41. Adds to our knowledge of Mondrian's early painting.

————, ed., *Mondriaan in de Collectie van het Haags Gemeentemuseum,* Catalogue (rev. ed., 1968). Since the Gemeentemuseum in the The Hague has the most impressive collection of Mondrian's work before 1920—and has fairly impressive holdings of the late paintings, too—this is obviously a significant catalogue.

Butor, Michel, "Mondrian: The Square and Its Inhabitant" (tr. William Brown), in Butor, *Inventory* (ed. Richard Howard, 1970), 235–252. Imaginative and eccentric.

James, Martin S., "The Realism Behind Mondrian's Geometry," *Artnews*, **LVI** (1957), 34–37.

————, "Mondrian and the Dutch Symbolists," *The Art Journal*, **XXIII**, 2 (Winter, 1963–1964), 103–111. Two responsible and informative essays.

Joosten, Joop, "Mondrian: Between Cubism and Abstraction," in *Piet Mondrian, 1872–1944*, Centennial Exhibition, 53–66. Clarifies the murky "middle period" of Mondrian's artistic career.

Loosjes-Tempstra, A. B., *Moderne Kunst in Nederland, 1900–1914* (1959). Survey of Dutch art in a period of decisive importance for Mondrian's development.

Ringbom, Sixten, "Art in 'The Epoch of the Great Spiritual,' " *Journal of the Warburg and Courtauld Institutes*, **XXIX** (1966), 386–418. Though mainly on Kandinsky, throws much-needed light on the place of theosophy in Mondrian's work (see Welsh just below).

Welsh, Robert P., "Mondrian and Theosophy," in *Piet Mondrian, 1872–1944*, Centennial Exhibition, 35–51. A very important essay. While I am disposed to take Mondrian's theosophy a little less seriously than does Welsh, my debt to this essay is considerable.

Wijsenbeek, L. J. F., "Introduction," in *Piet Mondrian, 1872–1944*, 25–34. Part biographical, part analytical.

4. The World of Art

Ashton, Dore, *A Reading of Modern Art* (rev. ed. 1971). An interesting essay.

————, ed., *Picasso on Art: A Selection of Views* (1972). A dependable, extremely useful collection of Picasso's pronouncements.

Barr, Alfred H., Jr., *Matisse: His Art and His Public* (1951). After a quarter of a century still the most useful book on Matisse.

Cooper, Douglas, *The Cubist Epoch* (1970). A splendidly written and thoroughly illustrated catalogue. See also Fry, Golding and Rosenblum cited below.

Fry, Edward F., *Cubism* (1966). A good anthology with an Introduction.

Gray, Camilla, *The Russian Experiment in Art, 1863–1922* (ed. 1971). Intelligent survey of an important movement.

Grohmann, Will, *Wassily Kandinsky: Life and Work* (1959). Useful biography with *oeuvre* catalogue.

Golding, John, *Cubism: A History and an Analysis, 1907–1914* (rev. ed., 1968). A splendid analysis, concentrated on Picasso and Braque.

Kahnweiler, Daniel-Henry with Frnacis Cremieux, *My Galleries and Painters*, (tr. Helen Weaver, 1971). Very illuminating interviews with Picasso's dealer.

Kuh, Katherine, *Break-Up: The Core of Modern Art* (1965). A bit frenetic but filled with valuable quotations from modern artists.

Leymarie, Jean, *Fauvism. Biographical and Critical Study* (1959). One of the best analyses.

Pissarro, Camille, *Letters to His Son Lucien* (ed. John Rewald; 3rd ed., 1972).

Enormously revealing for the two worlds of art at the end of the nineteenth century.

Ringbom, Sixten, *The Sounding Cosmos,: A Study in the Spiritualism of Kandinsky and the Genesis of Abstract Painting* (1970). Fundamental.

Rosenblum, Robert, *Cubism and Twentieth-Century Art* (rev. ed. 1966). A brilliant survey, moving beyond Braque and Picasso to Leger and other painters—including Mondrian.

Sandler, Irving, *The Triumph of American Painting* (1970). Has useful quotations.

Schmutzler, Robert, *Art Nouveau* (1962; tr. Edouard Roditi, 1964). Sumptuously illustrated but with good text.

Steinberg, Leo, *Other Criteria: Confrontations with Twentieth-Century Art* (1972). A collection of idiosyncratic essays; stimulating if not always convincing.

Index

Italicized numbers refer to illustrations.

ART DEPARTMENT
BOWDOIN COLLEGE
BRUNSWICK
MAINE 04011

ART DEPARTMENT
BOWDOIN COLLEGE
BRUNSWICK
MAINE 04011

ART DEPARTMENT
BOWDOIN COLLEGE
BRUNSWICK
MAINE 04011